Words & Faces

HIRAM HAYDN

For even the most avid readers, publishing is wrapped in a certain mystery. For its practitioners it holds a constant fascination. The mystery is described and the fascination is conveyed in *Words & Faces,* an entertaining and companionable book by one of the best-known editors and publishers of our time.

Because Hiram Haydn focuses on people, this is a chronicle thronged with a great diversity of men and women. Three of the most vivid are sharply contrasting publishers: Nat Wartels, president of Crown; the late David Laurance Chambers, president of Bobbs-Merrill, who seemed at times a Dickensian grotesque; and the ebullient cofounder of Random House, Bennett Cerf. The reader encounters authors as various as William Faulkner, William Styron, Wright Morris, Aldous Huxley, Ayn Rand, Anaïs Nin—and Pearl Bailey. In an account of his many years as editor of *The American Scholar,* Mr. Haydn writes affectionately about the members of its editorial board, among them Christian Gauss, Irwin Edman, Jacques Barzun, Harlow Shapley, Reinhold Niebuhr, Paul Robeson, Henry A. Murray, and Van Wyck Brooks.

(Continued on back flap)

a work of intellectual history, *The Counter-Renaissance.* He was the father of two daughters and two sons, and lived with his wife, Mary, on Martha's Vineyard, where he died on December 2, 1973.

Words
&
Faces

Other Books by Hiram Haydn

By Nature Free
Manh'attan Furlough
The Time Is Noon
The Hands of Esau
Report from the Red Windmill
The Counter-Renaissance

Editor of
The Portable Elizabethan Reader

Coeditor of
Explorations in Living
A World of Great Stories
Thesaurus of Book Digests
A Renaissance Treasury
The Papers of Christian Gauss
The American Scholar Reader

Words
&
Faces

HIRAM HAYDN

Harcourt Brace Jovanovich
New York and London

Printed in the United States of America

Library of Congress Cataloging in Publication Data

Haydn, Hiram Collins, 1907–1973.
  Words & faces.

  Autobiographical.
   1. Haydn, Hiram Collins, 1907–1973. I. Title.
PS3515.A934Z52 1974   070.4'092'4 [B]   74–7184
ISBN 0–15–198460–3

First edition

B C D E

To Mike *and* Jon

Part One

T HERE ARE MANY GOOD BOOKS of general and specialized information about book publishing. I have neither the competence nor the inclination to add one more. My purpose in this book is the more modest if self-indulgent one of relating my experiences in the American publishing field for the past thirty years—especially in terms of the many interesting people I knew and worked with.

Asked to write a book of memoirs, anyone except the self-admitted great must pause and consider. What do I have to say of interest to many readers? What about my experiences warrants adding one more book to the overstock in existence? Memoirs: memories of what?

In my case, having no desire to write an analytical, introspective account of myself, I considered the possibility in two related contexts: the nature of the work, and the people I have come to know in the pursuit of that work. The profession of editing—the study and sponsorship of texts in both book and magazine form—has, I believe, some general interest among literary-minded people. But it was my memories of the people I knew through following that profession that were decisive in my accepting the offer and writing this book.

I came rather late to editorial work; I was thirty-seven when I began it. Prior to becoming editor of *The American Scholar* in 1944 and entering the field of book publishing in 1945, I had been a teacher. Following my graduation from Amherst College in 1928, I taught at the Hawken Country Day School in Cleveland for thirteen years, during the last three of which I secured a master's degree from Western Reserve University and taught evenings at Cleveland College of that university. In 1941–42 I worked for, and secured, a doctorate in Comparative Literature at Columbia University, and from July 1942 to February 1944 I taught at the Woman's College of the University of North Carolina at Greensboro, North Carolina.

When, in February 1944, I moved "permanently" to New York, it was as executive secretary of the United Chapters of Phi Beta Kappa and, ex officio, editor of *The American Scholar*. The secretaryship baffled me: the job seemed to require the talents of a public relations man, an antiquarian, and a service station operator.

One of the immediate problems confronting me was that of the publication of the *History of Phi Beta Kappa*. Written by Oscar M. Voorhees of Rutgers University, the official historian of the Society, it was composed of equal parts of statistics, roll-calling, glue and sawdust. Dr. Voorhees was a man of impeccable virtue, William Howard Taft stiff collars, and unparalleled loquacity. He was a minister, but not a practicing one; he had released Christ in favor of Phi Beta Kappa.

He was a well-meaning but intolerable bore, yet it was my duty to receive him whenever he chose to come in the offices of the United Chapters, to attend his every word, and thus to extend Christian forbearance to the limits of martyrdom.

At this time Will D. Howe was active both in Phi Beta Kappa and in book publishing. A founding member of the editorial board of *The American Scholar*, the general quarterly published by the Society, he was also a member of Phi Beta Kappa's governing body, called the Senate. He had worked for many years for Charles Scribner's Sons, had been briefly a partner of the firm of Harcourt, Brace and Howe, and was now serving Crown Publishers, a young and vigorous publishing house, in an advisory capacity. Hence he had been able to sew together two of his hats when he persuaded Crown to publish the *History of Phi Beta Kappa*.

Will Howe was a Hoosier who came on like a cross between Will Rogers and someone out of Dickens. I never could decide just which Dickensian character he reminded me of, or even

4

whether there was just one. I have at least once uncharitably tried to imagine an individual compact of Sam Weller, Mr. Micawber and Uriah Heep.

He smiled and drawled, and at whatever point he considered climactic, winked portentously, maintaining always his hayseed persona. It was difficult to dislike Will; it was still harder to take him seriously. Although he was shrewd, he had an insinuating manner that suggested he was whining when he wasn't.

Will explained to me that we were not really doing Crown a disservice by having them publish the *History*. He knew as well as I did how bad a book it was; still, it *was* the official *History*. Institutional sales in the libraries, etc., together with sales to chapters and many individual members of the Society, would make it a satisfactory publishing venture.

Perhaps so. (I believe that Crown did eventually at least break even on it.) But at this point the editorial department at Crown certainly doubted it. I was soon visited by Bertha Krantz, assistant editor at Crown, who was currently enduring the hardships of copy editing the Voorhees manuscript.

I liked Bertie Krantz right away. A bit under five feet tall, she was bright, animated, capable—a small bundle of energy and humor. She and I laughed ourselves weak over various ponderosities, circumlocutions and pontifications that dotted the script like a bad case of measles. But we also worked very hard over it.

Dr. Voorhees was mortified. He reported to all the important personages in the Society that we were ruining his life's work. He fastened me with his bald eagle's peeled eye and demanded, "Young man, for whom are you working? For Phi Beta Kappa [in the old manner, he pronounced it "Phee"], or for Crown Publishers?"

He was unconsciously prophetic. Bertie Krantz apparently reported to Edmund Fuller, editor in chief at Crown, that the Phi Beta Kappa secretary was surprisingly human, aware of the book's inadequacies, and perhaps a potentially good editor.

Fuller sought me out, and we liked each other. In turn, he introduced me to Nat Wartels and Bob Simon, the partners of Crown. Before long I was offered a post there as associate editor, and I accepted. The one job at Phi Beta Kappa that I had thoroughly enjoyed was that of editing *The American Scholar*, and thanks to the generosity of Marjorie Hope Nicolson, then president of the Society, I was able to retain the editorship of the magazine on a part-time basis, although leaving the secretaryship for the job at Crown.

Edmund Fuller is unique. The cliché goes that everyone is. But if that is so, then Fuller is more unique. Although he has by now filled out, he was at that time wiry to the point of being skinny. And he was, in his own inimitable way, an ascetic. For a certain period he ate nothing but cereal and wore only black and white.

But he was a merry ascetic. I think he told the funniest stories I have ever heard, and his puns rivaled those of Bennett Cerf for sheer atrociousness. Throughout the years during which I saw him regularly, he literally overcame the more than average number of slings and arrows pitched his way by his unequaled gift for seeing the humorous side of almost everything that happened to him.

One of his great moments occurred during a lecture. He suddenly came to a full stop, and stared out at the audience portentously. "I suppose," he said sternly, "that you are by now aware that you are listening to one of the most bigoted men you have ever heard speak."

Laughter, the staff of life. We shared a lot of it in our daily work. If either of us was depressed on a given day he would cross the hall to the other's office, and in ten minutes, at the most, feel revived.

Edmund called me "Doc." I suppose the name originated in my Ph.D., which turned out to be a handicap in my first years at Crown. Tough-minded publishers were apt to think of one who had been a professor as a high-minded, unrealistic dude who must be carefully supervised in his signing of books.

But Edmund's "Doc" was a term of affection. One of his few unhealed scars at that time lay in his never having gone to college, but there was no bitterness or envy in his choice of a name for me. "Now, Doc," he would begin, "there is a grave disequilibrium in the amount of time you spend working. Remember the parable that provided equal recompense to whose who came to work at noon and those who worked from dawn to dusk. I shall therefore, I think, harass you for a bit now, to tune your

6

nervous system to a gentle hum, and bring your eyes back to their pristine clarity."

This is not, of course, a direct quotation, but that was the way he talked. And all the time, his eyes twinkled. Bennett Cerf's were the only eyes I have ever seen *flash;* Fuller's were unique in *twinkling.* The combination of the polysyllables and the ornately formal sentence structure for the production of a burlesque style floored many people. More than once I heard a reaction of this sort: "Say, what is he, some kind of a nut?" To such a person it was fruitless to reply, "He's the most marvelous court jester since Shakespeare's, and just as profound as the best of them."

Edmund and Bertie Krantz were a great team. They worked closely together in hilarious harmony. And Edmund and I supported each other at those crucial times when we did battle with Nat Wartels, who was something of an authoritarian in running his business. Of Nat, more later. But in this context, he had hired me to develop a "high-class fiction list" and then listened with a cold ear, and read with a cold eye, most of the novels I brought him with the hope that we might publish them.

Without Edmund's backing I should probably have left Crown much sooner than I did. But I had it, as he had mine, and together we could weather the Wartelian storms.

Occasionally I thought Edmund's editorial judgment a little eccentric and he once called mine "bizarre," but for the most part we came easily to a meeting of minds. (Who was it who once said, "His editorial judgment is superb; he always agrees with me"?) And there was an especial need for this in our setup; if we had both read a manuscript and both wanted to accept it, we had of course a stronger case to present to Wartels.

I remember a little-noted but strong and touching novel by I. S. Young, called *Jadie Greenway.* It was the story of a young Negro girl (as the phrase then went) and her struggle to make her way through high school and to escape the usual snares of poverty and prostitution. One character who coveted Jadie was always saying, "You O.K., Jadie," and this became a watchword for Fuller and me. Whenever one of us found the current Crown weather oppressive, the other was apt to comfort him with "You O.K."

This sounds rather adolescent to me now. But then it and a

7

dozen other like exchanges were the salt that did not lose its savor.

Fuller is so unusual a man that his story is worth retelling. Reared in Delaware, after high school he made his at first lonely way in New York. He worked for the Federal Theatre in the thirties, and flirted with the Communists, which resulted in his becoming that rare thing, a vigorous anti-Communist who did not turn into a radical rightist. He did, however, become a devout Episcopalian, and many of our most interesting arguments were about religion.

During the Federal Theatre days, he met Ann Graham, a young actress. They married and in time had four children, two boys and two girls.

Meanwhile, in the late thirties, Edmund met Nat Wartels through a friend, and went to work at Crown, where he remained until 1947. Then, with characteristic decisiveness, he bought a farm in Vermont and moved the family there. They had never lived on a farm before, to say nothing of working one. The Vermont venture resulted in one of the funniest and yet most touching books I know, *Successful Calamity*.

Eventually he gave up and sold the farm, to enter into a new and most fulfilling adventure. I have mentioned his curtailed formal education. This lack plagued him, although he was obviously a broadly educated man. I would harangue him about this *fact,* but he stayed adamant. "I am an ignoramus, Doc, that's all there is to it—a bright man, I agree [the Fuller laugh]—but one of the ignorant, afflicted with illiteracy and acquainted with squalor."

While he was in Vermont he became the official state historian, and produced a work that bore none of the infirmities of the Phi Beta Kappa volume. In some complicated way that I don't remember, this association led to one with the head of Kent School in Kent, Connecticut, and this in turn to Edmund's appointment there as a master in the department of English.

He was, as I had been sure he would be, a fine teacher. And meanwhile he was turning out several textbooks for the school text department at Harcourt, Brace & World. These were so successful that after a few years he was able to cut down his teaching load and give more time to writing. But now he has returned to teaching, as head of the department of English at South Kent School.

The laying of his educational ghost has been good for Edmund; he has come into a mellow, more confident maturity. And he has grown a beard, prematurely snow white, that he trims in a Shavian manner. It makes him look so much like GBS that I have seen people stop in the street and stare at him, muttering to themselves.

Edmund Fuller: a man who has nurtured his eccentricities to ripeness. He has not permitted them to dominate or disfigure him; instead, he has cultivated them to his own uses. They have become attributes of his distinctiveness, as are his matchless integrity and generosity.

In 1945 Crown Publishers was (it still is) at 419 Fourth Avenue, which has since come to be called Park Avenue South. In this plain large office building Crown occupied several floors. The offices were equally plain, to the point of severity, but no one could cavil at this, because the partners shared one large room that was probably the plainest of all—almost shabby. Their desks faced each other at either end, with about thirty feet between them.

When there are two partners it is always interesting, frequently surprising, and not always instructive to learn how they divide their administrative duties. In the case of Crown, Robert Simon was in charge of sales and promotion, Nat Wartels editorial work and advertising. This startled me, for it seemed evident that Bob was a much more literary man. Before long, I understood: Crown was not a literary house.

Nat ran the show. Of this there was no question. Bob Simon's rather easygoing, passive nature fitted into this situation. But I had not been at Crown long before I learned that approximately every six months things were reversed for a day or two.

At such times, an old hand explained, tension would have been building up over several weeks. Nat's naturally aggressive and dictatorial nature would have been in high gear; he would have been ordering Bob around as though he were some junior editor or salesman. Then the breaking point. No matter who was present, Bob would explode in a supersonic rage.

9

I witnessed one such occasion. The transformation of that gentle, smiling man into a quivering, shouting embodiment of fury was of a class with the phenomena of geysers and volcanic eruptions. Nat would literally bow his head before the storm. For a day or two he would say quietly, "Yes, Bob" and "Certainly, Bob" and "Well, all right, I'll give in." But soon the balance would be restored, with Bob apparently content now that he had had his violent say; gradually the old order would be firmly re-established.

I never came to know Bob Simon well. He was consistently kind and friendly, attentive when we had occasion to talk. We never had an unpleasant word. Yet that beaming, nodding, outgoing appearance concealed a totally reticent man, about whose real nature I learned nothing of any significance during my four and a half years at Crown.

A very different matter with Nat. I dealt with him regularly and found him extremely complex and interesting.

He is a sandy-colored man, profusely freckled and rather handsome. Of middle height, he has quick intense gestures, and it was only when, unobserved, I once watched him go by that I realized his hands were soft and small, and hung limp as he walked, and that he carried his head a little to one side. At that moment I thought I saw the little boy he had been, one who worked his way into the dominant gang by his wits.

He has never married; at forty-five or so he was still living at home with his father and mother, to whom he referred with obviously genuine affection. And this fact brought me to an early realization of what at first seemed a paradox. A man of violent temper, intolerant of all opposition, arbitrary and frequently highhanded, he was capable of real sentiment and had a very low tear threshold.

Eventually I decided that this was no paradox. He had a deeply embedded sense of responsibility and an equally in-grained deposit of authoritarianism. He was the classically good Jewish son at home, though the many descriptions I heard of his life elsewhere suggested not only wildness, but at times ferocity. He was a tough, impatient autocrat in the office, but also full of benevolent paternalism. Let the most insignificant employee fall sick or get into heavy debt, let someone in an employee's family die—Nat always knew before anyone else, and always acted generously and warmly. His loans were legion, his tears ready, his support unfailing. It was as though he had made a pact with life: just simply let me run everything, and I will take good care of everybody.

I saw before long what happened to the employees he helped through their troubles: they belonged to him. He owned them. The old adage about mixing business relations and "friendship" never had more force for me than at Crown.

Nat and Bob had begun their business a few years earlier as proprietors of a remainder house. They bought books that were going out of print, being "remaindered" by other houses, at an incredibly low rate, and passed them to low-cost or discount bookstores, or to secondhand shops, for a profit. If all else failed, and they were still stuck with several thousand copies of a given title, they would sell them, for something like two cents apiece, to toy manufacturers, who ripped out the contents and used the bindings to encase some jump-up toy!

Bob was brilliant, Nat was shrewd. The Outlet Book Company gave them their start. Soon they were on their way with books of their own, and Crown Publishers was founded. When I went there in 1945 they had established themselves as outstanding publishers of books on pottery and porcelain, American glass, furniture and decoration, etc., etc. They had a knack for finding the best person to write each of these, and they produced them handsomely.

A further big step forward came with their publication of *A Treasury of American Folklore,* edited by B. A. Botkin. (This was a project jointly sponsored by Simon and Fuller.) It was a massive best seller and led to the establishment of a very profitable series, including books of New England, Southern, and Western folklore, and then Jewish and Irish.

All these, and many others, were what were known as "money-in-the-bank" books, works on subjects for which there was a substantial and sustaining audience. Moreover, because they were of high quality, they enhanced the reputation of the firm for being exceptionally able at developing books of their own conception and finding the best writers for them.

But Nat was never content to pursue a single path if he could

11

find another ready and sure market. He founded two lines of "rental library" books (a genre that disappeared with the advent of the mass paperback). I forget the names he gave these "presses," but one produced two "hots" and the other two "sweets" per month. Trashy, cheaply printed and bound, they were turned out as though by some corrupt computer, written by a few "pulp authors," and doubtless rented and read with avidity by those who sought them out in drugstores. The ultimate irony was that the editor for these two lines was a cultivated young woman possessed of a valiant social conscience and active as a liberal in politics. "It's a living," she said.

Crown had published little other fiction at this point, and my presence there was occasioned by Nat's decision to build up a "high-class fiction list." This attempt was at first a bewildering experience for me. Fresh from academic work, I had never been at close quarters with anyone like Nat. He found me somewhat unfamiliar, too. He tried to make clear what he was after. He explained that he wanted nice, respectable novels. "You know. Class," he would say, with a rather thin smacking of his lips. "Things that make people feel good."

He had an obsession with gentility, which led him to defer consistently to one employee, the editor of Lothrop, Lee & Shepard's books for children, now owned by Crown, simply because she was "a lady." He was almost obsequious to her.

Nat's desire for "class" was tempered by an ardent lust for "blockbuster best sellers." His voice would acquire reverence and his eyes would glisten as he spoke the words. And I soon discovered that the more sex and violence in a given novel the better. Yet here, too, he had his peculiar taboos. Sexual deviance disgusted him, and he could not abide a book in which "the bad guy" won. "People won't like that, Hiram," he would intone gravely, as though instructing a third-grade class.

From the beginning I knew that there was no use trying to fulfill his contradictory prescriptions unless I was to abandon altogether my own judgment and simply study his idiosyncrasies of taste. I resolved to seek the best I could find, with Edmund Fuller's help and support.

Nat was a little skeptical about the necessity of my taking literary agents to lunch at his expense, but he was won over by

Bob Simon, and by Ed Delafield, the sales manager and much the most sophisticated man in the firm in his acquaintance with the general publishing scene. And so I began this new and interesting experience of soliciting manuscripts by entertaining agents in elegant restaurants. I look back on all those drinks and all that rich food with horror. Then, I suspect, I relished it.

Most of the agents were kind to the greenhorn, full of advice and friendliness, and tentatively agreeable to submitting manuscripts. But they were largely skeptical about the kind of fiction Crown would publish. Those two lists of "hots" and "sweets" were familiar to them. They also questioned Nat's willingness to pay the going rate on advances to authors. And they doubted that he would delegate any real authority to me.

Some told me that they would not submit until they had favorable evidence about these matters. Others were ready to give me a chance. But for a while the manuscripts that came in were novels by the young and unknown, frequently not very good, or rather shoddy scripts that were a reminder of the "hots" and the "sweets."

I persisted, and I had the greatest help from Mavis McIntosh. A founding partner of the agency of McIntosh and Otis, she was now running McIntosh McKee with Elizabeth McKee. I had first met her through Douglas Rigby, a friend of mine, a writer and a painter, whom I think of as *"le boulevardier sans peur et sans reproche."* She was his agent, and she consented to become mine*—I think it was in 1944.

Over the next half-dozen years I was constantly, and happily, in her debt. At that time I was the chief support of some five people, and always in need of money—a fact that led at one point to my having received advances on four books, none of which I had then completed. A splendid way to mortgage one's nervous system!

At any rate, it was Mavis who managed to find me commissions for articles in unlikely places, such as *Reader's Digest, Collier's* and *Holiday*. It was she who secured me fatter advances in book contracts than I had dreamed of. She proposed that I conceive an idea for a series of books to present to Scribner's, since she did a

---

* At that time, two novels of mine had been published, and I hoped to earn some money by writing for magazines.

good deal of business with them and knew of their interest in such a possibility. This suggestion led, in 1946, to the development of the Twentieth Century Library.

This series was designed to present to a general audience the work of those thinkers whose ideas had most strongly affected subsequent twentieth-century thought and life. Each book was to contain a short biography, give the substance of the man's thought and trace its impact. I proposed Freud, Darwin, Marx, Veblen, Einstein, Poincaré, Spengler, William James, Dostoevsky, Dewey, Keynes and Joyce, among others.

Three of us were to collaborate in selecting subjects and writers, and in sharing the editing. Three, because Charles Scribner, Jr., a young man just out of Princeton, was serving an apprenticeship in his ancestral house; his father felt that joining in this venture from its inception would be a valuable experience for him.

The "house" editor appointed to work directly with me was Burroughs Mitchell. Burroughs is of middle height, solid. His eyes are sharp and kind. He is unpretentious, honest, commonsensical. His sense of humor, wry, ironic, sees him through the puddles and muddles life pours before all of us.

Lest this sound too much like oatmeal and tweeds, I hastily add that Burroughs is a friend to laughter. I remember in particular a lunch that he and I ate while James Jones drank Martinis. Jones was in high gear, but Burroughs, with less obvious stimulation, not only kept pace in their witty exchange, but eventually won on points. It was a gleeful lunch.

Jones and *From Here to Eternity* were Burroughs's "discovery"; it was said that he had labored as mightily with this book as his famous predecessor, Maxwell Perkins, had with Thomas Wolfe's early novels. But Burroughs is modest. If pressed, he might have quoted Perkins in this context: "One does not praise a jeweler for telling a diamond from a piece of glass."

When Leopold Infeld's book on Einstein was turned in, Burroughs and I passed it to Charlie Scribner. At Princeton he had majored in physics, and seemed on the way to becoming a nuclear physicist. But *noblesse oblige* won out; he joined his father in publishing.

Infeld, a lean gray wolfhound of a man, had earlier collaborated with Einstein on a book called *The Evolution of Physics*. He was currently under fire at the University of Toronto. There were charges of a different sort of collaboration, and not with Einstein. Soon Infeld and a friend disappeared behind the Polish Curtain.

But at this point he came to New York to discuss revisions. Charlie talked to him as a proper prep-school student might address a master. His heavy emphasis on "sir" was genuine, a strand in the fabric of background and rearing.

The burden of Charlie's criticism was that there was a chapter that was oversimplified and therefore distorted one of Einstein's ideas. The following script, like others in this book, is a paraphrase.

INFELD: But I admit the oversimplification. This book is not for physicists. Why do you object?

SCRIBNER: To distort and then explain that it's necessary is condescending to your reader, sir. The book is not for scientists, true, but it is for intelligent people.

INFELD: So what do you propose?

SCRIBNER: I think it should be rewritten, sir, to correct the distortion.

INFELD: I don't know how to do that. (With marked sarcasm) Why don't you write it over?

SCRIBNER (genuinely delighted) : Oh, may I give it a try, sir? I would like that!

He gave it a try. Infeld not only accepted every change Charlie made; he wrote a warm acknowledgment of his help.

Charlie Scribner has moved on, through the years, to a prominent place in the publishing world. Still, I often wonder what he would have achieved if he had chosen the other road. And I will never forget the picture I had of him then. A radically thin young man, wearing round, steel-rimmed spectacles, he seemed an ascetic. There is a breed of scientific ascetics, very different from the religious sort, yet sharing a simple regimen, avoiding not only luxuries but even moderate comforts. This is only conjecture about Charlie, but that's how he seemed to me. Like those others, he would, I was convinced, find ecstasy in mathematical progressions, and otherwise live frugally. (Alfred Kazin once mentioned such young scientists to me. He found a certain kind of elevation in their faces, a purity of purpose and a dedication similar to what he believed to have been true of the young Unitarian ministers in Emerson's time.) . . .

It was through my work with Scribner's that I had my one meeting with Maxwell Perkins, who had expressed some interest in the Twentieth Century Library. It was in the last year or two of his life. As I approached and entered his office, I felt as I think many people must when entering the office of the president of the United States.*

I was put at immediate ease. A slender man who looked frail, much older than his years, he wore a green eye shade to protect his eyes. This gave him superficially the appearance of an old-fashioned clerk at the local post-office window, or pehaps someone totting up one of Dickens's ledgers. But the eyes were arresting, the voice cultivated, dry, quietly authoritative.

We did not talk long. He spoke with approval of the names on the list for the series. Then he looked at me quizzically. "But you've left out the one most potent force of all," he said. "Here. I've written it at the bottom of your list."

Lenin.

Not long after Maxwell Perkins's death I began to hear that his mantle had fallen on my shoulders, that I was considered the nearest thing to him to be found. In part this legend came, I suppose, from the fact that I was much interested in working with "new" young writers.

The legend had sufficiently persisted that when I eventually went to Random House in 1955, Bennett Cerf told me, "I know you're the Branch Rickey of publishing—that you have farm systems through a lot of writing courses and so on. That's all right with me. We'll need the best of them as our Faulkners and O'Haras and Warrens wear out. All you have to do is to see to it that two out of each twenty do develop that way. They'll pay the freight for the others."

Well. I told him that it should be interesting to have Branch Rickey working for Tom Yawkey.

At first I had felt uneasy about the honorary degree that had been conferred on me so quickly—guilty, because I had a pretty

* Written before 1972.

16

clear view of just how far short of Perkins's work mine must fall. Worried, too, lest I become self-conscious or smug about it.

One subsequent development adds an insight into Maxwell Perkins. As this loose talk continued, a series of Authors wrote me and came to see me at my office. (I was then already at Crown Publishers, but worked on the side with the Scribner's series.) I capitalize Authors because so few of them seemed to me writers. That is, they wrote little, if at all. But each—novelist, story writer, poet, playwright—would bring along a few pages of traditionally yellowed manuscript, and a letter or two of encouragement from Maxwell Perkins, dated five, eight, ten years back. Each, whether wistfully, petulantly or downright aggressively, would ask me whether, on the strength of his few pages and Perkins's endorsement, I wouldn't advance him some money.

At first I would ask my visitor if he was referring to an advance against earnings, and explain that he could hardly expect a contract when so little of his work had been completed.

But this was not what they meant. It soon became clear that over those years Perkins had given handouts from his own funds to a number of these waifs who seemed to him to show promise. And indeed some of the work was promising. But none of them, it seemed clear, had developed further.

In each case I escaped the snare of mendicancy and flattery quite easily. I simply didn't have money to give away. Presumably the word was passed on, for soon the procession of Authors ceased. . . .

But I have been distracted from my account of Mavis McIntosh. One incident that displays her radical ingenuity and her mischievous sense of humor concerns my submission (at her suggestion) of a short article to *Reader's Digest* as a possibility for inclusion in a department they were then featuring called "The Most Unforgettable Character I Have Ever Known."

When Mavis suggested that I try one it was in response to my recurring need to raise some extra money. This time my wife, Mary, was about to have our first baby, and I was worried about hospital expenses. But when Mavis made her suggestion I objected that I didn't know how to write their kind of stuff and I didn't want to learn how, either.

She pointed out that if they liked a first draft sufficiently well they paid the writer a nonreturnable two hundred dollars, and if under their guidance he completed the revision to their satisfaction he received eighteen hundred dollars more. She said, furthermore, that she would help editorially. If I'd go ahead with a first draft we'd rework it before submission.

I agreed. My subject was a man named Mortimer Smeed (I used a fictitious name), who had been headmaster of the Lower School (grades 1–6) at Hawken School in Cleveland, Ohio. My first job after college had been teaching under him at Hawken. I loved and revered him. Known to all the boys as Toughy, he ran a gentle but firm school. Just and imaginative, he inspired boys and teachers alike, so that many of us returned to the school in the evenings to get on with some project on which we were working.

To write about Mort Smeed took much of the pain out of "writing to order." I took the draft to Mavis; she made some excellent suggestions; then she submitted it to that editor at the *Digest* whom she knew best.

He responded with a check for two hundred dollars, and one specific proposal for a change in the text. But its tone, he added, wasn't really of professional *Digest* quality. He knew that Mavis, being a pro, could put me straight. We worked, and submitted a new draft, which neither of us thought as good as the first one but which we hoped would suit the editor.

Not for one minute. It was farther from the true *Digest* touch than even the first one had been. He suggested we leave it where things now stood: I keep the two hundred dollars and forget the article.

Mavis persisted. She had a new idea, she told him. Let us have one more chance. He finally agreed.

What was the new idea?

Her two-thousand-year-old eyes held merriment. "Simply this," she said. (She had a quiet, clipped voice.) "We'll leave in the only specific proposal for revision he's made. Otherwise, we'll submit a clean copy of the original manuscript."

I stared at her.

"Is he that much of a fool?" I demanded.

She chuckled.

"He's not a fool," she said dryly. "But the *Digest* does strange things to intelligent people, and he's been there a long time."

With proper awe, I did what she suggested. Two days after we resubmitted, she telephoned me.

"He called me up," she said, with mirth in every syllable, "and he said, 'It's perfect now. Why couldn't he have done it that way the first time?' "

My long association with Mavis included an enduring friendship. I spoke of her two-thousand-year-old eyes. Piercingly blue, they have always seemed to me to contain clear evidence of the existence of a rare extra-dimensional wisdom. And this suggestion of—age? reincarnation?—was the more piquant in a young and delicately boned face. She had studied Eastern thought and traveled some of the paths of occult learning. I listened to her about Gurdjieff and Ouspensky.

And this made a fascinating counterpoint to the efficient businesswoman she was. She was certainly one of the best literary agents in the country—cultivated, with excellent taste and judgment and considerable business acumen.

It's difficult to describe her cool, astringent manner without doing less than justice to her femininity. She is one of the few women I have known who used to favor hats, which she wore with a certain flair. I say "cool and astringent," and I think—in the Scot's way. I have never seen her in the slightest emotional dishabille, and I have seen her in a number of trying situations. She and her husband, John Riordan, an eminent mathematician, make a striking pair.

I gladly acknowledge the much that I owe her. I am reminded particularly of a situation when I had done something foolish and ill-advised. She knew about it, and came directly to me to tell me that she did. She was in a position to salvage me, and she did, simply and immediately. Gratitude was dismissed with the brief reply, "As you would do for me."

And so, when I took the job at Crown, as usual she helped me. The scripts she submitted were the best I received. One of them was a historical romance about Lord Bothwell and the court of Mary of Scots, by a young, then unknown writer named Jan Westcott. This novel made no pretense of being "literary,"

19

although the writing was good—vivid and simple. But it had a special appeal because its author clearly believed passionately in every word she had written, in every reference to the legendary Mary and the dashing Earl.

This observation holds good for me in terms of a number of our most popular novelists. I once drove myself to the reading of several religious novels by Lloyd C. Douglas simply because I couldn't understand why his sold by the carloads and most of the other religious novels I was acquainted with—presumably similar in subject and tone—didn't sell at all. What I found was this same passionate conviction that was there in Jan Westcott's work—a conviction, manifest on every page, that persuaded the reader. And when I met Irving Wallace the intensity of his seriousness about his work suggested this same quality.

At any rate, Fuller and I took the Westcott novel to Wartels. He read it, was doubtful, compared it unfavorably to Daphne du Maurier, Thomas Costain and other popular romancers.

I persisted. Finally, with a sly grin, he said, "All right, Professor. I guess this is as good a time as any for you to start learning the facts."

Much haggling over terms. I think that Mavis finally compromised in negotiating primarily to help me get my start. But in the end it didn't matter. The book sold extremely well; it was either a full or alternate selection of the Literary Guild, and the author made just as much money as though she had had a large advance.

This book and Walter O'Meara's *The Trees Went Forth* were two of my first half dozen. O'Meara, who had won renown and made a fortune in advertising work with Benton and Bowles, and then J. Walter Thompson, had decided at forty-five or fifty—I forget which—to confine his work in that field to serving as a consultant, and to keep a long-promised tryst with his muse.

He came to me through my wife's aunt, Worth Tuttle Hedden, herself soon to win national attention with her second novel. I shall never forget our first meeting. O'Meara is a tall, dark, broad-shouldered man of such distinctive physical beauty that one is apt to meet his like only two or three times in a lifetime. Intensely black hair even now, twenty-five years later, and a ruggedly handsome face. He is what is called "Black Irish," but there is a startling resemblance to the handsomest type of American Indian. Since he grew up in the timber country of the Northwest, it was tempting to suspect him of belonging to both strains—an exotic combination, but I learned it was not true.

The Trees Went Forth is the tender and moving story of a young boy growing up among lumberjacks. For sheer lyrical simplicity and honesty of feeling, it is almost unmatchable.

Nat was pleased with this book. I never discovered how much with the book, how much with its author's being a big man in the advertising world. As do most publishers, Nat looked benevolently on prestige. Had he not, I should never have had the pleasure of publishing Leo Stein. Leo's career was shadowed during his life by that of his sister Gertrude, but increasingly he has come into his own—as a connoisseur and critic of painting, and as a writer—and even then his name meant something.

The opportunity to publish him came through my friend Douglas Rigby, who introduced me to Leo's cousin, Fred Stein. At Crown we published two books by Leo: *Appreciation: Painting, Poetry and Prose* and *Journey into the Self,* a posthumous autobiography edited by Fuller. The second relates Stein's life-long self-analysis and is quite extraordinary.

One unusual feature of my friendship with Leo Stein was that we never met. We knew each other almost intimately, but only through our extended correspondence. One contributory factor was Leo's enduring interest in the psyche. For years, after analysis with Burrow and Brill, he had been vigorously engaged in self-analysis, and he had no patience with formalities.

Oddly enough, it was at this time that I had my first editorial experiences with psychoanalysts. I met Theodor Reik at Crown. He came to my office to talk about a proposed book. Negotiations did not prosper, and I saw him only the once. But he left me with an indelible impression of a Prussian officer. I found him cold, intimidating.

I had greatly admired several of Erich Fromm's books. We wanted a book on Freud for Scribner's Twentieth Century Library, and I made an appointment to see him at his then New York apartment. I spent an hour and a half with him. During that time I asked him three questions, said "yes" or some equivalent half a dozen times, and "no" once.

I could not believe that I was hearing this torrential monologue from the man who had written books replete with sensitive, thoughtful reflections on love, on fulfillment, on the creative interplay between personalities. He went on, eyes agleam, hair askance, talking about Freud and Freud's theories, Fromm and Fromm's theories—their concordances and their differences.

Since that time he has written for the *Scholar* and we have exchanged a few letters, all reasonable and pleasant, but I have never seen him again. I sometimes think that session never really took place, that it was part of a tedious nightmare—a sort to which I am prone.

The man finally selected to write the book on Freud was Gregory Zilboorg—and a fine book it was. But the author . . . something else.

To dignify further our invitation, Charlie Scribner went with me to Zilboorg's apartment. The Great Man was sporting a Czar Nicholas II outfit, and he pranced, postured and gamboled, and regaled us with Zilboorgiana for more than an hour.

Our mission accomplished, Charlie and I descended by elevator in silence. As we left the building, he said, "Whew! Good to be out."

Yet I have heard, or overheard, a half-dozen spontaneous tributes to Zilboorg from people he helped—"saved," said one.

I had several long editorial sessions with him. When at work, he was quiet, attentive, serious. The moment work was concluded, he was ebullient, exhibitionistic, even clownish. I remember well, and with horror, the way he played with his six-month-old baby, the product of a new marriage.

"See," he would say, tossing the infant some three feet in the air and catching it, "see this proof of Zilboorg's virility—at my age, this!"

I know this sounds improbable. But it happened—that way—once.

When our job was completed he invited me to lunch, to celebrate. He would be off to Europe in a few days.

"You will have," he said juicily, "zee famous Zilboorg Martini. You are a fortunate man."

I have forgotten his exact *new* address, of course, but let us call it 7 East Sixty-fourth Street. I arrived at the agreed time, but was forced to wait outside while movers carried a large sofa out to their van. After barely escaping the next load by pressing myself flat against the wall, I entered a large, luxuriant duplex apartment and asked one of the movers if he knew where Dr. Zilboorg was.

"No," he said, "they've all gone. They're on their way to Europe."

Free as the caged bird whose liberty Leonardo bought, I happily sought and found a French restaurant down the street. While eating, I mused on the vagaries of psychoanalysts.

But when I returned to the office, my secretary told me that Dr. Zilboorg had phoned three times. Heavyhearted, I dialed the number.

"Vere vere you? I vaited, and drank all zee excellent Martinis. You do not like Zilboorg, after all?"

I told him what had happened.

"Seven East Sixty-fourth? Seven East Sixty-fourth! But I am at Six East Seventy-fourth. Ah, I have caught you out. Freud and I have caught you out!"

Freud and he had caught me out. . . .

Reik considered himself Freud's only heir. Zilboorg assured me that he was the man on whose shoulders the purple mantle rested. So when Abram Kardiner began telling me of his intimacy with Freud I was hardly surprised. But Kardiner's style was quite different from those of his colleagues. He held the floor quite as long as they, but much more quietly.

I found him unusually *aware*. His dark eyes were always watching attentively. They seemed to belong to an entity separate from the rest of him. It was as though they were carefully observing not only you—me—but also his own performance as, entertaining raconteur that he was, he told story after story.

His control of an occasion was insidious. He had a soft, purring voice, all the more insistent for its low key. And he was insistent; he wanted total immersion. Should your attentiveness waver for only a moment his hand would reach out and grasp your arm, gently but firmly. And all the time, the eyes—alert sentries, whose guard was never changed.

We published a book of his, *Sex and Morality*, at Bobbs-

Merrill (to which I went from Crown in 1950). It required more editorial work than the others I have mentioned—so much that we arranged for a fine young editor named Adie Suehsdorf to concentrate on it. . . .

In only one case did I, in a similar fashion, take on a free-lance job myself. I had been much impressed by several books of Karen Horney's, especially *The Neurotic Personality of Our Time*. When in 1949 a common friend recommended me to her for work on her new script, *Neurosis and Human Growth,* I eagerly took the job. For some four months we worked together three nights a week.

Most of the psychoanalysts I knew, except for those in her school, tended to depreciate her work. Her deviation from many of Freud's ideas came, it was alleged, from her resentment of his convictions about women; she was, one said, a feminist theoretician. But I had not found this true of her books. Nor did I find them shallow, or her a popularizer—two other frequent charges. That of popularization developed, I was sure, from the fact that her books were so well written—or edited—that they were immensely readable, while almost all the others in the field were both turbid and turgid. Fromm seemed to me the only real writer among them.

I was curious to find out the origin of Horney's style. How much of it was her own, how much an editor's? I found that she had a vivid flair for words and phrases; her single important difficulty was sentence structure.

She was, I believe, the daughter of a Norwegian father and a Dutch mother. Her education and primary language were German, and despite her splendid English vocabulary she wrote a heavy Germanic sentence. It was to overcome these constructions that she needed an editor.

The first revised chapter that I took to her had been prepared hastily because of an overload of work at Crown. I never made that mistake again. In a low, quiet tone, she took me right over those legendary coals. And they were hot! The knowledge that she was completely right found me speechless and ashamed.

My next work—redoing the first chapter and editing the second—was meticulous. Very soon her uneasiness disappeared, and from then on we had one of the happiest collaborations I've known.

Karen Horney had sea-captain blue eyes, a husky, almost guttural voice, and a sturdy, squarish body. In her sixties, she was vigorous and forthright. I remember with happy amusement the night she came to a party at our house, wearing a filmy evening dress and Ground Gripper shoes!

"My feet hurt," she said when some audacious person commented on the shoes. And that was that.

After the self-conscious, guarded presence of a Kardiner, the posturing of a Zilboorg, the frosty majesty of a Reik and the obsessed insistence of my nightmare Fromm, Horney was a blessing. She had genuine, simple human dignity; I never saw any evidence of a need to impose her "importance" on anyone.

Characteristic was the situation in which I found her one evening. This time her apartment door was open to admit me, for she was on her knees, presenting only her broad backside as she struggled to find her little dog's ball, which had rolled under the couch. Clutching it, she struggled up, her face red from the exertion.

"So," she said cheerfully, "we cannot always present our best side."

We usually worked from eight to ten, had a beer or sherry, and parted. One night, when we had carried on longer than usual, the doorbell rang.

It was Paul Tillich. I had never met him, and when Horney (everyone who worked with her seemed to call her just "Horney") invited me to stay, I was delighted.

What a dialogue! Soon they apparently realized that my happiness was in listening to them, and ceased trying to draw me in. I cannot remember the details, but the quality of their thought and expression was unforgettable. They tossed challenges and responses at each other; ideas bounced in the air. And however masculine Horney seemed to many people, she was utterly feminine in this exchange. It was a meeting of profound minds; it was also a loving exchange between a man and a woman.

I learned later that this was a frequent occurrence: Tillich often broke his evening walk by stopping in to see her about ten-thirty.

The sequel is sad. Karen Horney died of cancer, and, I was told by one of her close associates, died angry, fiercely protesting in the manner of that famous poem by Dylan Thomas. (In fact, I was told by several of her group that she was a very difficult woman, full of violent moods. I never encountered them. Even the tongue-lashing she had given me that first evening had been low-pitched.)

I went to the funeral and saw Paul Tillich for the second time. He conducted the service. When he spoke of Horney, he was so restrained, so remote, that the effect was depersonalizing, peculiarly sterile. I could not understand it.

Then he came to the benediction. He never finished it. He broke down. . . .

My editorial sessions with Nat Wartels remain my most vivid memories of Crown, except for those of Edmund Fuller. Nat had scant patience with another's argument, once he had made up his own mind. I wish for no more than a penny for every time he cut me short, lifting that soft hand, fingers tight and palm extended obliquely toward me in a slicing motion, saying in exasperation, "Now wait a minute—Just a moment—Let me tell you—" And he opened every discussion, "I'll tell you . . ."

I have experienced more than my share, I think, of men in charge, whether in academic life or in publishing, who were always irritated, sometimes infuriated at interruptions, yet themselves constantly interrupted others. In my publishing encounters, Nat was their prototype.

Another of his characteristics that interested me was his manner of awarding praise. If the occasion was more or less public, as in a sales conference, he would roll out smoothly and resonantly his praise of books he rated highly. "It's a winner," was usually his culminating line, "a real winner, boys."

But this, after all, was endorsement of a book. Praising a colleague or an employee, especially if alone with him, was a very different matter. He would adjust his face to an expression of pleasure, say rather rapidly, "That's a good piece of work, Hiram," and look away. There was little danger of being spoiled.

When Nat looked away, it was usually at his desk. Its appearance would have been terrifying to most people, but it didn't bother him. Not even a patch of its upper surface was visible. Piled at least eight inches high in random, overlapping fashion were pieces of paper—in all sizes, colors, shapes and states of preservation. To anyone else the realization that this rubbish heap constituted his files of correspondence, estimates, contracts, budgets, etc., would have been desolating. But this extraordinary man could reach out his hand at any time and burrow and tunnel without hesitation to the single sheet he wanted. He relished his control over apparent chaos.

Nat, I found, was a driver. He drove himself and everybody else. Much of this, of course, was simply his temperament, but there was an economic factor contributing to his frenetic pace, as well.

As is common knowledge, book publishing is so constituted that huge investments are made in printing, producing and promoting a whole season's list months before two cents' return will be coming in. So the banks make seasonal loans to book publishers. And Crown was no exception. Indeed, being a young publisher, with little opportunity to build up a strong back list as yet (though one was definitely on the way), Crown was often short of cash. But Nat performed an intricate juggling act, and with some help from Bob Simon and others he brought it off.

Nor was he in any way niggardly; on the contrary, given a book in whose sales potential he believed, he spent heavily. He was a gambler, and a shrewd one. I learned much from him about the commercial possibilities of particular subjects for books. And frequently his hunches about fiction were impressive, revealing to me aspects of a given book that I had overlooked.

I think what most upset Fuller and me about our meetings with Nat was, first, the abrupt way in which he'd summon us (till we finally admitted to each other that we felt like schoolboys on our way to the principal's office), and, second, the scant respect he seemed to have for our opinions.

"But how do I know that it's really as good as you say?" he'd demand. "I'm not a literary man. I can't be sure. Who would be a good person to send it to to find out? Do you know Clifton Fadiman?"

On the bald face of it this may seem incredibly naïve. But not so. Nat's attitude is not unusual—simply more bluntly and radically expressed than those of many, many colleagues (most of them working in the sales and business aspects of publishing) in all the houses in which I have worked. Whatever an editor's credentials as a man of literary taste and judgment, they are given scant weight by the sales department or, frequently, by the administrators of the house.

The latter fact has its built-in ironies. The editor is with the publishing house for the purpose of selecting and securing books. The editors of any trade department are eventually responsible for the large majority of the books the house publishes. Does it seem sensible to entrust the selection of the product you are to produce, advertise, and sell to people in whose opinion of those projects you have small confidence?

The reasoning among sales managers and salesmen, at least at sales conferences, frequently goes like this. This editor chose this book. Naturally he's going to try to sell us a bill of goods. He wants to look good to the partners (or the president or other executive). So he tells us this is the greatest new young novelist to appear in some time. How do we know? That's no handle to sell a book. We need first novelists like we need holes in our heads. Editors! I suppose they're necessary, though I sometimes wonder.

And in most houses, at the second session of the sales conference editors are excluded, while the others decide the number of copies to print, and the salesmen are instructed how many copies to try to place in the bookstores in advance of publication.

Now it is certainly true that there have been and are editors who have a tendency to oversell, to praise each book as a rare jewel. But the majority of us can recognize a suicidal pattern when we see one. Honesty about one's judgment concerning a book is of crucial importance.

Let me put aside the usually fairly good-humored cold war between the editorial and sales departments. Whether with Lew Miller at Random House or with George Vay and Ed Hodge at Harcourt Brace Jovanovich, I have always felt happily free to punch and get punched. These three marvelous men I have often called "formula-ridden old pros" to their faces, and they have responded with various versions of "egghead" and "Professor." I think in this connection especially of George, who would never want you to know how independently sensitive an intelligence he has. He and Ed Hodge brought to my active time at Harcourt Brace Jovanovich an almost daily joy.

But the sort of confrontation I have described between Wartels, on the one hand, and Fuller and me on the other, is a different matter. And it is not uncommon, though usually more covert. But I remember one publisher I barely knew confiding to me that all his editors were "rotten. Pathetic."

"Why don't you fire them?" I asked him.

He looked at me pityingly.

"For what? More of the same." Then he poked me in the ribs to show me it was all good, clean fun.

To return to Nat Wartels. One season Edmund Fuller and I were tremendously impressed by a novel we had under contract. We considered it stunning. It was *The Other Room,* by Worth Tuttle Hedden. It was the story of a young Southern white woman, a recent college graduate, who went to teach in a predominantly black school in Louisiana. Her experiences, including falling in love with a young black man, bordered on the radical for 1947. We felt it had a fine sales potential as well as being a really good novel.

But Nat couldn't see it. "Now wait a moment—Listen—Let me tell you."

Then, only two weeks before its publication, Aaron Sussman of Sussman and Sugar, Crown's advertising agents, called Nat up and urged him to read a report on *The Other Room* written by Nina Lowenstein, one of Aaron's readers. Nat did, and called Edmund and me to his office. When we finished reading the report, Nat, who had been watching us intently, said, "Now we have confirmation. What shall we do?"

This report did indeed confirm what we had been saying about the book. But the authority in this case was a young woman working at her first job in an advertising agency. Just so that it was not an intramural judgment!

Convinced, Nat acted. He took a full-page advertisement in the first Sunday *Times* book section with available space (costing then about two thousand dollars), exclusively for *The Other*

Room, with the heading "We Almost Missed This One." This sort of (usually) disingenuous confession advertising was a specialty of Simon and Schuster, whom Nat greatly admired. But as best I can remember, the idea for this particular advertisement was Aaron Sussman's.

The Other Room "did" moderately well after its late start, although, in my opinion, not nearly so well as it could have if it had been handled with confidence from the beginning. It found its large audience in the Bantam paperback version. In this edition it sold more copies in the first month after publication than any previous Bantam title.

I tell the story at this length not to show Fuller and me right and Wartels wrong, but to illustrate the extreme to which this curious anomaly about editors may go. . . .

At its worst, Nat's temper was vicious. I had been at Crown only a couple of months when he let me have it broadside, including some pretty insulting language. I had a rather well developed temper myself. I stood up and said, "If you ever talk like that to me again, I'm through."

I knew right then that I had won the argument. I knew it because I saw, with some amazement, that at least for that moment Nat was afraid of me. And he never did talk that way to me again.

So I learned something that I now think I should have learned soon after puberty: men in authority who bully subordinates are probably cowards. And as a tangential generalization: men in authority who are tough and hard but basically sound like subordinates who fight back when they have legitimate grounds. And finally, if you stand up and deliver the truth as you see it, however tactlessly, you are likely to be treated with respect by those you work with.

These quaint precepts came to me, as I have said, belatedly, and largely through working under Nat Wartels, D. L. Chambers, president of the Bobbs-Merrill Company, and Bennett Cerf—in widely different contexts and widely different ways.

But I found it corrupting knowledge. When, fresh from sixteen years on a campus, I first stood up to declare myself, and continued to say in this new publishing world just what I meant, they were innocent acts. I was ingenuously doing what I had been doing up to then. But in this business world, the reactions seemed to me unfamiliar: surprise, fear, respect—in different quotas from those of the past. I had left academic life partly because I felt untested; I wanted to come out from the shelter of that desk. And I stumbled naïvely on the knowledge I have just been describing. Now I knew; I had eaten the apple. How could I follow these courses spontaneously any longer?

I am not sure that I could—or did. . . .

Crown was a fairly tough apprenticeship in publishing—especially for someone coming from academia. As for me personally, there were two scores against me: I had been a professor, and I was not Jewish. Fuller had only the second one to live down, as had Ed Delafield, the sales manager.

A study of Jews in publishing could make fascinating reading. It is quite true that the old-line houses were anti-Semitic in muted, Ivy League, button-down-collar ways. Publishers as outstanding as Cerf and Klopfer of Random House never would join the Publishers' Lunch Club because they knew they had been excluded in the earlier days for being Jewish.

But by the time I came into publishing, the leaders in the business were Jews: Alfred Knopf, Richard Simon, Max Schuster, Bennett Cerf, Donald Klopfer, Ben Huebsch, Harold Guinzburg . . . I could go on and on. Yet even then the old-line houses (they shall be nameless) seldom had Jews in key positions. In counterpoise, though not necessarily in retaliation, there were apt to be few non-Jews in positions of importance in "Jewish" houses.

And this was true of Crown. Delafield, Fuller and I were the exceptions. Nor do I mean to imply that there was conscious antigentilism. It was simply that none of us was one of "the boys"; none of us belonged to "the gang." I remember a genial moment when Nat said to me, "You're our goy; by now Fuller's a Jew. So I want to try something out on you. Read this."

I took home an advance copy of a book called *The Old Country*. It was a translation into English of a selection of Sholom Aleichem's stories, an excellent translation by the Butwins, man and wife. I read it, entranced. I came back to Nat and said, "It's simply incredible. He's one of the greatest writers I've ever read. And I'd never heard of him."

We met fully in that moment. As we talked on about the stories, I saw a Wartels new to me—sensitive, loving, open. And it is of that talk I think when I remember Nat with affection, which I do, as a matter of fact, quite often. Not just on this unique level, but in those lighter moments when he was actually relaxed. Then, his charm was authentic.

The second score against me, that of being "a professor," was the harder to overcome. Many of the people I worked with in these first years seemed to feel a certain respect for my having a doctorate, but simultaneously tended to place me, respect and all, on a shelf, or in a corner, while they went on conducting business with regular people.

This way my experience at Crown was a little like that I had had years before when entering high school. I didn't belong; I was an outsider; I became a loner. There was a conviction that I wasn't a regular, one of the guys—a conviction I shared. And I remember now one violent session Edmund and I had with Nat. When I met Nat in the corridor the next morning, he said, "What! You here? I thought you'd be home sulking."

But all this passed, and by the time I left, in July 1950, to go to Bobbs-Merrill (Fuller had left for Vermont three years before) I felt fairly much at home at Crown. One of the friendships that grew there was with Ed Delafield, a man racked by fierce tensions but full of warmth and kindness.

My decision to go to Bobbs was ultimately determined by the promise that, as their New York editor, I could choose my own books without consultation. I wanted that freedom and that responsibility. So I left an authoritarian regime, little aware that I was entering a more absolute authoritarian regime, one with a long-standing tradition.

My earliest experiences with the old Indianapolis firm of Bobbs-Merrill had occurred in the late 1930s. One of their editors had expressed a more than passing interest in one of those unwanted novels of mine that I kept peddling.

Nothing came of this at the time, but in the fall of 1941 I sent Bobbs an outline for a new novel, together with a long opening section. At last, after twelve years of rejections, I received a contract. The president of the firm, David Laurance Chambers, had been persuaded to risk an advance of four hundred dollars on this project.

Never has human hand squeezed a dollar bill tighter than did Mr. Chambers's. A sure thing had to be a sure thing had to be a sure thing before he would give it more than token promotion and backing. My first novel, *By Nature Free,* published in 1943, was supported by inclusion in several "list" advertisements, and went its way to quiet death. The reviews were staggeringly good, but Mr. Chambers's response to my request for more advertising was to assure me that the budget was used up and I should be content with such good reviews. He furthermore sent me now—and only now—a copy of a pre-publication review in one of the trade journals, praising the book as "the best novel about small-town life since Sinclair Lewis's *Main Street,"* and predicting a large sale. Finally, he enclosed a copy of his letter to that reviewer, stating that the praise was welcome, but the prediction way off the mark. "I see no large sales possibility for this book," he wrote, "and we do not intend to promote it in that fashion."

You could call it candor.

A much more startling example of Mr. Chambers's penuriousness and stubbornness involved another novel Bobbs published that year: Ayn Rand's *The Fountainhead.* Despite an unmistakable groundswell of excitement over this book, DLC, as we all knew him, gave it only the most perfunctory advertising support. Solely through "word of mouth" (enthusiasts urging others to read it), *The Fountainhead* became a runaway best seller.

In 1945, I finally met DLC, and found him in person a type familiar back in World War I days, with a rather pale soft face, pince-nez and a straw skimmer—all reminiscent of Woodrow Wilson* and Walter Hines Page. But though he was courteous and cultivated in manner, I had had several bristling letters from him, alternated with gracious assurances of esteem, and should by now have realized that there were steel teeth in this trap.

Indeed, in 1945 and '46 we exchanged unfriendly letters and one phone call during which we both shouted. The issues were

* Incidentally, Chambers had done secretarial work for Woodrow Wilson at Princeton.

lack of advertising for my books and my request to be released from the firm option he held on my next book, through an outdated clause in the Bobbs-Merrill contract. My first contract had specified that I should submit my next two books, and if they were accepted, I should receive *the same advance* against royalties that Bobbs had accorded *By Nature Free:* four hundred dollars! Now that I was in New York I had discovered what advantage he had taken of my ignorance of contractual matters.

He finally released me, in a fit of temper during the telephone exchange to which I have referred. I assumed that my relation to the firm was permanently ended.

Hence I was surprised to have a phone call, early in 1950, from Ross Baker, the sales manager, who worked in the company's New York offices, only a couple of blocks from Crown. He and I had been friendly, but it had been a long time since we had been in touch with each other.

Our first two lunches mystified me. Ross made cautious references to being on the lookout for a new editor, saying that the present one, John L. B. Williams, a quiet gentleman I knew and liked, and DLC were having trouble, and it was clear that Williams was going to be fired. All this was very confidential. I waited for him to ask me if I would be interested in the job, but he didn't.

I liked Ross even more than before, but I was also beginning to understand him better. He was then the wariest of men. He could be confidential about a necktie, cautious about the selection of a salad: "But does it come with romaine or real lettuce? Does the Roquefort dressing cost more than the other kinds?"

For, whether or not through his association with DLC, Ross was, *it seemed,* stingy to a heroic degree. He had no children and a wife of independent means, yet he scrimped and saved astonishingly. We once stood on a street corner for half an hour, arguing whether I should take a cab (on the expense account) to my luncheon appointment, or the subway. He was headed in my direction, but he would not share the cab I eventually took. We were both, of course, late for our appointments.

One evening he chose a dinner spot for us because it was the only restaurant he knew where if two people chose the same entree, they could get two meals for the price of one and a half!

He knew every shop in New York that undersold its competitors. He purchased furnishings from wholesalers he had cultivated. He bought excellent secondhand cars from a dealer he had once done a favor. His life seemed to be one obsessive pursuit of bargains. When I came to know him really well, I finally asked the inevitable question: "Why?"

He looked at me shrewdly. "You never know when it'll come in handy."

This story has a happy ending. But first, an account of the warm heart under this inscrutable "miserliness." Twice, during the years we worked together, I was in financial straits and much worried. Neither time did I say a word to Ross, but each time I found a sealed note on my desk, my name on the envelope in his spiked Gothic hand, and inside a personal check for one thousand dollars. The first note read, "Will this tide you over?" I accepted gratefully, and paid him back in a few months. The second time I had just solved my problem and so thanked him but refused.

Ross's politics were somewhere to the right of Calvin Coolidge's. Yet one of his best friends was the distinguished editor Angus Cameron, who was an ardent leftist. When Angus was fired from Little, Brown for alleged Communist leanings,* during the McCarthy days, Ross promptly wired him, "Bring your family and stay in my town house till you've made new arrangements. We'll be in the country."

A handsome man, Ross, with bright-blue eyes and red hair and mustache. Square-shouldered. I was only momentarily surprised when, watching a Bastille Day parade in Paris, I saw Ross at the head of a battalion, resplendent in plumed hat and blue uniform. I realized then that I had always known he was really a

---

* Amusing and appropriate irony: soon thereafter, Angus, whom I know and greatly respect, was hired by Alfred A. Knopf. Congratulated for his action in that timorous era, Mr. Knopf is reported to have replied, "It's a lot of nonsense. I don't believe any of it. And it's not brave of me when everyone knows that politically I'm right of the right-field foul line. As for Cameron, he's simply one of the best editors around. I'd be a fool not to take him."

captain of cavalry. And yet, though often dashing in appearance, he is most affectionately memorable to me as I used to see him on our trips to Indianapolis, with a suitcase in either hand, trudging resolutely from railroad station to hotel, solid, tenacious, somehow a symbol of reassurance.

And now back to "You never know when it'll come in handy." Ross retired early, when new powers came into control at Bobbs. He and his wife, long estranged, had a friendly divorce; she, British, returned to live in England.

He was alone. He went to Europe and stayed several years, traveling in a camping Volkswagen. I received occasional long letters that made him sound determined not to be lonely. Then a different kind: he was marrying a lovely woman (confirmed by Angus Cameron one day at lunch). And now they are living in that country house; we have been there: they're a great pair.

Of all these matters, of course, I knew nothing when we were lunching together in 1950. It was only at the third lunch that he cautiously hinted that Bobbs might be interested in me if I was interested in Bobbs. And it was another month or two before we finally worked it out. I insisted that I would come only if I were given a free hand editorially, with no consultation with DLC required.

Ross had friends at court out at Indianapolis, and it was probably through them that he at last persuaded Mr. Chambers. So, along about July 1, I said good-by to Crown and went to work at Bobbs.

The editorial department was undergoing a clean sweep, and Ross arranged for me to have a series of appointments with applicants for the post of assistant editor. It developed that I needed only one; I appointed the first man I met.

This was Louis Simpson, who was to become one of our finest poets. I have deleted the page or two I wrote about him since reading in his recent *North of Jamaica* of the distaste and contempt with which he viewed his publishing experience—he worked only at Bobbs—lest his more than nominal appearance in this book offend his sensibilities.

Louis began his work at Bobbs-Merrill the very day I did; he was the first member of the small editorial staff I built there. The second was Elizabeth Bragdon (later Easton, and now an established editor at the Book-of-the-Month Club), who was in charge of publicity when I came to Bobbs. Tall, shy, not wholly recovered from an upbringing that had taught her to accept a subordinate place in the scheme of things, she was strained by her job, for it required going out and "selling" our books to reviewers and book-review editors, as well as squiring authors to interviews and radio and television programs. She yearned for the putative privacy and stimulation of editorial work, and when the chance came I secured it for her.

Betty is intelligent and industrious, and her primary interest in general (I will go to all lengths to avoid that nonword, "nonfiction") books, especially on topical subjects, nicely balanced Louis's concern with fiction, poetry and belles-lettres. But both had little or no editorial experience, and when I finally added a third young person to our staff, I compounded this disadvantage.

I did not do so ingenuously or haphazardly. I had a theory that what mattered most in an editor was intelligence, sensitiveness to a variety of stimuli, and a reasonably rich intellectual background. I believed that I could act as a guide to professional skill, despite the meagerness of my own experience in less than five years with Crown.

I was mistaken. Coming to Crown as I had, after an almost exclusively academic life, there was a great deal that I did not know about the all-around editor's job. I knew next to nothing about book production; I found the "cost sheet," the careful inquiry into how and at what point one could "come out" with a given book, as obscure as the Eleusinian mysteries. I had a fine disdain for the salesman's commercial emphasis, and I resented any curb on the acquisition of *good* books, regardless of the limited sales they could command. Worse still, I fondly believed that I could, on my own, transform the mediocre Bobbs list into an outstanding one, and simultaneously find the time to instruct these young people in the fine art of editing. The result—let us be moderate—was less than satisfactory. My assistants were, I see now, generous; they did not complain. I have always been a poor administrator, delegating work but never really relinquishing it. And the overload I was carrying led me to alternate periods of gentle benevolence and paternal assurance with—to their appar-

37

ent bewilderment—ones of intolerance and impatience. Assuring them of the freedom I wanted them to feel and assume, I would then supervise even the smallest details of their work—to make sure that everything was as it should be.

This was harder to do with the third assistant editor than with Louis and Betty. They must often have shaken their heads sadly; *he,* erratic and willful, bucked and objected.

John J. Maloney had a brilliant mind and an extraordinary gift for the writing of fiction. A great devotee of Scott Fitzgerald, he surpassed the best of his master's work in his own. But his own was a dismally small output, measured quantitatively.

I first encountered John at the New School for Social Research, early in the twelve-year stretch during which I conducted a novel workshop. Among the students in this course who later became practicing novelists were William Styron, Sigrid de Lima, Thomas Gallagher, Mario Puzo, George Mandel, Daniel Stern, Bel Kaufman, Nancy Hallinan, Leonard Bishop, William Michelfelder, Diana Chang, Sonya Arcone, Hamilton Maule, Morris Renek, Diana Cavallo, Florence Cummings and Jefferson Young. Yet none of them blazed so spectacular a path across my consciousness (and some of theirs) as John Maloney.

It became evident in class almost immediately that this blue-eyed, sweating, stiff-jointed Irishman had an unusual critical mind. Speaking in jerky spurts, muscles tightened with the effort and perspiration three-dimensional on his forehead, he would reach unerringly for the elusive kernel of whatever fictional problem and grasp it, show it to us. At the end of his first semester with me, I went to my friend Clara Mayer, the dean of the New School, and said, "I have in my workshop a student who should be teaching a course."

In characteristic fashion, she saw Maloney several times, quizzed him dryly, then appointed him to the faculty. I believe that he did well for a while, but I had been unrealistic in my expectations. For John was a drinker, and became a prodigious one.

I have mentioned his own writing. When he was in my class, I read about one hundred pages of his first novel, a work derivative from James Joyce yet possessing an unmistakable originality and demonstrating his magical gift with words. He had only one copy of this manuscript, and it disappeared when he paused too long, in the process of moving from one apartment to another, to have several Martinis in a tavern.

For he was not only an alcoholic, but what is known as a "loser." The undertow of defeat, loss, death overcame the rhythm of the waves of his life. Let there be only the smallest possibility of making a promising venture go wrong, and he would find it.

Long later, in 1960, he made his second try, and submitted only thirty-five pages of a new novel to me at Atheneum, hoping for a contract. By then I had become so involved in his life that I did not trust my own judgment (that it was superb) and passed it over to Michael Bessie, who had some reason to distrust and dislike John. Yet the very next morning Bessie came in and said, "What can you do? He'll probably never finish it, but how can you turn it down?"

We gave him the contract; he wrote very little more. He settled, probably only half-consciously, for a "literary life." All the young writers who had enrolled in the novel workshop came to know and like him: especially De Lima, Styron, Puzo, Mandel, Gallagher. Through them, he extended his circle of literary acquaintances to include, among others, Norman Mailer and Joseph Heller. For a while he and Styron shared an apartment, later he and Bob Loomis, the solid, reliable Random House editor.

I stress those qualities (Bob has others) because they were so alien to John. Yet he was poignantly lovable—exasperating, at times wild to the point of endangering those about him, but compact of such warmth and imagination and wit that one could forgive and forget, it seemed at the time, almost endlessly. And in the talk, the interminable, delightful talk, about writers and writing and life and living and other small discreet topics, he was a peer and colleague of the first order to all of us.

He and I shared another passion, which added a special zest to our conversations: baseball. I have read several pieces that purported to explain the predilection of eggheads for this sport, but not one writer has satisfied me that he has a definitive explanation of this frenzied obsession. And I have been an addict since the age of seven.

John was a Giant fan. New York? San Francisco? If the

Giants had moved to Singapore, his allegiance would not have suffered even a tremor. The Giants were the Giants. And Willie Mays was Mr. Baseball. I would urge on him the superior qualities of Tris Speaker or Joe DiMaggio, simply to force him to more superlatives and more statistics substantiating the unequaled greatness of Mays.

But the golden days became tarnished; John's condition worsened; he would meet you for lunch and have two double Scotches before, literally, feeling able to talk at all. One by one his devoted friends became unavailable. There was no diminution of affection. But this one had small children, who had watched several drunken scenes; that one went to work early and could not keep John's hours; another was outraged by the way John alienated his other friends, who began to avoid *him*.

I shared at least the first two reasons, but our (temporary) break came after an attempt to persuade him to "take the cure." Alone, I could never have succeeded, but I had expert aid from William Michelfelder, a novelist who wrote two heartbreakingly disillusioned novels about Roman Catholics, and who was an active worker in Alcoholics Anonymous. Bill was a long, quizzical man whom I thought of, for some reason, as a wizard. And he knew what he was talking about, was authoritatively convincing. He made all the arrangements, and one desolate rainy night, the three of us took a cab to Roosevelt Hospital.

At one red light we had to restrain John physically from climbing out. He had the fierce strength of the terrified and drunken, but we managed. We finally entered the hospital and started down a long corridor, John lurching in advance. Suddenly a big, tough nurse stepped out of a doorway, saw him, and with a swift practiced blow knocked his glasses off, sending him reeling against the wall.

The brutality of the act and the pitiable, frenzied terror to which John was now reduced were too much for me. Despite Michelfelder's rational protests I took John away. Took him back to his apartment, where for hours he threatened me with a knife for having tried to betray him.

I did not see him for some time, and heard little about him. Then came a call, in 1961, asking me if he could bring a friend out to see Mary and me in Westport. We agreed uneasily, but the friend turned out to be Giosi Lippolis, an Italian writer and translator, a gentle and sensitive woman obviously devoted to John.

They were married and before long moved to Rome, where he died of the second of two heart attacks, in 1968. We had had a further estrangement, but during the last couple of years had resumed writing to each other. I cannot believe that life with him during those years was much easier than before, but Giosi's dedication apparently overcame all obstacles, and after his death she wrote a very moving letter about what *he* had done for *her*.

I like to think exclusively of the John who loved baseball, who intoned *Finnegans Wake* like scripture, who wrote those dazzling fragments, who was so gentle and *simpatico* with little children. But I am, I fear, a sentimentalist. For his *whole* story is prototypical for so many artists, and a cardinal letter in the lexicon of life. . . .

At any rate, in 1952 I hired John at Bobbs-Merrill. I, a sentimentalist? A madman.

He did some excellent work, but his perfectionism (a contributing factor to his scant creative output) was so extreme that he would sometimes make three or four drafts of a "reader's report" advising me to reject a certain manuscript before he would turn it over to me! And his other difficulties slowly became more prominent right there in the office. It was with immense inhibited relief that I wished him well in a new job with one of the television networks. . . .

I have described at some length my staff at Bobbs because I want to suggest our parochial intimacy (Louis and John and I took into our gang that fine woman, Lillian Brahms, who moonlighted as a secretary) before I move on to the different world of the home office in Indianapolis, and to my four-year struggle with D. L. Chambers.

Others in the New York office were, of course, equally aware of the radical discrepancies between the conduct of business in New York and in Indianapolis. The New York office was cozy and very homely: Miss Knox, an octogenarian whose sole duty was to dispense petty cash, had approached my wife, when she worked at Bobbs, to ask if she could hang her stockings (wet) in *her* office, since they dried better there. They flapped, comically dismal, above the glass partition.

Before I left, Ross Baker was in charge of the office, but when I arrived in 1950, he and Walter J. Hurley, a ruddy, pleasant man in charge of production, shared responsibilities and to some extent a competitive rivalry. Each had his girl Friday, each his supporters. The gingerly balance of power, however, created the effect of a benign cold war rather than overt friction.

Over us all hung the elongated shadow of DLC, but the threat of a Calvinistic deity six hundred miles away caused only a subdued uneasiness rather than (as I was to discover) the desperation of finding oneself directly under the surveillance of his terrifying Eye. Technology had produced the telephone and the dozens of varieties of memorandum pads, pink, blue, yellow, white and green, that DLC dispensed with an overgenerous hand, but we were spared his Presence.

History was frightening, too. The New York publishing populace would have been drastically reduced had the Bobbs-Merrill alumni been removed from its ranks. Almost every week I encountered yet another highly successful editor, sales manager, production chief, who had been fired by David Laurance Chambers. There was a joke tirelessly repeated: "I owe everything to DLC. If he hadn't fired me . . ."

It was, then, with something less than exhilaration that I made my first trip to Indianapolis for a conference with Mr. Chambers, an expedition scheduled to recur on a bimonthly basis. I remember arriving in the grimy Indianapolis railroad station on a steaming September morning and being transported to a hotel that bore the imprint of Middle America, that flatland of bigotry and nasal infelicity from which I had fled in 1941, hoping for a permanent exile. Then on to the office. At that point, all the visits of the next four years merge into a montage of dread, ordeal and renewal.

Yet I can remember separate incidents, climactic moments of confrontation, nightmarish sequences of threats and conspiracy. I am writing soberly: to me, the Chambers Affair was a painful melodrama.

That first morning I entered what reminded me of a large old-fashioned department store. Desks and offices were distributed in horrid rows over the first floor, which stretched away from me, it seemed, into that dim distance where parallel lines meet. The store analogy came, I suppose, from my having encountered a similar perspective in my early years in Cleveland's vast department stores. One of them had, as did the Bobbs offices, a break in the center of its vast plain of office equipment and busy robot-clerks—in the form of a long flight of broad stairs, shaped like inverted parentheses, swelling on either side at the top into a balcony that overlooked, from three perspectives, the milling activity below.

The balcony corridors were also filled with desks, swarming with clerks and secretaries. I looked in vain for an overhead trolley down which little metal boxes, containing bills and change, would sing on their way back to clerk and customer. (I found *that* a few blocks away, at J. C. Penney's.) In retrospect, I am glad that I had not yet read Kafka.

Up there were executive warrens and, I was to discover, another long vista leading through the mid-floor business offices to the law department. But for the moment I was not looking. To my right, at the head of the stairs, behind a small desk, sat a large, grave woman who was Lois Stewart, Mr. Chambers's secretary. Lois was—is—made of superior stuff: she has survived DLC and is still there.

His office was in marked contrast to that rough workshop shared by Wartels and Simon. It was immaculate, old-fashioned and quietly elegant. And behind a large mahogany desk sat the Great Man. He had removed his jacket and necktie and opened his white, white shirt at his skinny veined neck. His gray hair was very neatly combed to one side, his face, bent over his work (for he did not look up), a small grayish oval. In fact the only living color I saw was a narrow line of pink scalp that marked the part in his thinning hair.

Then he did look up, and I saw where all the color was. In his blue eyes. Pale Alexandrian eyes. Yet I knew, even then, capable of incandescence.

It must be apparent by now that I am obsessed with eyes, and especially blue eyes—with their range from fierce sea-captain blue to the pallid, shallow periwinkle of the magician *manqué*.

To put it in the naïve traditional way, I believe that one's soul is in one's eyes—that if you know someone's eyes, you know him. There are dead eyes, drowned ones, numbed ones, sly and joyous and furtive and wounded ones. Rodent eyes, lion eyes, serpent eyes, those of deer and fish and dogs—all in human faces. And those of D. L. Chambers are among the most memorable in my experience.

But for now, as he rose in patent surprise and delight at my presence and extended his gnarled and liver-spotted hand, his were guileless, a little watery behind his pince-nez, affecting a jollity echoed in the strange *O* his lips formed as he gurgled a welcome. (I suppose he intended it to be a chuckle expressing his pleasure at my arrival.)

He was all courteous solicitude. Had I had a good trip? Was my hotel room satisfactory? Had I been to Indianapolis before? Were they treating me all right in the New York office? This last was Jocular, a vein that did not become him.

But the first hour or so was undeniably pleasant. I had been right in recalling him as a cultivated man, one of good breeding, taste in literature and intellectual competence. Forgotten were the hostile letters, the violent telephone call, Ross Baker's warnings.

The strategy the old man (he was old—at once brittle and pinched—frail, I thought with easy compassion. He was then about seventy-one, and he lasted to over eighty)—the strategy the old man selected was to introduce me to the history of Bobbs-Merrill. Founded in 1838 by Samuel Merrill, the firm was unique: the oldest of the two or three significant publishing houses in the Middle West. I learned of William Conrad Bobbs, and of the Merrills, into whose exalted *ambiance* Mr. Chambers found his way. I heard how he had, step by detailed step, risen to the presidency. All modestly put, in his voice with gravel in it, all in good taste, even a little dry when talking of self.

I was hearing the story of a life, I thought respectfully: the life of a truly dedicated man. I noted the acceleration of pride as he spoke of his relations with Booth Tarkington and Mary Roberts Rinehart, told of the golden list of the twenties, when Richard Halliburton and Bruce Barton and Julia Peterkin were

44

on his roster, and they and John Erskine's *The Private Life of Helen of Troy* made enormous profits.

He did not go on from there. There was a silence, during which I indulged a sentimental fantasy of restoring past glories to the company and winning his enduring gratitude.

"And so," he said at last, "that is the past. We must now speak of the present and the future, of the working relation between you and me."

His voice became soothing, hypnotic. He spoke of his pleasure in securing an editor of my caliber. He stressed the crucial importance of our intimate collaboration, assured me of the priority I would have on his time when, believing I had found a worthy manuscript, I sent it on for his approval.

I was duly mesmerized. Once or twice I tried feebly to interrupt: "But, Mr. Chambers—" He rode quietly over me, elaborating the details of our joint program to bring Bobbs once more to the front rank of publishers. In conclusion, he laid a comrade's affectionate hand on mine.

The dismay that had been building in me was close to desperation by this time. In this situation, a strong firm man, confident and sure of himself, would have had difficulty in asserting himself, so devious and finely meshed was the net that had been cast. And I was not that man. I would not let myself be browbeaten by a Wartels, but I knew myself no match for the subtleties and innuendoes, the beguiling play upon my emotions that I had just undergone. My childhood had undermined any capacity for resolution in the face of such masterful dialectic, such disarming flattery.

Yet I must. I must resist. And I blurted out with awkward assertiveness the conditions under which I had accepted the job. I would not be submitting manuscripts for his approval; the terms of our agreement stipulated that I had the right to accept or reject on my own.

The transformation (which was to prove only the first of hundreds) was devastating. Those eyes took on the deep color of a wild rage; they seemed to me to protrude as though issuing from their sockets on stalks. The palsied hands shook. The voice, grown suddenly sonorous, must have made the whole building tremble as did the withered, turkey-cock wattles under his chin.

45

I was an ingrate, an upstart, arrogant and fatuous.

To this I could respond better. Coldly, I told him that these seemed strange charges to fasten on a man guilty only of wanting to stand by an established arrangement and expecting the other party to keep his word as well.

Another instant change. A softening. A pleading note from an old man who had given his life to a task that was now to be stripped from him. In his physical infirmity. Within sight of the goal, the grail. He had been Bobbs-Merrill, had guided it through all the treacherous shoals and channels of decades. Night and day, always at the tiller. Why could we not work together, in the twilight of his life? Hand in hand. Why?

The Old Man of the Sea. This Protean changing of shape, of form, that was always to elude one's grasping hands. Here? No. There? Which way did he go?

I answered simply that we had an agreement that included the only terms under which I had been willing to come to Bobbs.

He sighed, spread out his hands. Then his face, his whole body tightened until it seemed that he would twist himself into a corkscrew.

"We will talk of this another time," he said coldly. "You are lunching with Mr. Berger and me. We will meet you at the front door. Miss Stewart will show you where the washroom is."

Shaken, I waited at the front door for half an hour. Then he reappeared and introduced me, as though in afterthought, to his companion.

This man seemed to my unsophisticated eye the embodiment of a Mississippi riverboat gambler. Like Mr. Chambers, he carried a broad-brimmed skimmer. His jacket and trousers did not match. But they bore no resemblance to conventional sports jacket and slacks. They were, in some elusive way, reminiscent of a morning coat and formal striped trousers. But below, two-toned brown-and-white shoes. Above, dominating this strange costume, a loud silk necktie, sprouting monstrous varicolored blooms. Fruit? Vegetables?

Lowe Berger grinned at me. That smile compounded my distress. For it was not a legitimate smile or grin; it was a tic, a reflexive action. The second time it occurred, it seemed, in my feverish state, more like a wound.

I was miserable. In what Halloween farce had I been assigned a victim's role? We walked down North Meridian Street to the Athletic Club, they side by side, hands clasped behind their backs, faces set, attending only the unpropitious prospect before them.

No. Twice, Lowe Berger turned to me and said something. I became aware of *his* eyes (I refuse to mention their color). I became aware in that instant of a man of dignity, sympathy, acute sensitiveness, and self-respect. Above all, a man to trust. And I was right. Never even a shading of the truth as he knew it: constancy, integrity and understanding. I think of him always with love and respect; I mourn his early death.

On that day of initiation, his presence sustained me. I felt relaxed and cheerful throughout the dreary lunch of long silences, which DLC would occasionally break with a routine question to Berger. Me he never addressed; for him (resolutely) I was not there. But it did not faze me, for there, on my other side, was Lowe Berger. We talked from time to time, but not for long. We didn't force it.

After the return voyage, which they navigated with hands clasped behind their backs, Mr. Chambers left without a word to me.

"Come into my office," Lowe suggested. "Let's get acquainted."

I spent most of the afternoon with him. I learned about the power structure. The law department, with a monopoly on the printing of all state records and documents, provided the company's largest source of revenue. Its head was subordinate to Mr. Chambers, but, since his field was technical, one about which DLC knew little, he was substantially independent. Lowe himself headed the school textbook department, and was vice-president of the company. Without his saying as much, I could see that he had built, in the few years since he had come from Appleton-Century, a department record now rivaling the success of the law department, and thereby entrenched himself in a very strong position.

There was no equivalent executive in the trade department, for that was Mr. Chambers's field. And its profit, as is so often the case, lagged far behind those of the other two divisions. This was a sore point with DLC, and made the task of a trade editor the more onerous.

Lowe, I found, spoke in elusive and even elliptical paradoxes. I had a difficult time translating them into simpler, more direct terms. But when he saw that I was floundering, stammering in response, he abandoned his peculiar idiom.

I found myself telling him in full of the morning's encounter. He listened, his grave eyes intent, and I learned to keep my eyes on his, above the nervous smile that flicked on and off. When I had finished, he said, "Good. Good for you, Hi. Stand there."

That was where High-Low began for us. Each evening of the sales conferences, all of us who had attended those dreary, droning sessions protracted almost beyond endurance through Mr. Chambers's insistence that each book must be reported on for a minimum of twenty minutes, each novel's plot fully adumbrated—all of us who had survived would play poker at the hotel. Lowe sometimes wore his "poker vest"—a garish affair with three small pockets on each side, cut to form a vertical row. As the evening progressed and raises grew larger, he would ignore the usually large piles of chips before him and begin flipping coins from these pockets. There were two pockets for nickels, two for dimes and two for quarters, but to increase the optical illusion that they were spurting from all directions, he would alter the locations of these denominations from evening to evening.

"Raise you twenty," he would intone in an even, cheerful voice, and with deft thumb and forefinger flip a nickel from pocket two-left, another (with his other hand) from three-right, and a dime from one-right. The coins would land with precision in the center of the pot.

When we were at the same table and his turn as dealer came round, he would usually grin at me and announce, "High-Low." After a while I ceased to wonder that we so often split that pot. There could, after all, be no connivance, no sleight of hand, no shenanigans. Lowe was in touch.

In touch, I thought that first afternoon, with every quivering nerve end of life, including my own. He seemed to know intuitively the nesting places of my doubts, fears and hopes about my

48

new job, and without asking any questions related them to Bobbs-Merrill realities, obliquely but lucidly.

He felt sorry for that old devil, Mr. Chambers. He respected his learning, his achievements, his dedication. But he lunched with him every day, kept fully abreast of "the old sinner's" fantasies, because he knew that he was no longer to be trusted—that ancient griefs and frustrations and hatreds, long pent, had corrupted his judgment. Offering no specific examples, he spoke of the Chambers family in a way reminiscent of the House of Atreus. It was long later that I learned some of the details, most painfully when a son-in-law I knew, Julius Birge, a big, gentle, eager man, went to the basement of his house and blew his head off with a double-barreled shotgun. I was never invited to DLC's home; I am grateful for that.

Lowe told me that one could measure the energy potential of hate by the fact that DLC, suffering acute prostatitis, refused an operation and would, he knew, continue to refuse it so long as he lived, which Lowe predicted would be another decade. Fear could kill, he believed, but it could also engender a hatred that was sustaining, could enable some to live simply for revenge on life.

"And now," he finally said, "I want to make it clear to you that you must not be intimidated by all this. You will never be alone in your fight to build a real trade list."

He commended Ross Baker to me; he assured me that he would himself be constantly vigilant, and see to it that I was forewarned whenever Mr. Chambers mounted an attack.

And that was the way it was. Three times DLC sought to fire me, taking his complaint to his board of directors. Three times Lowe checkmated him, for by now the board, originally in Mr. Chambers's pocket, had come to be aware of, and to distrust, his irrationalities, his vindictive hostilities. They had learned to turn to, and rely upon, Lowe's calm voice, his level scrutiny, and his measured judgments.

The first charge against me was that of "sexual obsession," referring to my championing of William Styron's *Lie Down in Darkness*. The second charge, based on my publishing Benjamin Appel's *Fortress in the Rice*, held that I was, if not an active

49

Communist, at least a fellow traveler. And the third, with reference to my expense account, held me "extravagant and irresponsible." (This had a whiff of validity.)

Whenever a storm was brewing, my phone in Connecticut would ring, always in the evening, and a familiar and heartening voice would say something like, "Hi? Lowe. It's going to rain hard tomorrow, but don't give it a thought. I don't think you'll even need an umbrella."

On such occasions, I would remember again that first afternoon, and Lowe suddenly turning almost severe. "I want you to understand that I am not disloyal to Mr. Chambers. Tomorrow, if I so chose, I could succeed him as president. I never will, so long as he lives and is able to work effectively. I owe him my opportunity, and he has my loyalty. Only now it must take the hard form of opposing him over and over again, protecting him from himself."

At last I asked him, "Why have you told me all this, the first time we've met?"

He smiled his strange smile; his strong chin jutted out; his eyes held mine insistently.

"Because I can trust you. And I want you to know this little world the way it is. Then it can't hurt you, hobble you. I want you to be free to get us good books. We need them."

I saw Mr. Chambers the next day. There was no mention of our previous talk. We discussed the few books I had already signed; I told him of some others for which I was negotiating. Our tone was level, impersonal, polite. I left for New York. . . .

Oddly enough, the first book I had ready for Bobbs was *The Grand Portage,* by Walter O'Meara, whose *The Trees Went Forth* had been my first at Crown. Walter is an impeccable craftsman; he has always turned in to the copy editor the cleanest "copy" of all the writers I know.

Hence his manuscript made an enormous hit with Mr. Chambers (probably the finest, most precise trainer of copy editors in the country), who assumed that I was responsible for its near perfection. "I can see," he wrote me, "that we have at last a professional editor, who is neither too self-important nor too lazy to deliver a script in its properly finished state."

This alarmed me, and I replied that I could not guarantee such "professionalism" consistently. It was O'Meara who was the unusual professional. My disclaimer was adjudged a case of undue modesty. But not for long. No other manuscript won such praise from him, and the Cold War was resumed.

Our next contretemps occurred in his office on one of my early trips to Indianapolis. I had just signed a contract with Saunders Redding, the distinguished scholar and writer, for a book entitled *On Being Negro in America*.

DLC listened in silence to my comments about its possibilities. At last he looked up, pursed his lips, and said, with marked distaste, "Your entire list seems to consist of Jews and Negroes."

I exploded. Standing, I delivered my first real philippic to him. I can remember few other occasions on which I have found without hesitation precisely the words I wanted to express my anger. When I finished, I walked out.

Later, Leo Gobin, Lowe Berger's close friend and the treasurer of the company, sought me out to tell me that DLC had described the incident to him, expressing astonishment at the "degree" of my "fury," and at the way I had "sprung to [my] feet."

Leo chuckled.

"And I said to him, 'And isn't Hiram big?' "

Leo, one of those refreshing redeemers of the Middle West, open, generous and shrewd, is now president of the Bobbs-Merrill Company, and I think of this fact partially as evidence of the persisting influence of Lowe Berger. . . .

But more often I could not parry Mr. Chambers's thrusts effectively, particularly when—as often happened—we would fight to a draw in his office, only to have him, by innuendo and slur, have the last word about our issue in a general meeting, where to reply would have been to induce open civil war.

His presence hung over these meetings, particularly the sales conferences, like a vast, dark, sagging canopy. He would never hesitate to spew forth his acid comments on the presentation of books by his editors. He seemed to consider his responsibility as chairman of these meetings a mandate to cut down to minimal size any expression of passionate belief, or even any presentation deviating from his norm of hardheaded, impartial exposition.

I remember the exhaustion I felt on finishing my account of *Lie Down in Darkness,* a book I believed in profoundly.

Mr. Chambers intoned in his powdery voice, "If a quarter of what Mr. Haydn has said about this book is true, we are about to publish an extraordinary work. But the crucial word is 'if.' "

The salesmen were in a state of perpetual uneasiness at these meetings. Most of them, as commissioned men, served other houses as well, and DLC's tactics offended their sense of professionalism. In accordance with their various personalities, they were severally intimidated, embarrassed, amused, disgusted. But they were unanimous in one respect: they were silent unless he directly addressed one of them. Then, the reply was exaggeratedly respectful, but brief. Even George Vay, a blithe spirit who convulsed all of us with his sallies when out of the range of DLC, maintained a mask of polite composure at the conference proper. It must have cracked the skin of his face.

The salesmen "let go" only in the fifteen minutes of allotted freedom between the end of the morning session and the gathering for lunch. The meal was always held at the Athletic Club, and was really a dinner. Copious, heavy, the food was stultifying. Mr. Chambers was a rabid prohibitionist, and no alcohol was served. But during those "free" fifteen minutes, most of the men hurried out of Bobbs to the hotel bar next door, and had two or three drinks before appearing at the Club. The result was disastrous for the afternoon session. The dark, paneled board room, the liquor, the heavy lunch, and the drone of editors' voices induced an irresistibly somnolent atmosphere. Heads nodded, eyes blinked, feet shuffled, and catalogues covered yawning mouths. I remember the almost incredible case of one salesman, whose respect for me I attributed to his fondness for my wife when she had worked as an editor at the New York office prior to my arrival. He was determined not to let me down, to hear my every word at one of these afternoon meetings. So he sat there, elbows on the table, thumb and forefinger of each hand literally holding open his eyelids! The effect was more nerve-racking than undisguised sleep would have been.

I also remember the look of fury on DLC's face when a salesman snored. Yet he never altered his program: Maryland fried chicken, prime ribs of beef, pot roast—even in June. For so sharp and so constantly, meticulously observant a man, DLC had curious blind spots. Perhaps this one was related to his own meager appetite.

At my first of these conferences, I realized that there were really no commissioned officers; there was only a general and a roomful of privates. Ross Baker, Walter Hurley, the "star" salesman Bill Finneran—all were reduced to a common level.

Nat Wartels at least officially shared his leadership with Bob Simon. And he established a hierarchy amongst the rest of us. But DLC reigned in monolithic splendor. The somber portraits of his predecessors watched from the walls as this *roi de l'ombre* proposed and disposed. He was as truly persuaded that he *was* Bobbs-Merrill as was *le grand* Charles that *he* was France. And DLC had reached a point at which he found tact expendable; only the year before I arrived he had so insulted Charles Denhard, the respected head of the Denhard, Pfeiffer and Wells advertising agency, that Charlie never returned to Indianapolis. After all, he once told me huskily, he was not "the old bastard's employee."

To be sure, when alone with this one or that (including me), DLC could be not only charming but so flattering that one's head might swim with reassurance. Woe to him who took as dispassionate and spontaneous this expedient prologue to the requesting of some extraordinary service.

And double woe to him who did not maintain a constant vigilance. Sometime in 1952 I sent the manuscript of *Fortress in the Rice* on to Indianapolis. (All our books were copy edited there and then returned to Hurley, to pass on to the printer.)

In only a day or two, Mr. Chambers began a staccato hailstorm of blue memos. (This was the fateful color, the warning of impending eruption.)

1. He found this account of the Huk uprising in the Philippines a Communist tract. 2. Had I checked out Appel's political affiliations? 3. Why had I not altered such and such a scene? 4. Did I realize what, in the present national political climate (he meant Joe McCarthy), publishing such a book would mean

to the reputation of the Company? 5. If I remained recalcitrant, he would take the problem to the board, who would, he was sure, refuse to honor the contract, invoking the clause that said the author must deliver a final manuscript "satisfactory to the publisher." 6. Why did I maintain this obdurate silence? 7. I might have the courtesy to reply, in whatever disagreement, to his questions. 8. He had still heard nothing from me about this urgent matter. Etc., etc., etc., etc., etc.

The fact was that I had answered every memo. For instance, at one point Ben Appel, sensing the sort of trouble I was having, volunteered the information that he had never been a member of the Communist party, and I duly passed this information on to DLC in answer to his second question. But there was never an acknowledgment of my replies, and toward the end of our exchange I began to receive only those mystifying notes demanding that I explain my "silence."

As I look back on that situation I marvel at my naïveté—no, my stupidity. It never occurred to me that this progression of notes was more than another campaign of harassment. Hence I did not consult Ross Baker beyond a passing comment on Chambers's irascibility about this book, and I did not get in touch with Lowe Berger at all. Nor he with me, which further allayed my doubts. I was going out to another sales conference before long. I endured the barrage and waited for a showdown in Indianapolis.

I was, therefore, completely unprepared for my lack-of-reception when I arrived for the sales conference. Mr. Chambers was not available; Mr. Berger was "out." I had reason to doubt this statement, for I was sure I had seen his back disappear into his office only a few minutes before.

Lowe's inaccessibility really upset me, and throughout the long conference day that followed I was haunted by a sense of something ominous to come. When the afternoon meeting broke up I stood alone in the vast "department store," irresolute, lonely, frightened. My feelings must have been evident. A hand on my shoulder. Julius Birge, DLC's kindly, beleaguered son-in-law.

"I want to speak to you alone," he said earnestly.

I followed him to some dim and unfamiliar cubbyhole.

"Hiram," he said urgently, "why haven't you answered him? Any of those memos?"

As I slowly recovered from my amazement, what had really happened finally reached me. I felt a complete fool. But (angrily) even Mr. Chambers—and had Lowe believed this?

I told Julius the facts: that I had answered every memo, thoroughly and, I thought, effectively. I saw conviction, then anger mount in his usually calm, thoughtful face.

"It's repulsive," he said, and hurried off.

I had a quick few minutes with Lowe before the evening poker game.

His eyes searched my face. No, he hadn't lost confidence in me. He simply couldn't understand my silence and decided to await my arrival. Moreover, he was gravely worried and had made a number of futile appeals to DLC to drop the matter, not to bring it to the board. For, he pointed out to me, this was not like the ridiculous accusation connected with Styron's book; in the Middle West, the mere charge of Communism sufficed to kill a man's effectiveness and to black-list him. He could not prevail over the board on this issue at their meeting next week.

I told him of the talk with Julius Birge. His eyes narrowed.

"Do you have copies of your memos?"

"In the New York office."

"First thing tomorrow, have them sent on." His face cleared. "Thank God. Now we have a chance." . . .

Late in the poker game, Julius and DLC's only son, David Jr., lawyer and a director of Bobbs-Merrill, who had led his discussion with me over cocktails that afternoon to the subject of Communism, with what he apparently fondly thought subtlety— Julius and young Chambers suddenly appeared and converged on Lowe. After a brief whispered conversation, he left with them.

The next morning, Lowe told me what had happened. Julius had stayed late at the office. A most unlikely burglar, he had rifled all DLC's files and found, tucked way at the back of one, my missing memos.

The pent-up frustration of years, his share of humiliation and impotence in dealing with the old man, had triggered him. He sought out other directors for much-needed support; then he went to DLC's home, awakened him and confronted him with the evidence.

The case was closed. Only now, when I realized that this was not the recital of some soap-opera melodrama, did the full force of DLC's malevolence hit me. I have seldom felt more shaky.

Before I left Bobbs-Merrill, Mr. Chambers retired "upstairs" to the chairmanship of a board he could no longer control, and Lowe Berger was duly installed as president. The incident involving me was only one of a series that had literally forced Lowe's hand and made him take the step he had forestalled as long as he could. Thereafter, working for Bobbs-Merrill became a recognizably realistic proposition.

Looking back, I think I understand better now the course of things at Bobbs. In the twenties and even thirties, the trade department was riding high after the successes of John Erskine and Bruce Barton and Richard Halliburton, that intrepid latter-day Munchausen, and a number of others. Thereafter, for a variety of reasons, the road led downward. Bobbs was unable to compete for leading authors with New York firms as the business became increasingly agent-oriented. True, there was a New York editor in the New York office who had equal access to these agents. But he worked under two heavy disadvantages. He could not negotiate with authority because he had to submit everything to Mr. Chambers, and his competitors either had such authority or at least could confer with their superiors on the spot. Moreover, DLC was unwilling to offer an advance of the size becoming customary in New York.

Another important factor was that he found the work of the new generation distasteful. I do not believe that he would have signed John Dos Passos, Ernest Hemingway, William Faulkner, John Steinbeck or Nelson Algren if he had had the chance. He looked back with painful nostalgia to the genteel tradition in which he and Bobbs had flourished. He never tired of telling about his association with Booth Tarkington. He found what comfort he could in his two consistently best selling authors, Alice Tisdale Hobart and Inglis Fletcher. They wrote decent, inspiring books, *and* they sold. So he continued to insist on his standards. But the other books did not sell. For many years the trade department was primarily supported by a strong children's list (the Childhood of Famous Americans series, in particular) and that hardy perennial, Irma Rombauer's *The Joy of Cooking*.

In rationalization, he fell back on a favorite generalization. "Gross volume," he would say. "That's the answer: gross volume. You can't expect most good books to sell today."

The older he grew the surer he became that he knew the answers, despite staggering evidence to the contrary. And the surer he became, the more tyrannical. It was the old story of a man trusting almost no one else. The more he came to doubt the adequacies of those who worked for him the more he insisted on being in total charge of the list. The less he was able to command the new writers the more he indulged his prejudices. It became DLC against the world, and he would not relinquish the practices that had worked in the past. In my time with Bobbs, he and George Brett of Macmillan were the last two publishers to hold out against selling books on consignment. He would not take books back from the booksellers, and so they were naturally disinclined to place as large orders for Bobbs books as they would with comparable books from other publishers.

I was not aware of all these factors when I went to Bobbs, but I could not remain uninformed for long. And, even more than with Crown, I was confronted with a situation heavily weighted against success. As I look back now, I believe that the list I built at Bobbs, in the face of these odds, represents the best editorial work I have done. But I could never have done it without the generous, unfailing support of Berger and Baker.

The early success of Styron's *Lie Down in Darkness* was of enormous help. The reviews were splendid; the book sold well; the author was established almost overnight. And for Bobbs and me it meant that agents had tangible proof that we could launch successfully a real *contemporary* literary talent. It suggested to reviewers and book-review editors that Bobbs was building a serious, up-to-date literary list that would deserve their scrutiny.

Another early success came with the publication of H. M. Tomlinson's *The Face of the Earth,* a book of essays by a master of prose. Then in his eighties, the once famous author of *The Sea and the Jungle, Gallion's Reach* and *All Our Yesterdays* had not had an American publisher for fifteen years. After the successful publication of *The Face of the Earth* Tomlinson wrote, "You have rescued me from where I have been interred, as the last footnote of the textbook *From Beowulf to Thomas Hardy.*"

No other novelists in my time at Bobbs received attention equal to that accorded Styron, but we did publish with real success a number of other good "new" ones: George Mandel, Thomas Gallagher, Jefferson Young, William Michelfelder, among others. All of these received wide and respectful attention from reviewers, and most of them also made the firm money, whether through book-club selection or paper reprint leases. In 1953 we had a Book-of-the-Month Club sole selection for the first time in Bobbs-Merrill history: Robert Raynolds's *The Sinner of Saint Ambrose.*

Raynolds had had a strange career. Long before, his first novel, *Brothers in the West,* had won the Harper Prize. Although he continued to write, and usually well, his books commanded progressively less and less attention, and their sales dwindled to one or two thousand copies apiece. Finally he could not find a publisher to take him on, and printed one novel privately.

I met Bob Raynolds at a large party in Newtown, Connecticut, sometime in 1952 or '53. We were introduced by Kyle Crichton of *Collier's* magazine, who added, "You'll remember *Brothers in the West,* Hiram—Bob's Harper Prize novel."

I saw on Raynolds's face what looked to me to be a flicker of anguish. I guessed.

"Why go back there?" I asked. "What are you doing now?"

Raynolds plunged into a rapid but broken account of his long descent into hell. I want to stress that this was not the usual author's enjoyment in talking about himself. He blushed, stammered, now and then broke off altogether and stared at me helplessly. It was simply that no one had asked him this question in a long time; people had avoided inquiring about his work, lest they embarrass him.

Finally, I learned about his almost completed new novel, *The Sinner of Saint Ambrose.* I asked to see it.

"You'll turn it down, like everybody else." Even his beloved agent, Henry Volkening, who had seen him through all his vicissitudes, had finally released him—literally because he was persuaded that Bob needed a completely new *ambiance.*

In a few weeks Bob sent the novel. I read it, accepted it, and we worked for a while on revisions. When the incredible news came from the Book-of-the-Month Club, Bob was in Spain. Full of elation, I cabled him, adding as an unimportant postscript that they had made only one condition—that he change the title, which they considered "wrong for our audience." Then I sat back, enjoying daydreams about his getting the news, feeling that I was experiencing his joy, his tears, his pride and sense of redemption.

Two days later, I received a cable from him. It went something like this:

UNDER NO CONDITIONS WILL I CHANGE THE TITLE REPEAT UNDER NO CONDITIONS STOP APPRECIATE YOUR EFFORTS THOUGH.

BOB

It was one of the great moments in my publishing experience. Old Invictus. The Book-of-the-Month Club yielded. . . .

Every writer I have known seems to me to have experienced despair at one time or another. This sentence written, I reject it as jejune. Why not every *person* . . .? But it is writers I am concerned with here, and the writer's despair in connection with his work.

The most gifted have moments when they feel they have lost their touch, that they will no longer be able to write. The most successful commercially are often enraged over being ignored by the literati. They feel dismissed as popular hacks. Young writers despair that recognition will ever come; old writers mourn becoming *déclassés*. More or less established, regularly practicing writers suffer torment over reviews or the lack of them. Those who are outstandingly successful in one genre are distressed that no one appreciates their work in another. All writers are hurt by the failure of publishers or editors or reviewers or friends to grasp the *true quality* of their work, however many compliments are offered them.

I think I have felt the most sympathy for those who have chosen or—more often—been forced by political or economic misfortune to migrate to a new land and even to learn to write in a new language. One of the ironies of this situation is that whether the immigrant tries his hand at the alien language or continues to employ a translator, he usually finds it much more difficult to secure a publisher and an audience in his new land than does his counterpart who remains in "the old country" and whose books are imported. The latter's books are often acquired through competitive negotiations that proclaim his importance, while the former frequently seems to be considered in advance a failure, if not an outcast, simply by virtue of having become a transplant. And this, ironically enough, even when his status as refugee demonstrates his loyalty to the very political and social values professed by those who are suspicious of him.

This tendency has been marked in the cases of Europeans who have fled Hitlerian or other tyrannies and come to the United States. To be sure, if it is the question of someone who has already become entrenched as an important figure in world literature, like Thomas Mann, the argument does not hold. But the more usual experience, even for people with some established reputation in their own country, is that described by Carl Zuckmayer in his recent autobiography, *A Part of Myself.* He arrived in New York, was made much of by a group of literary folk and intellectuals, offered every kind of help, extended numerous unspecific invitations, and then, after some two or three weeks, left wholly alone, ignored.

It seems preferable to come quite unheralded and know from the first the bitterness and loneliness of a totally new start. But for one who has been published in Europe there are bound to be some links in New York, whether with those who have made the same passage earlier or Americans encountered in Europe.

At the risk of oversimplification, I find three prototypical ways in which European writers (and here I would add publishers and agents) have resolved the problems of migration. One is to avoid assimilation, as far as possible: to maintain one's European habits, attitudes, circles of friends—in short, to live as an exile. A second involves overassimilation—going American, so to speak.

The first course is effective only in the case of an extraordinary writer who is thought of as winning his right to isolation simply by his ability. Otherwise these unassimilable enclaves are apt to engender a group-sustaining contempt for the vast alien country to which its members have been "sentenced," and to contrast at every turn its infelicities with the grandeurs of the past in the fatherland. Hardly inducive to finding fulfillment. Those who remain productive tend still to seek a European market.

The second group often lose their individuality in the process of becoming Americanized. Since there is nothing more integral, more central to a writer's development than the nurturing of that individuality, this course may be even more disastrous.

The third way of meeting the challenge must be obvious already, from the traps into which the other two fall. It is to follow the middle ground, of course, to enter the new society and learn from it without in any sense trying to ape its style, attitudes, etc. It involves the retention of one's self, one's peculiar and distinctive qualities, while being open and receptive to the new experience.

Two men (though neither is primarily a writer) come immediately to mind: Martin Gumpert and George Salter. Gumpert, who had been Thomas Mann's doctor, settled down in New York and built up a good practice, specializing in geriatrics. Salter became our pre-eminent book designer and jacket artist. Both were cool, sagacious men.

I think, too, of Robert S. Rosen, whose parents were butchered in a German concentration camp and who himself barely escaped capture by the Nazis. Once in New York, he worked during the day for many years, while at night securing successively his high-school and college diplomas, his master's degree and his doctorate! Beyond this bare recital of an incredible achievement, I want to point out that Sam (as Mary and I have always called him) accepted the American scene he found without giving up even a fragment of his rich European heritage.

Even following this middle course provides no guarantee of regaining in the United States the degree of esteem one commanded previously in Germany or Hungary or Italy, or even through all of Europe. And I am writing of this here because it was primarily at Bobbs that I had extended experiences with European writers.

Early in my days at Crown, we had decided to publish a novel, translated from the Hungarian, by a writer named Ferencz

61

Kormendi. Only a few months before, a fellow Hungarian named Lajos Zilahy had made his debut under similar sponsorship, and his book had become a best seller. But this was not to be Kormendi's experience. The novel in question, *The Happy Generation,* was a long family novel more or less in the *Buddenbrooks* tradition, and an excellent book. It received respectful reviews and sold some five or six thousand copies. In Europe Kormendi had been accustomed to publication in a half-dozen countries and languages and a total sale in the hundreds of thousands.

Knowing the record, I watched with interest his reaction to his American baptism. It was an unforgettable lesson in civility, self-respect and fortitude. Ferencz Kormendi is a most urbane man, but his response to this ordeal transcended urbanity. He did not treat his wounds with the ointment of imperturbability. He would inquire from time to time about the fate of his book, and receive the lukewarm news with an ironic flicker to his expression, but one conveying more the sense of his own human vulnerability than any conviction that the ways of the world were cruel or meaningless.

Nor was there any diminution of his steady friendliness and courtesy as a second (published at Bobbs), then a third, book failed to achieve a secure place for itself in American letters, or even significant income. By now he was writing directly in English, and while his work suffered as a result the loss of some of his peculiar stylistic flair, he accepted this hurt, too, with grace and courage.

During this period I went once to a party at his house and met his charming wife and his European friends. They were all writers, or at least associated with matters literary. I remember one especially, who was much looked up to as a distinguished poet and novelist. His attitude about exile was in marked contrast to that of Ferencz. He was aloof, slightly bitter, seemed suspicious and even hostile to me and the one or two other Americans present.

I do not think that I am deceiving myself about Ferencz Kormendi. He is neither a saint nor a doctrinal Stoic. He is, I think, a man who has made his own terms with life, suffered, and accepted without the slightest loss of self-respect. I remember how on occasion his eyes would glitter and the pulse in his forehead beat perceptibly. I knew then what a struggle he was undergoing, but I knew also that this finely tempered man would not, like many of us, compensate in private in some miserable way for what he must endure silently in public.

His lovely and aristocratic wife ran a superlatively successful bakery; Ferencz secured a post with Radio Free Europe; they made their way to Washington and still another life. I published at Bobbs a novel about the coup in Hungary, called *The Seventh Trumpet,* under a pseudonym, because at the time Ferencz's mother was still in the old country. But he had no better luck with a pen name than with his own. And finally the day came when I could no longer justify to my employers the presence of his books on our list.

I dreaded telling him. But I should have guessed what would happen: *he* supported *me* through this ordeal. And the book in question, a novel with a Roman setting at the time of Christ, written in English by a Hungarian, has only recently been translated into German and accepted enthusiastically for publication by a German house! God moves in a mysterious way.

A large part of Kormendi's troubles in America was the result of neither being able to afford a translator nor having his books sell sufficiently to persuade his publisher to underwrite the costs. This was not the case with a distinguished German writer, Walter Mehring, whose marvelously delicate satiric work, *The Lost Library,* was splendidly translated by Richard and Clara Winston.

Its publication came early in my stay at Bobbs-Merrill, and lent an unwonted exoticism to that homely Midwestern list. A book more allusive and elusive than Virginia Woolf's *Orlando,* it presented the translators with an almost insurmountable task. But blithe Richard and brooding Clara were equal to that task. Very few of the reviewers were, but there was something about the book's Heinesque quality that awed them sufficiently to force them to respect it in a gingerly way. It was too saturatedly European to find a large American audience, but I look back on its publication with pride.

Mehring himself was not to stay long in this country. I saw him only a half-dozen times over a period of two years. But I shall never forget his gaminlike presence, his shrewd eyes, his endless cigarettes, his drawling comments on the bizarre American scene. Barely over five feet tall, thin to the point of scrawniness, he lived on wine and tobacco and presided over the revels of daily life with a sardonic zest. It was inevitable, I think, that he and his frail, charming wife should slip off as soon as possible to Paris, where, I suspect, they disappeared into a *cave* and transformed it into Oberon's kingdom.

America barely touched Walter Mehring, though he was electrically in contact with it. Quite a different story with René Fülöp-Miller. René wallowed in America, played with it, laughed at it, was in turn exalted and abused by it, rejected it, adopted it, tried to reshape it.

A man in his late fifties when I first met him, René already had run through several lives and careers. Of Carpathian and Macedonian heritage, he was generally designated a Hungarian and thought representative of the wild richness of that national temperament as it is stereotyped. Tall, he wore his gray locks to his shoulders before ever a hippie swayed in the breeze. Those gray curls circled the bald center of his pate, his eyes gleamed greedily and his lips were wet with the love of life as he bent over an American matron's hand to bestow upon it an unwonted kiss.

He was extravagant in gesture and in speech: he seemed to be trying to inhale his listeners as he related adventure after adventure; his hands would roam possessively to hold his audience closer. He spilled over with love, love, love, and his tales were frequently of his own escapades.

This tall gypsy cavalier from central Europe was truly smitten with love in all its aspects. He loved his children with a devouring, relishing, caressing devotion that stifled. He loved his friends with what seemed to most of us, with our varying degrees of American inhibitedness, an indecently embarrassing lavishness. He never addressed me without beginning "Dear Hiram." I kept silently imploring him to say something crisp, astringent, even outrageously rude.

He never did. He saved all that accumulation of sour bile that inhabits most of us for his books, in which, drawing it through some distilling retort, he transformed it to health and meaning.

His handsome wife, Erika Renon, a poet with striking Delphic eyes, seemed to find his stories equally fascinating. While he burbled on, chuckling liquidly, pausing now and then to relight one of his collection of deep-bowled pipes, she would stand erect, eyes shining, black hair parted directly in the middle and drawn tightly over her skull—like Grant Wood's *American Gothic* woman brought back to youth and vitality.

Shortly after René came to the United States, in the twenties, he had a tremendous success with his book on Rasputin, *The Holy Sinner*. It had a huge sale and led to a film. Later his study of anesthesia, *Triumph Over Pain,* another best seller, was a Literary Guild selection and was also followed by a film.

Yet the hundreds of thousands of dollars made in New York and Hollywood didn't last long. He spent them, he would tell you gleefully—where? how? who knows? He was by now poor and dependent upon friends for access to publishers, contracts, money.

I met him through friends who lived, as we did, in the Sullivan-MacDougal Street Gardens, below Washington Square. Before a single evening was over, he and one of those friends had persuaded me that I wanted to give up writing the book on Dostoevsky for the Twentieth Century Library series at Scribner's and instead let René do it.

I don't, of course, remember the details, but I know enough about my own compulsion to be the Helper, the Salvager, to feel sure that I was not conned. Despite an enormous interest in and considerable knowledge about Dostoevsky, I foresaw a formidable task, when combined with my other responsibilities, and I suspect that relief was one of my emotions.

But the point about René was that he somehow managed to bring, or—perhaps more accurately—to *magnetize* opportunities to himself, not really extending himself in seeking them actively beyond letting a word fall here, a hint there. I could never detect any scheming or planning behind this phenomenon: he was not an ordinary egotist, but a successful narcissist, whose conviction that he was the center of centrifugal forces was unmarred by any conscious manipulation.

At any rate, I thereafter published several of his books and had a minor hand in the publication of others. He was lavish with his gratitude, as with his other emotions. I was at once exasperated and acquiescent in our relations. Some corrupt passive strain in me prevented me from cutting loose.

But something positive was involved, too. René's work was first-rate. His book on the Jesuits, his study of Lenin, his *The Saints That Moved the World*—all these were books at once possessed of scholarship and of a dervishlike intensity of insight. His knowledge of matters literary, philosophical, psychological and, in some areas, historical was vast. Many people found it tempting to dismiss him as a popularizer; some even considered him a charlatan. I think them wholly wrong. Here, in my opinion, was one more illustration of confusion of personality with writer.

At any rate, it is his last works, two novels, that impress me as staggeringly good. *The Night of Time* (Bobbs-Merrill, 1955) is a macabre and powerful satirical fantasy of war. *The Silver Bacchanal* (Atheneum, 1962) is an equally compelling and equally bizarre treatment of occupation, the "peace" that follows such wars.

Both these novels display the full force of René's complex nature. A gleeful demonic humor plays over their scenes like spasmodic lightning, alternating with a heavier, rowdy laughter that was new in his work. Yet they are also infused with a tenderness, an unobtrusive compassion, that is very moving.

And it is this quality, and only this, that sets them apart from the black humorists, the giddy fantasists of the generation of Vonnegut, Pynchon, Heller, Southern and Barthelme. He anticipated their antics, their blithe sardonic distortions, their *opera-bouffe* satanism—actually, with his much more richly stocked mind, far surpassed them at their own game. But at the same time, he never lost his essential humanity, never let himself be seduced into the easy nullity of total naysaying. A truer comparison would be to the work of Günter Grass.

Am I contradicting myself? I do not think so. René was a radical example of that recurring, almost ubiquitous split between the man and the writer. The man who so irritated me and many others was almost a parody of the man who wrote the books. That Middle European flourish, with its cloying effusiveness, was completely absent from those stinging, withering and yet deeply humane books.

I risk one generalization about writers. People are often much disappointed to meet someone whose books they have read with pleasure, sometimes even with reverence or adoration. "But that can't be the man who wrote that book!"

It isn't. The man or woman who wrote the book, often enough, expends all his human richness on the writing, has only the least of himself left for people. I suspect that many writers, sensitive and lonely as children, "outsiders," are driven increasingly to their desks because they find the daily impact of simpler and more forceful personalities too bruising. In turn, free when alone with the tools of the trade, they pour out their lives on the blank pages before them and leave their studies, drained, to present only their superficial outlines to the world around them. Here is the reverse of those public personalities whose reputations as writers exceed the actual substance of their productions.

As for René, it must be said that in his last years (from the time he was sixty-five until he was seventy or seventy-one—the period in which he wrote these two novels) he came into a quieter strength and a greater dignity. The early death of his oldest child had, I believe, a profound effect on him. And his final years of teaching, at Hunter and Dartmouth, were apparently very rewarding, to students and teacher alike. When his temporary appointment at Dartmouth was not renewed, his students staged a demonstration in protest, long before such actions became common.

Working with him in those last years was a happier affair, too. He and Erika, his devoted translators the Winstons, and I had sessions that were full of hilarity and stimulation.

If Walter Mehring found the United States (or perhaps I should say New York) a sort of George Grosz circus, René (with a much greater acquaintance with the country as a whole) saw it with the eye of a Gulliver, was vitally interested in all its vagaries, equally aware of its absurdities and its strengths, and eager to participate in it. Without losing a particle of his cosmo-politan European style, he plunged directly into American life, holding aloft one discovery after another, crying out, "Look! Look, everybody! You do this. Why?"

Not only did Bobbs give me my first substantial introduction to European writers; it provided me with my first "publishing trip" to England. In 1953 I went over to see what I might procure for our firm. I was to make only one other such publishing trip. Most chief editors dash back and forth a couple of times a year, reading manuscripts, making deals, dining and wining and exhausting themselves for three weeks. But for the most part I have been employed either by a house that already had an established visitor, or one that found the practice expensive and unrewarding.

Even at this long remove I cannot feel confident of the objectivity of my first reaction. Given my prickly nature and the British tendency to hide defensiveness (of this much I *am* sure) under a suave mask of more or less courteous condescension, it was, I suppose, inevitable that my initial rounds of their publishing houses should be less than happy.

At the end of the first week I was bewildered and angry. It seemed to me that I had been found guilty before putting in an appearance. Guilty? Of the crime of Americanism. It was clear to me that I was wearing a star-spangled vest, yet I could not remember putting it on. Oh, business was conducted, manuscripts were offered, polite inquiries were made, but this undercurrent was visible in all but two or three places. And the exceptions—I remember John Murray, William Collins, Jamie Hamilton and, most notably, Roger Machell—reinforced my interpretation of the attitudes of the majority. And yet never an openly rude reception.

Toward the close of the second week I was continuing my schedule grimly, reminding myself each day that Mary and I would be free together in the evening. Only one or two of the British publishers entertained us at dinner. I remember one at the Warburgs' apartment. Fred and his wife Pamela were most hospitable, yet I had the feeling that they were trying to make it an *American* evening. The Martinis were stationed all over, like road signs.

Finally, the climactic moment occurred on an afternoon visit at Cassell's. The editor I sat with was one of the most sympathetic men I'd met on the trip, and I overstayed a while. Then, realizing that it was late, I stood up.

He objected.

"Stay for tea. You won't have another appointment this late. It's a curious thing, Haydn. You're not a bit like an American."

I realized eventually that this was intended to be a compliment. And this incident ends happily, for we have remained friendly, although we haven't seen much of each other. But at the time it seemed to me that the whole game was now transparent, that this man, more open than most, had "let everything hang out."

Where was my sense of humor? Deficient, I'm afraid. It is easier in retrospect. I remember a story of Bennett Cerf's about Laurence Pollinger, the well-known literary agent. Twice on Bennett's trips to London Pollinger had invited him to lunch in an expensive restaurant. Twice Pollinger had somehow managed to be occupied when the check was brought. Twice Bennett picked it up, expecting a hospitable rebuke. It did not come, on either occasion.

So, as Bennett told the story, the third time he went to London he was determined to make Pollinger pay. As before, an invitation to lunch was received the first day. But this time Bennett insisted, on grounds of curiosity, that they meet at the most expensive restaurant in the city. Lunch progressed in the usual way, and then Bennett looked at his watch, announced he was late for an appointment, and apologized for having to leave instantly. Pollinger put a hand on his arm, explained that he must go to the men's room but that Bennett must wait, for he had something very important to tell him. He would be just a moment. Then he disappeared as the check arrived.

Fuming, Bennett sat there, determined not to pay but also forced to stay, lest Pollinger, who had many desirable clients, really *did* have something important for him. Five minutes passed, ten. In rage and despair Bennett finally paid the check and rushed for the door. To meet Pollinger, smiling cordially.

"I just wanted to tell you," he said, "that from now on I want you to feel free to call me Pollinger."

There it is. Telling the story to me years later, Bennett roared with laughter. "But at the time," he said, "I could have killed the man."

Clarification is needed, however. This sort of chicanery is not at all characteristic of British publishers. They are mostly careful gentlemen. Yet there were some who were blunt, and when rude, bluntly so. I think of Victor Gollancz and Fred Warburg. On one of Fred's trips to New York I invited him out to Connecticut for a party in his honor and to stay overnight at my home. He accepted with evident pleasure and asked if we knew Jean Stafford. We did, and he asked us to invite her, too, which we were glad to do.

I was amazed when, during the cocktail hour, he was directly, specifically rude to her. It seemed a strange way to woo a writer. I asked him why he had spoken to her this way, and rather rudely asked him why he was frequently, openly rude.

He looked at me sadly.

"It's because I'm shy," he said. And he was not "putting me on."

I think I understand. Fred, despite his fine record as a publisher, was never accepted in the London "establishment." He remains an outsider. The fact that this was also true of Victor Gollancz makes one wonder if a discreet anti-Semitism is involved. But there have been Jews fully accepted there; I doubt that this is the case. I think it is rather a matter of personality. I know that both Alfred Knopf and Bennett Cerf were denied admission when presented for membership in the Century Club in New York. Yet a number of other Jews have not been; it appears to be the traditional matter of men with strong personalities making fast enemies as well as friends.

So it would have been for Victor Gollancz. A monolithic, strenuous man, he was something of a law unto himself. He liked to play with people, string them along, let them expose themselves. But when he was played with he would roar like an enraged bull. An immensely shrewd publisher, he had a penchant for American books, and he bagged a great many prize winners. But he also had a gentle and imaginative side, and never seemed to hesitate when he found a fine, sensitive novel that wouldn't sell; regularly he took it. One year when he appeared in New York on his annual visit, Ken McCormick remarked, "Here comes Operation Vacuum Cleaner."

His wife Ruth usually accompanied him, and they were a most harmonious team. When Victor became his bluntest and most insistent, she would gentle him. "Now, Victor." But she was fiercely loyal to him, and looked askance at anyone else's criticizing him.

He invariably got the better of me in our encounters. The only time I ever topped him was on one of the last occasions on which I saw him. He was leaving the Café Argenteuil as I entered. Ruth and an author were with him. After the amenities he said to me—with some pride, I thought—"You know John Updike, I suppose."

"Well, I've met him," I replied, turning to Victor's guest, who was looking surprised, "but this is John Cheever."

To return to London in 1953. The day after I was congratulated for not being like an American I went out to Oxford, to New College, to pay my respects to Lord David Cecil, who was published in America by Bobbs-Merrill. I was still seething.

Mary took a walk while I visited Cecil. When we met, three-quarters of an hour later, she looked surprised.

"Why, you're well again," she said.

Yes. I had just spent that time with a fine gentleman. Shy, rather painfully self-conscious, he extended to me his hospitality with the unpretentious courtesy I so badly needed. We talked of books; I literally had to force myself to leave. I would have been content there for the rest of the day.

The final week in London was much pleasanter. I felt fortified, and then we saw Roger Machell again, too. He, Jamie Hamilton's right arm at the firm of Hamish Hamilton, has been a joy to know. An intrepid man who performed heroically in World War II, he is equally modest and thoughtful. His rather prominent eyes, behind shining spectacles, put me off the first time I met him. They seemed to smile in a strange way. I first interpreted the smile as conveying cryptic knowledge, and felt vulnerable. But I soon learned that the expression was simply one of enjoyment of life, and through the years have found him

71

an incomparable host, a delightful companion, a sensitive judge of books—and uniquely distinguished as an Englishman who drinks bourbon.

The second time around, in 1963, when I represented Atheneum, was a much pleasanter experience. I had a few encounters of the 1953 sort but they were obscured by many delightful ones. A dinner party given by Norah Smallwood was a high point, as was my meeting with her and Ian Parsons and Peter Calvocoressi at Chatto and Windus, in the middle of which a door opened and a gnostic gnome entered, addressing a question to Norah. He stayed only briefly, but I was delighted to have seen Leonard Woolf.

I much enjoyed also a lunch at Peter de Sautoy's home, a meeting with Dwye Evans of Heinemann, a visit with Victor, another with Bob Lusty, a renewal of friendship with Mark Longman and the making of a new one with Michael Hoare . . . on and on: too many pleasant memories to recount.

So what's the reckoning? That British publishers include a great many delightful people, that I am a very thin-skinned man, that as a whole the British are genuinely reticent and distrust instant intimacy—as do I. That between the two London trips I had of course seen many of these people in New York, dealt with them, come to know them. When I went over in 1963 I was no longer a newcomer, to be proved. That that proving was probably justifiably of special importance with Americans, for—at least in those years—there was abroad a regrettably large number of my fellow countrymen whose manners and taste were atrocious. I saw them—worse, heard them—all over, in London and on the Continent.

But—

More Americans than not find Parisians rude and disagreeable. Not just the cab drivers—most Parisians. I do not. Perhaps it is simply temperament, but I enjoy arguing with them, when it seems necessary. I far prefer them to the tight-lipped Londoner of shops and theaters and restaurants, who says, "Thank you veddy much," when he/she obviously means, "Blast you bloody Americans."

I like, respect, even am devoted to many British men and women in publishing. But I end as I began. Two stories. On the

72

1953 trip, David Higham, a literary agent who resembled Colonel Blimp, took me to lunch. I was inquiring about the chance of seeing Edith Sitwell. Something about a book.

He was at pains to put me straight. Not Edith Sitwell, Dame Edith Sitwell. Do not address my letter to Miss Edith Sitwell. In addressing her directly, use My Dear Dame Edith. "I," he said in conclusion, smacking his lips, "as her agent and friend, call her Edith. But you do not."

Thanks.

Sometime between 1960 and '64, George Weidenfeld appeared at Atheneum. He had not made an appointment; Mike Bessie was out. George was disgruntled. It was suggested he see me instead. So he appeared in my office, fixed me with his popeyed stare. After shaking hands, he said abstractedly, "Hiram, I suppose you're really the finest editor in America," and looked at his watch.

For me, the culmination of my work at Bobbs was the spring '54 list. From the beginning I had been sure that I could build an adequate fiction list through my usual channels—the young people who thronged to the New School, my friends who conducted writing courses in various universities and colleges, and my own willingness—no, eagerness—to publish writers who had already made their way but been dropped by their publishers for commercial reasons.

In the third category I have already mentioned Tomlinson. A comparable case was that of Mark Harris, who could not find a publisher for his fine semifictional treatment of Vachel Lindsay, called *City of Discontent*. I published that book and then his first great novel about baseball, *The Southpaw*. It has always made me indignant that this really splendid book, worthy of Ring Lardner at his best, played second fiddle to Bernard Malamud's *The Natural*, a muddy allegorical tale that delighted the ruling elite but made porridge of baseball.

I have already written about the many good young writers who appeared at the New School; others came to me through their undergraduate teachers. Notable among the nurturers of young talent was William Blackburn of Duke University. I had first met Bill, a genially crusty, highly perceptive man a few years

73

my senior, when I was teaching at the Woman's College of the University of North Carolina at Greensboro (1942–44). We had visited each other's classes, and I soon discovered the extraordinary gift he muffled under a quiet, plain-man exterior. Eventually he introduced me to Styron, Bob Loomis, Mac Hyman, Reynolds Price and Fred Chappell, among others. He has made, unquestionably, a great contribution to American literature, as a friend, guide and teacher of young writers.

So the fiction list grew, it seemed, without much effort. But the other books, needed for balance—history, biography, belles-lettres, current affairs—these were harder to come by. While I was interested in finding young hands in these fields, too, I reasoned that a list as undistinguished as that of Bobbs needed authors with resonant names, people who had only to produce a book to be sure that it would receive wide attention.

One such whom I approached was Orville Prescott, the prominent daily book reviewer of the New York *Times*. In my experience, no other reviewer exercised so much influence on the sales of books as he did. For his reviews were electric: they crackled with the energy of his convictions.

Many readers thought and said that "prejudices" would be the more accurate word. Never mind: he said what he thought; he said it pungently and directly. As a result, he had no apathetic readers. And often he did as much to accelerate interest in a book he loathed as in one he fiercely admired—so provocative were his strictures.

Only in the case of his reviews could a publisher watch the "ticker tape" and measure the impact on orders of an exuberant or bristling Prescott review. The phone would ring and the jobbers would reorder: fifty copies, one hundred, even five hundred. He was the only book reviewer with a power comparable to that of the *Times* theater critic.

When I approached him about writing a book for Bobbs-Merrill, he was obviously, modestly pleased. I published *In My Opinion,* a book about the contemporary novel, and later, at Random House, a semiautobiographical book. He has since gone on to write about various aspects of his lifetime love affair with the Renaissance.

74

What both he and I could have feared in signing a contract was that his reviewer's treatment of Bobbs-Merrill books might be affected. But we weren't, and it didn't. He laid about him as before—praising, rejecting, denouncing in about the same proportions. He was what he was, bless him—and still is.

Obviously, most well-known writers already had publishers, who guarded them jealously. But there is a practice in the business that speaks to this problem. Almost every reputable publisher will release any of his authors to write for a competitor one book that he is eager to do, *if* the other publisher has proposed the idea for the book. With the blessing of Baker and Hurley, I set out to conceive and acquire such books, constantly adding to a list of subjects and linking to each an established writer to whom it might appeal.

A variation on this approach was to plan and publish a series, comparable to the Twentieth Century Library at Scribner's. Bobbs was strong in American history, and, in collaboration with a young Columbia historian, Donald Bigelow, I innovated the Makers of the American Tradition series. Each book would have representative selections from the writings of the American in question, and an interpretive analysis of his contribution to the tradition.

The first three volumes were *Roger Williams,* by Perry Miller; *Benjamin Franklin,* by I. Bernard Cohen of Harvard; and *Andrew Jackson,* by Harold Syrett of Columbia. A fourth appeared after I had left Bobbs: *John Dewey,* by Irwin Edman— his last book. I have never been able to analyze successfully the reason that this series did not "get off the ground"; perhaps our intramural problems played a large part in its relative failure, for American history was another precinct over which DLC exercised a proprietary (and effective) guardianship.

Perry Miller's *Roger Williams* was the exception; it is still in demand. And his name, and Edman's, were the sort I coveted in my attempt to bring more prestige to the firm's list. But the series was only one special device I used in my general attempt. The two releases I was most happy to secure were from Knopf and William Morrow, to enable, respectively, Louis Kronenberger to write a book on the state of American culture and manners, and

Joseph Wood Krutch to write a twenty-five-year-later sequel to his notable *The Modern Temper*. These two books were published in the spring of 1954 as *Company Manners* and *The Measure of Man*.

Both were very well received in every way, and the following spring *The Measure of Man* won the National Book Award for nonfiction. But considerable as their success was, there was another book on the list that far exceeded their records. This was Elmer Davis's *But We Were Born Free*.

Davis, one of our really great journalists, had been a Bobbs author for a long time, but had not written a book for years. Now he had been persuaded by Anne Ross, a part-time editor in the Indianapolis office and an old friend, to put together a book of essays, partly articles he had already published, with a new lead piece that was a frontal attack on Senator Joseph McCarthy's intimidation of America, then at its peak.

This book caught on and ran its course like a forest fire. For months the two competing books for the number-one place on the nonfiction best-seller list in the New York *Times* were Davis's courageous one and *The Second Tree from the Corner*, by E. B. White. Now one, now the other would take over first place. But they were always one, two. I look at that best-seller list today and mumble, "There were giants in those days."

Our triumvirate of Davis, Krutch and Kronenberger created quite a stir in publishing circles. This was clearly a new Bobbs-Merrill. I had had no real part in securing or editing *But We Were Born Free;* indeed, I did not meet Mr. Davis until a couple of years later. Herman Ziegner, at first in charge of publicity at the Indianapolis office, and thereafter an accomplished editor, both at Bobbs and Atheneum, had collaborated with Anne Ross in the editorial work. But to New York publishing circles, I was *the* Bobbs-Merrill editor, and despite my disclaimers I was given the credit for the Davis as well as for the Kronenberger and Krutch books.

That spring—I think it was in April—my phone rang. A secretarial voice said, "Mr. Haydn? Will you hold a moment, please, for a call from Mr. Cerf."

And then—breezy, ebullient, "Hiram Haydn? This is Bennett Cerf. I called you in Indianapolis. What are you doing in New York?"

Long later, I told Bennett that he had hired me on an uninformed hunch—that he had not even known enough about me to be aware that I was Bobbs's *New York* editor, and that he was convinced that I, singlehanded, was responsible for the triumph of Elmer Davis's book. But, on the latter score, I reminded him that at each of our first three meetings I had repeated that the Davis had not been my book. I felt it important to stress this, because both he and Donald Klopfer reiterated their hope that, if I came to Random House, I would build their nonfiction list as I had that at Bobbs-Merrill.

Oddly enough I cannot remember clearly my first telephone conversations and meetings with Bennett. I do remember that he asked me right off whether I would consider coming to Random, and I had replied that I thought not. I had worked so hard on the list at Bobbs that I didn't want to relinquish it now that things were really "coming our way." I believe he suggested that I think about it some more and, if I decided I was at all interested, call him back.

It itched, and I called him back. After some more talk he set up a lunch at Donald Klopfer's apartment, for just the three partners—Cerf, Klopfer, Bob Haas—and me.

That lunch I remember in detail. We had barely started eating before Bennett began to quiz me. I had decided, he said, that I wanted to come to Random House. Now what sort of terms did I have in mind?

I was as dumfounded as I had been at my first meeting with Mr. Chambers. To be sure, Bennett's upsmanship was much more direct, but this also meant that one had no time to prepare oneself for it. And another difference was that I was now being inspected with close scrutiny by six eyes—not just two, however piercing.

I underwent once more that agony of having to speak up, risk conflict, that has dogged me since an exquisitely miserable childhood first falsely taught me to fear the retribution that self-assertion might set in motion.

I managed. I said that I could not see why I should suggest terms and conditions. I had not sought out Bennett; he had sought me, to ask if I was interested in a job at Random House. It seemed to me appropriate that he propose terms, if he was serious about his invitation.

Bob Haas giggled. That grave, distinguished gentleman giggled with obvious glee. And Donald Klopfer's long, melancholy face lighted with amusement, perhaps even with approval. I relaxed.

Bennett seemed a bit annoyed for a moment, saying rapidly, "Well, you did call me back, didn't you?" But he then, with customary resilience—reverting, as I was to learn he almost always did, to his natural honesty and fairness—began to laugh at himself.

Thereafter it was a very pleasant meal; we parted with the understanding that the three of them would draw up a proposal and then get in touch again.

It was about two weeks before I heard from Bennett. In the meantime I felt unsettled. The offer was bound to be much better than my present arrangement with Bobbs-Merrill. To go to Random House, one of the several best houses, was an obvious step upward, in terms of both prestige and money. And my family had expanded; Mary and I had three children now.

Why then did I feel so unsure about the move? Was it a lack of confidence in myself? Did I feel inadequate to so imposing an organization and title? For Bennett had made it clear that they were seeking a new editor in chief. Or was it simply that, with DLC inactive, the job at Bobbs was very secure? I had won my place there, and shouldn't I now enjoy it?

One evening in those two weeks I was working late. The radio was buzzing away; I seldom heard it. Suddenly, however, I gave it alert attention. Someone had said, "Bennett Cerf."

The program was one called "Conversation." On it this time were Clifton Fadiman, Louis Kronenberger, Oscar Levant (the well-known panelist from "Information, Please"), perhaps one or two others, and Bennett. The topic was "What are you most afraid of?"

The talk was brisk, full of interruptions, sallies of wit, and laughter. The consensus was for "annihilation by the Bomb." There were occasional variants, but that was *it*.

At last Fadiman said, "Bennett, you haven't said a word. Are you ill?"

Bennett's voice sounded uncharacteristically small, even diffident. He said that he hesitated to answer this question truthfully because he was aware that his reply must seem trivial, self-obsessed, beside the vast matters that had been discussed. Yet the point of the program surely was to say what you really thought and believed. Anyway, what he feared most was not being loved.

That was the moment I decided definitely to go to Random House if the offer was satisfactory. The man I had just heard say those words with unmistakable genuineness was a man I could talk to, a man I could work with.

And so, a week or two later, I sat beside a swimming pool in Mount Kisco (feeling a little as though I had been transplanted to Hollywood) and listened to Bennett. The salary offered was more than twice the one at Bobbs. The marginal benefits—their retirement plan, the profit sharing for employees, the major medical policy for which they paid half, the Christmas bonuses—the "marginal" benefits were staggering to a man whose present employers had only once in four years made a gesture beyond the paying of his moderate salary: a Christmas bonus in the form of a twenty-five-dollar government bond!

I remember the moment when Bennett stipulated the salary. I sat there in silence, astonished and afraid to betray my awe. He misread me.

"That wouldn't be all," he said hastily. "It would be difficult to go any higher without going well beyond the range of editors' salaries and coming close to what Donald and I take from the business. But there are other ways of raising the ante."

He proceeded to outline an "incentive plan," whereby I would get a certain commission on every copy sold of each book I brought in, regardless of whether the book made a profit. The percentage of the commission, however, would be raised once a book had broken even. Furthermore, I would get a cut of all reprint leases and book-club deals.

I still find this offer incredible, one that my contribution to

79

Random House never justified. It took all the self-control I had to confine my response to saying it was certainly a good offer, and now I must find out what the reaction of the Bobbs-Merrill people would be.

Bennett suggested dryly that he was ready to wait for the verification of what he considered certain—that Bobbs would be unable or unwilling to match his offer.

He was right, of course. Almost two months passed before Ross Baker finally made his trip to Indianapolis to confer with Lowe Berger, and came back with a proposal that came nowhere near that of Random.

Soon I was sitting with Bob Haas, going over the final details of my five-year contract (the first I had ever had for my editorial services). The news that I was going to Random House had led to daily advice from "friends" who all counseled me to be tough and "get everything" I could in this deal. "They're out of your class," one said. "You need a lawyer."

This advice affected me more than I realized at the time, and I quibbled (in retrospect, I think, greedily) over small advantages. I remember Bob's fine eyes fixed on me questioningly; I remember my shame. I'm glad that this was the last time I ever saw him look at me that way.

I signed in August '54, but I stayed on at Bobbs till the end of the year—a dry season during which I could only mark time. It was an enormous relief when, early in January 1955, I for the first time turned north from Grand Central to go to work.

On that first morning, I arrived early. At the receptionist's desk I asked, as instructed, for Donald Klopfer, and was told to go up to his office. The vast spiral staircase between the first and second floors of Random House must have persuaded as many courted authors to join the firm's list as the partners or any editor. It was majestic, as was the whole house, from its stately courtyard and front door onward. Built for the Villard family of railroad fame, it was bought by Joseph Kennedy while he was ambassador to Great Britain. Bennett and Donald acquired it by winning the favor of Cardinal Spellman for their publication of Étienne Gilson's work on Thomas Aquinas. The Cardinal "instructed" the Ambassador to sell it to them! Or so Bennett told me.

For this old stone mansion at the corner of Madison Avenue and Fifty-first Street shares a large cobbled courtyard with the Archdiocese of New York. Now that Random House has moved to a new building on Third Avenue, the north wing of the mansion has been reclaimed by the Church.

At any rate, that first morning the stairs awed me, as they had on earlier visits. I proceeded to Donald's office and paused in the doorway. He was in the midst of what sounded like an emotional telephone conversation.

"No, no, Dorothy," he said. "You tell Saxe that nothing has changed, that we love him just as much as we always have. I'm terribly sorry about the ulcers kicking up again. We'll have his new office ready in a couple of weeks and we want him all well by then. Now, Dorothy, make him see sense. You know we really love him." He was manifestly upset, even pleading.

When he hung up, he turned and saw me. For a moment of eloquent silence, his dark, mobile face expressed surprise, embarrassment, sadness and chagrin. Then it lighted up into a smile, and he spread his hands wide in that immemorial gesture that confounds both the tragic and the comic.

"So you heard." Then, more briskly, "Life must go on. I'll call Bob."

It was not clear why both Haas and Klopfer were needed to escort me to my office halfway down the hall, but I decided that they felt I needed support after our conversation of the previous week. It had been only then that I had learned I was to have Saxe Commins's office, and he was to be moved up to the fifth floor, into a new one. I had protested; Bennett and Donald had charged me with undue sentimentality. I had replied that I was not being noble, but practical. My taking over Saxe's office would prejudice his friends and colleagues here against me: it wasn't fair to force me into such a position.

They insisted. They were being practical, too. If I was to be their head editor, they must have easy access to me; my office must be on their floor. Moreover, no one would blame me; everyone would know it was their decision. I capitulated because there was nothing else I could do.

Bob and Donald escorted me those thirty or forty steps, as firmly as policemen, to the office I had not wanted to occupy.

We entered. A small, neat, silver-haired man was seated at a table.

Bob Haas spoke his piece.

"Bill, this is Hiram Haydn, our new editor. Hiram, this is William Faulkner. You'll share the office just for two weeks; then we'll move you upstairs, Bill, to Saxe's new office."

Mr. Faulkner gravely acknowledged the introduction. The two partners tumbled out, perfidious dissemblers, and left me alone with William Faulkner.

Now I understood why Haas had been summoned: to break the news to Faulkner. It was he who had been Faulkner's publisher before they both came to Random. And I was particularly angry that they had not told me that when Faulkner worked in New York he shared this office with Saxe.

After a few polite remarks, Mr. Faulkner turned back to his work, and I was left to simmer in silence. My files had not yet arrived from Bobbs-Merrill; I had no desk work to do. There were many useful telephone calls to be made, but how could I talk naturally to anyone when the greatest novelist in America was sitting a few feet away, working on a new book?

Bennett had no such scruples. A half hour later, he came in, moving in three-quarter time, and saying, "Hi, Bill! Welcome to Random House, Hi!"

Then his manner abruptly changed. Ten days before, I had deposited a manuscript with him, saying that I was not recommending it to him but that it seemed to me an interesting one over which to get acquainted with each other's publishing judgment. I thought it a quite salable but trivial and vulgar story.

Now Bennett plunked it down on my desk and said sharply, "Here's that miserable piece of trash you gave me to read. I'm surprised at you, Hiram," and left the room. His staccato heels beat a forced march away. I listened to their diminishing echoes while a slow but devastating heat mounted to my head.

For another three-quarters of an hour I sat there in alternate rage and despair. I doodled fiercely; I wrote my resignation twice. I felt humiliated, furious and desolate.

Then at last William Faulkner slowly turned around in his

swivel chair—a progress so slow and deliberate that it seemed to me I watched for minutes.

He looked at me; his eyes were clear and kind.

"Why, Mr. Haydn," he said, "I don't reckon you're doin' hardly anything."

I acknowledged the truth of this with a strangled gurgle.

He smiled, and asked me if I was concerned about disturbing him at his work. He assured me that, whether he was at home in Mississippi or here in Saxe's office, no amount of talk or noise affected his concentration.

I made some feeble response, and he looked at me thoughtfully.

"Are you troubled," he finally asked, "about being here in Saxe's office? You don't suppose that I think you wanted to take it away from him, do you? Why, Mr. Haydn, no man in his right mind would want to come in and do that. I never have considered such a thing. It's those great monopolists down the hall—" he pointed—"they arranged it this way because they're sensible men. Now you forget all that—especially about my work—and do the things you're here for."

All this in the gentlest of Southern voices. I felt healed. And for two weeks I did what I was "there for," what he had suggested, except that I did still lower my voice—I hoped effectively but not conspicuously.

I was, of course, intensely curious about Faulkner at work. (The new novel was *The Town*.) Several times that week he left for lunch before I did. Each such time, without shame—as I report it without shame—I went over to study the sheet left on the table at which he worked or in the typewriter on the nearby stand. For he wrote in longhand at the table, then (it had seemed to me) rose when he finished a single page, and carried it to the typewriter, where (apparently) he rewrote it. Surely his *furor poeticus* was not submissive to such quantitative measurement!

Yet it was—if that's what it should be called. Twice the evidence was unmistakable. In each case the page in longhand had ended in the midst of a sentence: once with the word "and," once in the middle of a prepositional phrase. I pondered these breaks and became aware of the possibility that I was being preternaturally naïve: that it was not a question of Faulkner's being the slave of a quantitative slide rule, but rather being so open to the dictates of what Montaigne called *"le patron dedans"* that he could leave off anywhere and regain the flow simply by waiting and listening for that master voice to resume.

It was early in the second week that I finally managed the temerity to ask him about this process. Every morning, punctually at eleven, he would lay down his pencil or still the typewriter and swing around to face me. He would light a cigarette and begin to talk. It was our social hour, and, in anticipation of it, I would carefully clear away in advance whatever interruptive debris might interfere with it. I even arranged with the switchboard operator to take all calls between 10:45 and 11:15. Had Faulkner known this, I think it would have amused and pleased him. A hint or two suggested to me that he enjoyed veneration if it was not explicit or vulgar.

He would talk for no more than ten minutes, and although he made polite attempts to draw me out about myself and my work I preferred listening to him. As a result, neither of us said much that would gracefully survive repetition.

But on this Monday or Tuesday morning I blurted out my confession about peeking, and asked my question. He laughed.

"Why, Mr. Haydn," he said, "haven't you ever heard that I wouldn't know a sentence if I saw one? I don't read those reviews, but I hear about them. And I just suppose that it's more interesting this way. If you stop at 'and,' why, you can go anywhere. And that's what we all want, isn't it—to feel that we can go anywhere?"

It sufficed, and we continued our polite and casual acquaintance. Only on the very last day he shared the office did I really secure another insight.

I had an appointment for lunch that day with a young woman named Charlotte Payne. I had published her good first novel, called *Milo,* at Bobbs-Merrill the previous year. Charlotte had come north from Mississippi to write novels. She had discovered that there was more to the process than writing if one desired also to eat. Being naturally gifted, she became a Powers model.

She was announced, and I asked the receptionist to send her

84

up to my office. As her heels clattered through the small coat room that led to the office proper I witnessed a transformation in Mr. Faulkner. I swear that the small hairs on the back of his neck bristled, and in instant reflex he began the slow movement of the swivel chair that would bring him around to face me.

I rose to greet Charlotte, who burst into a stream of rapid chatter. I interrupted her.

"Charlotte," I said, "I want you to meet William Faulkner. Mr. Faulkner, Miss Payne."

She acknowledged his bow briefly, turned back to me.

"But Hiram," she said, "I want to tell you—"

Then she froze, and in obedience to the classic double take, swung back to face that small elegant man. She gasped.

"Why, Mr. Faulkner," she said. "Mistuh Faulk-nuh. Why, I guess this is the proudest moment of my life."

He bowed again, courteously, and smiled.

She rattled on, reciting a list of all his novels, interjecting sighs and "why" and "oh my goodness" from time to eloquent time. Then she finally stilled herself and looked at him with unmistakable reverence.

"I know I'm making a fool of myself," she whispered, "but you can't know what this means to me. Mr. Faulkner, I'm from Mississippi!"

That debonaire man inclined his head again.

"So am I," he said. . . .

That afternoon he returned from lunch, smiled at me and showed me a copy of the paper-bound edition of *Milo*.

I missed him badly when he moved upstairs.

Although I had come to Random House as editor in chief, there was no announcement to that effect, and no departmental organization. I couldn't discern any way in which my status was different from that of some four other senior editors.

Finally, I asked Bennett about the matter. He explained that he didn't want to make Harry Maule uncomfortable. Harry would retire in a year or two (as it turned out, he stayed on for some seven or eight years!), and then the new order would be openly established. Instead, at the end of the year Robert Linscott, another veteran, did retire, and Albert Erskine was moved down to his office, between Bennett's and mine. Soon it became apparent that Bennett didn't want to offend Albert either: perhaps Albert had some expectation that must be nursed along. Bennett, I decided, had reassured too many people.

At that time there were, as I have intimated, three partners. The third was Robert K. Haas, whose firm of Smith and Haas had been merged into Random House some years before. Haas had brought with him a splendid list, including William Faulkner, André Malraux and Isak Dinesen. In his middle sixties, Haas was an impressive man. Kind, just, quiet, he gave the word *gentleman* a renewed force. And it was he who solved my problem.

In fact, he brought it up, saying that he didn't feel sure that I was altogether happy in my new job. When I had said my say, he smiled. "We must rectify that," he said. "I'll talk to Bennett now."

Half an hour later, he reappeared.

"The three of us will meet with you and Albert tomorrow," he said, "and straighten everything out."

At the meeting, Bennett was evidently on edge. As always when he was irritated, his eyes flashed (he was, as I have said, the only man I have ever known whose eyes *did* flash) and he talked at an accelerated pace, beating out a staccato volley of words. He concluded his summary of the situation, "So Hiram's a four-star general, and you, Albert, are a three-star one."

I told Albert then that I had no illusion that I was his superior officer, that I hoped we could be equals, sharing the command, and each in charge of different aspects of the whole editorial task. He responded in a friendly way, and we began and continued a really harmonious relationship. Slowly we worked out a program of meetings planned exclusively for the editorial department, dealing with whatever were, at a given time, its most serious problems. These meetings were also attended by the younger, assistant editors, the copy editors and the readers. We did achieve, I think, a pretty good morale for a while.

Albert Erskine is a tall, rangy, unusually handsome man. Of Southern birth and rearing, at Vanderbilt he came early into the *ambiance* of the Agrarians, a group including Allen Tate,

Andrew Lytle, John Crowe Ransom and Robert Penn Warren. Katherine Anne Porter was Albert's first wife.

I sometimes called him the last of the Confederate leaders. Pessimistic and ironic, skeptical to a point not always short of cynicism, he yet had (still has, I'm sure) a gentleman's code, reminiscent in its courtliness, its fine-tempered loyalties and its self-respect of the best of the Confederate generals. In our time, when screaming hostilities, name calling and backbiting are often taken for granted or, as sources of amusement, even admired, Albert's concern for personal honor is rare.

I remember an incident in a restaurant. Six of us had barely been seated when the restaurateur accosted one of the women at our table. He did know her, but he was very drunk and without inhibition. She was embarrassed. I told him to leave her alone. He lurched up to me, yelling, "I'll throw you out of here, you professor, you."

Instantly Albert rose. "You'll have to throw two of us out then."

I was his host and his friend. While everyone else at the table was either amused or embarrassed at the attention we were causing, Albert was, as usual, embodying his code.

The restaurant owner retreated rapidly. But the incident was not over. Albert turned to me. "After that, we cannot eat here," he said.

The others remained, but he, the woman involved, and I left. I remember feeling bemused but full of warmth over such a loyalty.

That quality was a constant in our relation at Random House. I don't recall any spectacular incidents, but I never received a crossed signal, never heard of a word spoken differently in my absence from what had been said to me. When I began taking on too much young talent, whose books were unlikely to sell, he warned me that Bennett and Donald, for all their compliance at first, were beginning to be restless.

I found Albert a very private man. He tended to be a loner. Hence his friendliness meant the more to me. And when he remarried and moved to Westport, we saw him frequently. There I discovered a different Erskine, one with a passion for working the land. I remembered with amusement the Agrarians, and wondered if any other of them had been manually agrarian.

Proud, stubborn to the point of intransigence (no one, including the partners, told him *what to do*), he was devoted to his work. And able. Of this I had—to be sure, at second hand—ample evidence. Red Warren, Ralph Ellison, Edmund Fuller and many others have told me how much they liked working with him. And I believe that he is the only editor who ever persuaded John O'Hara to make a change in one of his manuscripts.

After Saxe Commins's death, Albert was "assigned" to William Faulkner. To be Commins's successor was a formidable assignment, because he and Faulkner had been inseparable for many years. But the new arrangement was bound to turn out right: the two men had been born into the same tradition; they apparently understood each other from their first session.

I happened to be in Donald Klopfer's office the day that first editorial session was going on down the hall, and I was surprised when Faulkner entered.

"I don't mean to interrupt you," he said to Donald, "but I feel I must tell you what has just happened." He went on to describe Erskine's proposals for revisions in a new edition of an early novel, and wound up, "I got more help from Mr. Erskine in an hour than I've ever before experienced."

I have suggested that the meetings Albert and I arranged gave some coherence to our large department. But the existing editorial arrangement meant that there was no danger of our program hardening into a bureaucracy. The partners of the firm believed in giving each editor a real autonomy. The resultant process went something like this: if an editor decided he would like to sign up a book, he took it either to Klopfer or to Cerf, described it, and explained the reasons he believed it should be accepted. Sometimes the partner in question agreed, and terms were discussed. Sometimes he chose to read the script before giving consent. If there was disagreement, the script might be passed on to the other partner. Or the merits of the disagreement would be worked out on the spot. And I cannot remember, in all the cases of which I knew, either partner's using his authority arbitrarily. Bennett would come on hard in disagreement,

Donald soft, but both were impeccably fair, and big enough to yield if the editor's argument was sufficiently impressive.

However inconvenient this system sometimes was to Erskine's and my supervision of a department, the theory behind it is to me sound practice. You give your man a chance to prove himself. He has a freedom and a responsibility far beyond those usually assigned individual editors. Either he makes his own way, or he doesn't.

The chinks in this reasonable plan were Klopfer and Cerf themselves. They were almost incapable of firing anyone, including editors who did not live up to their responsibilities. I remember one astonishing case. They felt that a particular editor had failed not only to produce a profitable list but also to justify *that* failure by sponsoring really distinguished books for a small market. It was evident that he must go if their plan was to have serious meaning and force.

They tossed a coin to decide which of them would tell the editor the bad news. Klopfer lost, but agreed to carry through only if Cerf would sit in on the session and break in whenever it was clear that he was weakening. Just before this meeting they rehearsed their discussion in my office, across the hall from Bennett's. Then, like conspiratorial high-school boys, they crossed over to the meeting place.

I saw the editor come down the hall, enter Bennett's office, and close the massive door behind him. He looked distraught.

Abandon hope. . . .

I could not work. I sat there, identifying with that man until identification became a physical pain. I cannot remember that even a twinge of self-congratulation stained my sympathy: there, but for the grace of God—

A half hour passed, an hour. I did not see the editor when he left, but I heard the closing of the door and then his rapid footsteps. They were not those of a defeated and humiliated man. But then I had known *that*. Bennett and Donald would have been kind.

I waited for them to come in. Ten minutes. Twenty. I crossed the hall and knocked. Bennett's voice, admitting me, sounded as though he was gasping.

I found them weak with laughter. I stared at them.

"What's so funny?" I demanded.

They quieted down, looked sheepish. Finally Donald explained. They had not only never gotten around to firing the editor; they had raised his salary and lent him money for the down payment on a house!

This relation between the partners and their editors, as I have said, made it difficult for Erskine and me to exert any real authority over the department. And the setup was too pleasant to push hard for centralization. Moreover, there were three senior editors who would have understandably resented being subordinate to younger men. These were Saxe Commins, Bob Linscott and Harry Maule.

Commins was renowned as the editor of Faulkner and O'Neill. It was he whom I was succeeding as editor in chief; he had had a heart attack and could now work only on a part-time basis. Maule had come to Random House from Doubleday after some trouble there, bringing Sinclair Lewis with him. He was widely known as the Old Pro. Linscott, formerly of Houghton Mifflin, was another highly regarded editor, who worked with a number of Random's most successful writers. But all three men were, it seemed clear, near retirement. And all three were decidedly worth knowing.

Saxe Commins was pleasant and friendly to me; we lunched together a time or two.

In his postcoronary period, he was clearly a defeated man. He could not accept his diminished schedule, and he complained about having too much time on his hands at home in Princeton.

I suggested that he turn to writing. Memoirs? He had known intimately many famous writers—people about whom the world likes to hear.

Saxe was not unreceptive, but lukewarm. He didn't feel he had it in him. He wasn't a writer; he was an editor. That was a prime distinction for him.

When people in publishing spoke of great editors, they cited, with reason, Maxwell Perkins, Ben Huebsch, Eugene Saxton, Saxe Commins. Saxe had given his life to his work, and with the work radically curtailed, so was his life. He had already spent much of it on O'Neill, Faulkner, Auden, O'Hara, James

Michener and Budd Schulberg and Irwin Shaw—on many and various writers.

In serving them, in letting them absorb him, in so totally identifying himself with them (the stories of his attending Faulkner twenty-four hours a day during one of his "bad periods" are legion), had he perhaps lost his separate identity, and with it his capacity for distance—so important to an editor? Was this the meaning of Faulkner's statement about Erskine's help? Had Saxe become so devoted to Faulkner that he had been immersed in him?

The dangers of the author-editor relationship have been cited countless times. Being made, or making oneself ("some achieve greatness"), a father figure, a therapist, a confidant, a seer, a love object—these are the perils of the editor who needs to be first, who thinks and speaks of "my authors." Now consider the opposite tendency. Becoming an extension of great men and women, and thereby losing objectivity about them and their work—these are the snares and traps for the editor who needs totally to subordinate himself, even to be assimilated. This one wants to be introduced by the writers with whom he works as "my editor."

I am of course exaggerating. No one goes all the way in either direction. And I am not saying that this second sort of tendency was even partly true of Saxe Commins, for I do not know. I was not there. But I am saying that his attitude on one occasion incited these speculations.

The other two senior editors at Random House in my time there were equally interesting men. Bob Linscott was as much an individualist as Saxe seemed to me a self-denying editorial priest.

A tall, rugged man, Linscott actually looked like the Great Stone Face of the White Mountains. There also seemed to be an Indian cast to his features, but I never discovered whether there were Indians among his ancestors. I found him a fascinating and admirable man.

I had been warned against him by several people. He would resent my coming in as editor in chief; he would take every opportunity to knife me; I must stay as far away from him as I could.

My fate with people against whom I have been warned has, on the whole, been a happy one. There have been one or two exceptions, but otherwise the alleged villain has eventually become a much valued friend. The most notable example is William Jovanovich, who was at the time of the warning the president of Harcourt, Brace & World, and is now the chairman and chief executive officer of Harcourt Brace Jovanovich. When I accepted his offer to become his copublisher, as he called it, the telephone throbbed with forebodings. I shall be grateful all my remaining days for the chance to work with Bill and for our friendship.

Though in a less crucial way, my experience with Bob Linscott followed this pattern. No one could have been kindlier to the new editor in chief than he was. Soon after my arrival, when he invited me to lunch, I found him a delightful raconteur, a wise and original man. He was shy, spare with words, but when he leaned into a story or an opinion it was always worth listening to. Most interesting of all, he talked very little about others at Random House. Advance notices had called him a gossip, a backbiter and an infighter. I observed none of these qualities.

After that first year he was in New York only from time to time, in connection with special editorial projects. He and his wife had a farm near Northampton, Massachusetts, which he cultivated and where he chopped wood and did other arduous chores with relish, although he must have been close to eighty.

One incident before his departure from full-time work at Random House stays in my mind. William Styron had come with me from Bobbs-Merrill to Random House. The brilliant young Southern novelist had a deep reverence for Faulkner's work. I mentioned this on one occasion to Linscott, who was Faulkner's close friend. They lunched together with regularity, and I would have given a great deal to have been able to hide in the woodwork and listen to their talk.

Linscott responded immediately to my mention of Bill Styron's devotion to Faulkner. "Let's set up a lunch," he said enthusiastically. "You and Styron, Bill [Faulkner] and I."

It was arranged, and of that occasion I retain indelibly two impressions. One was Faulkner's immediate courtesy and friendliness to Styron. Contrary to the stories about his aloofness and inaccessibility to other Random House authors, he was open and gracious. My other vivid memory is of Bob Linscott's face. He brooded over the scene like a wizard: mostly silent, scrupulously attentive, and with a relishing gleam in his eye. There was something of the magus in him. I thought of Merlin, advising Arthur in advance of his meeting with a likely young knight, and finding a magician's pleasure in the fruitful outcome of the elixir he had brewed.

No two men could have been less alike than Linscott and Harry Maule, the third senior editor. Harry was of middle height, sharp-featured, with bright eyeglasses and carefully combed white hair. His tone was dry and matter-of-fact, and this effect was reinforced by the nasality of his voice.

Many people found him incredibly literal-minded. He was explicative, not implicative. Moreover, he belonged to an order of editors who were proud of being "old pros." He talked more about markets and sales figures and "women books" and "men books" than all the rest of us put together. He was apt, at sales conferences, to go into greater detail about any given book than most salesmen wanted to hear. And until Lee Wright came to Random he edited most of the mysteries and suspense novels we published, even an occasional Western. He was intolerant, to the point of indignation, of anything he considered *avant-garde* or precious.

But this is a very superficial portrait of the man who was Sinclair Lewis's friend and editor, and who, with Melville Cane, Lewis's friend and lawyer, edited *The Man from Main Street, a Sinclair Lewis Reader*. Indeed, a parody, perhaps, for I never came to know him well. By the time I met him he was already rather holding off from all his colleagues. But I did come to respect him, with his "tailor-made list," his strong prejudices, and his gentle way with plants. His office came close to being a greenhouse, and I remember the affection with which some of us would watch him putter about, filling his watering can, peering down closely at some stem or leaf. All his plants flourished.

And so, for that matter, in its own way, did his list.

Bennett Cerf and Donald Klopfer were an extraordinary team. They tempt me to the risky generalization that two is the essential number for a really successful publishing house. But, of course, exceptions to this statement flock instantly to mind.

At any rate, these two made an unusually happy combination. Opposites in temperament and taste, they complemented each other with rare symmetry. Bennett was volatile, energetic, dynamic, Donald quiet, deliberate, thorough. Bennett was in charge of advertising and publicity, and played a dominant part in all deals with people in film and theater. He was also an ingenious innovator: it was he who turned the old Liveright Modern Library into the great forerunner of today's paper-bound editions of the classics, and it was he who conceived the spectacularly successful series for children, the Landmark Books.

Donald had an outstanding administrative head, and it was he who studied, from one boundary to another, the many different units of publishing work that must mesh for efficient functioning. During my time at Random House he actually visited every department of the firm at least once every day. Moreover, it was to Donald that any employee with a grievance or a problem or an idea came, rightly confident of a full hearing. That long, sad face, those expressive eyes, were not deceptive; he had a capacious reservoir of sympathy and understanding.

Twice this quality affected me intimately. The first time was at a dinner party in our home. Late in the evening our youngest child, Miranda, then only four or five, woke up and came downstairs. She stood there in her nightgown, blinking, shy, a little cross.

Various people addressed her in that jargon that is neither baby talk nor intelligible English, and she ducked her head and looked away. I asked her if she'd like to sit in my lap, and she suddenly was fully awake.

"No," she whispered to me. "I want to sit in his lap," pointing, and went directly to Donald, settling there happily until she fell asleep in his arms. . . .

When our twelve-year-old son Michael was badly injured in a car accident I did not go to work for three days—until he was declared out of danger.

When I finally re-entered my office, Donald was there within five minutes. We shook hands, and I assured him that Mike was going to recover. Then we sat there for several minutes more, in a silence that I found uniquely peaceful. At last I saw a large tear leave his eye and literally roll slowly down his cheek. He made no effort to check its course; he said nothing. He simply smiled painfully, rose, and left the room. . . .

I realize that I am painting him as a kind, sensitive, thoughtful man, but predominantly sad, melancholy. Yet I have seen him hearty, ruddy, excited with life, and his laughter has resonance. I think I never saw him younger or more exuberant than one morning when I was in the hall and watched him run all the way up the long marble stairs to stand at the top, exultant, laughing, vital. It was only later that I remembered—wondering—that Bennett was away on a lecture tour.

There was no question but that he stood in Bennett's ebullient shadow—publicly, at least. I suppose that ninety per cent (or more) of the people to whom Bennett Cerf was a household name did not know the name of his partner, or even that he had one, but in the publishing house it was Donald who was paterfamilias to most of us. And in their relationship as partners, so far as I could know at first hand, they were true equals, sometimes in amity, sometimes in conflict.

I had been at Random only a little more than a week when the partners entered my office, wrangling in loud voices. When they quieted down, I learned that they violently disagreed about a manuscript recommended by Gerry Gottlieb, one of our young editors. Both of them had read it. Donald found it uproariously funny, and was eager to publish it. Bennett thought it cheap, a vulgar attack on the Catholic Church. They finally made it clear to me that this was one of my responsibilities: to make an editorial decision when the partners disagreed.

They left, still brawling, and I heard Donald say, "Come on, Bennett, you're just afraid that Spellman will raise hell with you. If you refuse to publish this book, don't ever call yourself a publisher to me again!"

I read the script; I delighted in it. It was published as *The Straight and Narrow Path,* Honor Tracy's first book to appear in the United States. When I somewhat apprehensively presented my findings to the two partners, I learned what I was to rediscover over and over again: there was no resentment, no reproach, no bickering.

Bennett said, "I predict we'll all be sorry." And that was that; in a minute or so, he was carrying on with some new and particularly outrageous pun.

Donald, then, could have as good a time as anyone else. But his prevailing timbre *was* melancholy. I don't pretend to understand the cause; he was also an intensely private man. Without being persuaded of the infallibility of the study of handwriting, I do find it somewhat revelatory. Donald's signature is wholly indecipherable.

Nor was he prone to the personal about himself. People often confided to him their most intimate aspirations and fears; he would listen gravely, attentively, and—to judge by the few times I was fully aware of the details—counsel wisely. It seemed to me that his very detachment from his own life (this is the way I saw it) freed him to be the more dispassionate and perceptive about the lives of others.

I often wondered whether he was aware of the frequency with which he opened his comments, in an argument over a writer, a deal of some sort, or a matter of general policy, with "Frankly" or "I'm going to be frank with you" or "In all frankness." If ever phrases were designed to arouse suspicion and guardedness, it is these. Yet such an interpretation always turned out irrelevant in Donald's case. What followed that introduction was straightforward and well reasoned. This led me to associate these phrases rather with his privacy, his emotional withdrawal. I suspected that when he said, "I'm going to be frank with you," he meant literally what he said, but he was also admonishing himself to "come *out* with it."

Such mannerisms and idioms of speech have always fascinated me. Lewis Miller, then sales manager and later vice-president of Random House, was perpetually saying "I for one . . ." It was tempting to an amateur psychologist to find the hidden springs of such a phrase in an egotism so pervasive that he recognized a need to put a formal check on its expression. But to know Lew was to find this interpretation, in turn, inapplicable. He had a certain flair, an idiosyncratic style that was at once formal and genuine, a manner that would have seemed appropriate at the court of Louis XIV, yet about which there was nothing meretricious. And far from being arrogant, he was thoughtful and considerate beyond the norm. So I learned, however belatedly, to temper these observations with a little skepticism.

Among the opposite charges that sparked Donald and Bennett were those of privacy and openness. Bennett was so open as to make it seem sometimes that he wore his entrails on his sleeve. Those who didn't like him often found him a brash exhibitionist, a show-off. Those who did like him (including me) found the ready accessibility of all his emotions, his almost total lack of reserve, refreshing and endearing.

His self-knowledge and his freedom to be himself, wherever and whenever I saw him, were truly extraordinary, if not always comfortable for others. I learned very soon to avoid him, if possible, in the mornings. Frequently, he seemed to have spent his last waking moments of the previous night counting and listing everything at Random House that currently displeased him. He would march in filled with a bill of indictments, and his angry voice would roll out across the hall into my office. But almost always, after lunch, he would return in good spirits, and his laughter would ring out for most of the afternoon.

He always recognized, and eventually acknowledged, the times he had been arbitrary, bad-tempered, unfair. I remember vividly one occasion when my son Jonathan, then only eight or nine years old, had come up to the second floor, unannounced, to join me and go home with me.

Jon had met Bennett at our house, and thought him the funniest and one of the "nicest" men he knew. Hence he acted with the forthrightness that Bennett himself practiced—with disastrous results. The first I knew of his arrival was when Bennett, in a fury, appeared in my office, dragging Jonny by one arm. He was so angry that he was almost incoherent.

"Do you know—this boy of yours—he opened my closed door without even knocking and walked right in. I'm having a very important meeting with some people from Hollywood. This is not a kindergarten, Hiram."

By now I had risen, equally angry over the way he had hauled my boy into the office. But Bennett didn't even see me. He turned back on Jon: "Didn't you? Isn't that what you did?"

Jon, to my surprise, did not even seem frightened.

"Yes, I did," he said. "What's wrong with that?"

I don't believe that I have ever, before or since, watched such a rapid succession of emotions seize and release a human face. And then Bennett, suddenly relaxed, was drained of tension.

"Not a thing, son," he finally said, shaking his head. "When you come right down to it, not a goddamn thing. Will you come back in with me?"

Jonny declined, but he seemed largely unshaken. He accepted the sudden transition; everything was all right now, for this was the Mr. Cerf he knew.

Since both Bennett and I were "trigger men," as Lew Miller liked to point out, we tangled frequently. I think it is accurate to say that we did not have arguments or disagreements; we had fights. Interestingly enough, the other partners approved of this. On one occasion, they came together to see me, and with some tact and reserve, commended me for "standing up to" Bennett, saying that there were too many "yes men" in the organization. This conversation surprised me, for as a rule Bennett and Donald seemed inseparable comrades, and Bob Haas, as the latecomer to the partnership, held at a little distance from their intimacy.

Only twice in the more than four years I worked at Random House did Bennett and I go home unreconciled. In neither case can I remember the precise cause of our trouble; what I do remember is the look on his face when we parted. It's hard to describe, but I think I would call it darkly, sweetly malicious. Yes, those are the adverbs. Yet by nine o'clock in the evening, on both occasions, my home telephone rang, and it was Bennett.

"Hi," he said, "how do you feel? I feel lousy."

A charge frequently leveled at Bennett was that he was predominately a playboy—a celebrity hunter who cared much more about his puns and joke books, his lecture tours, his Hollywood friends, his television show and the entertainment world in general than he did about Random House. He was no publisher; he let Donald do all the real work while he concentrated on getting himself in front of as many cameras as he could.

"Just answer this," I remember one man saying insistently to me. "Suppose Bennett Cerf had to choose between all his other

98

activities and his work at Random House. Wouldn't he give up Random?"

This time I had the right answer ready.

"No," I said firmly, "he would keep Random House, give up all the other things, and die."

For Bennett not only loved that publishing house foremost and fiercely; he worked at it, planned for it, and found in it the central meaning of his life. Yet so restless and energetic a man needed other outlets as well, and through them became the prophet of laughter.

He made no attempt to conceal the glamour that the entertainment world and association with its celebrities held for him.

"I just love it," he told me once, almost fervently, "and I love being a celebrity myself."

I remember walking back with him from lunch at Toots Shor's (the only time I have ever been there—and Bennett was the only person who could have persuaded me to go) a few days before he was to leave on his first European trip in years.

"I don't want to go," he said suddenly.

"You don't want to go?" I was astonished.

"No." He paused, looked theatrically guilty. "You see, Hi, I know it's childish, and I should be ashamed of it, but I love having people recognize me. Over there nobody will know who I am."

He was equally candid in confessing an error that had been shaped by prejudgment or simple prejudice. I remember asking him to read a manuscript by John Clellon Holmes, a novel called *The Horn.*

"I don't want to read that kind of crap," he announced a little angrily. "I can't even understand why you would bother with a book about a lot of jazz musicians."

I answered that I thought it a remarkably good novel.

"Well, I won't read it," he said darkly.

"All right," I replied. "Then I'll just accept it on my own."

He read it. A couple of days later, he brought the script to my office.

"It's terrific, isn't it?" he began. "I'm astonished. Of course we'll have to take it and lose a lot of money on it."

He paused in the doorway.

"I was kind of silly about it, wasn't I?"

I found that another outstanding quality of Bennett's was his courage. As a publisher, he had the garden variety: the courage of his convictions. But he carried it even further in his willingness to undertake the "test case" that resulted in Joyce's *Ulysses* being found not guilty of obscenity.

And in Bennett the quality extended to the physical. Back when Norman Mailer was submitting *The Deer Park* simultaneously to a number of publishers, after Rinehart had backed out of their contract, we turned it down. I was primarily responsible for our decision (I now think it was a mistake), as Mailer acknowledges in *Advertisements for Myself*. Yet he insisted on blaming and ridiculing Bennett, whom he kept referring to as "Sally Cerf."

Soon thereafter all three of us attended a party at the Styrons' in Roxbury, Connecticut. Mailer was his most pugnacious self that night. Throughout dinner he kept goading Cerf with "aspersions" on his manhood. He challenged him to "step outside." Finally, to everyone's astonishment, totally ignoring the twenty-five years' difference in their ages, Bennett marched to the front door and went into the yard. Norman did not follow; he contented himself with ridicule.

As I look back now, it seems to me clear that Bennett was that rare individual who made every relationship intensely personal, yet who seldom allowed this practice to alter his judgment about administrative decisions. His stance was frequently: yes, I'm fond of you and I sympathize with your point of view, but I'm responsible for this business and I don't think your proposal is right.

This sense of firm responsibility, I was to find, deserted him only when he felt rejected. That he could not bear. Every key situation involving such a possibility established all over again the centrality of what he had said on the radio program, back before I had come to Random: "What I'm most afraid of is not being loved."

Early in 1959 I was debating daily with myself the advisability of leaving Random House to become a founding partner of a new firm. Pat Knopf and Mike Bessie had invited me to join them, and by now various potential investors, including several friends of mine, were also weighing the possibilities. Developments began to accelerate, and by mid-February I was sure that I would make the move.

One semiholiday (either Lincoln's or Washington's birthday) I went to my office to catch up on a large stack of work. Within an hour or so Donald Klopfer arrived and sat down to chat. Before long he was telling me confidentially of Random's new plans. The firm was "going public." He discussed what this would mean, in general and to key executives like myself—the certainty of our having stock options, for instance.

I kept trying to think of some way to interrupt him. I was pledged not to reveal to anyone the plans for the new publishing house, yet how else could I tell Donald that he ought not to be giving me this intimate information?

I made up my mind hurriedly, with a makeshift compromise. I told Donald he must not tell me any more details, since I was going to leave, to take part in founding a new firm. But I withheld any other information about the new venture, and asked him to honor this confidence because it was premature to tell him even as much as I had.

He agreed, but shook his head.

"I think you're making a big mistake, Hiram," he said. "You'll be giving up the editorial work you really like, and suffering all the headaches of trying to run a business—the headaches I know only too well."

I told him that what I wanted was a chance to be on my own, to collaborate in running "our own business," and that I'd have to risk the headaches.

He grinned sadly and said, "All right. But someday you'll admit I was right."

That day came.

Bennett was out of town when Donald and I had our talk, but I had, of course, agreed that he should tell Bennett.

Three days later Bennett stormed into my office and told me off with articulate heat. I was guilty of a betrayal of trust and friendship, and he didn't want anything more to do with me. In fact, the sooner I got out, the better. This was a Wednesday; he wanted me out by Friday.

I told him I wouldn't go, that he had no right to treat me that way, that he knew about the move only because I had thought it would be dishonorable to let Donald go on revealing to me *their* plans, and that he was acting unreasonably and unfairly.

Setting his lips, he strode to the door, then turned around for a final salvo.

But what he said was, "To think you'd rather work with those other people than Donald and me!"

That was it, as Donald further said in a quiet talk we had later.

"He has never before been left by anyone he wanted to stay. He'll get over it, but it will take a while."

It did. Several days later he offered, as inducements to stay at Random, the stock options Donald had mentioned, and a vice-presidency. "But," he added, "that probably won't mean anything to you, since you prefer working with those other men."

Even a year later, having lunch with my wife, of whom he was fond, Bennett said plaintively, "But why would he rather work with Pat and Mike than with Donald and me?"

She loyally suggested that, as he had in his time, I had the understandable desire to be my own boss. But I know that on the whole she agreed with him. . . .

Several weeks passed after Bennett's outburst; his anger underwent time's attrition. Every now and then he would explode again, but only briefly. When he and Donald and I sat down to discuss the problems attendant upon the future affiliations of those Random authors for whom I had been the editor, Bennett was as fair as Donald. Only once did he break the speed limit. This was when he said, "Of course we're not going to release Loren Eiseley. He stays with us."

Donald pulled him up short.

"Come on, Bennett," he said. "We can't do that. Hiram faced us all down at the sales conference that *The Immense Journey* would sell forever. And that's what it promises to do. We all dragged our feet on it and we were wrong. Of course Hiram gets Eiseley, if Eiseley wants to go."

With some writers, of course, there was no problem. The writer decided on his own, and immediately. The most notable case was that of Jerome Weidman, whom I had come to know when I went to Westport to live, and whom I eventually persuaded to come to Random. His first book for us, *The Enemy Camp,* was a Book-of-the-Month Club selection and very successful.

Jerry learned of my imminent departure late one evening. The next morning he broke the record for the Olympic fifty-mile dash to awaken Bennett before dawn and assure him that he would stay on at Random.

Cerf and Klopfer laid down very decent ground rules. If an author was *under contract* to them, and they wanted to keep him, they would not grant a release. But those who were simply "under option," that is, according to the prevailing clause, had agreed to submit the next book to them for publication on "terms to be arranged"—these were free agents and might sign as they chose.

Horace Manges, who was Random House's attorney as well as the attorney for the American Book Publishers Council for some years, had long been seeking a "test case" about this clause. It was his position that, so long as the clause read "on terms to be arranged," it was simply an agreement to try to reach an agreement, and would not stand as binding in a court of law.

Still, few publishers at that time would have accepted this position, made so generous an interpretation. Donald and Bennett did.

By mid-March the story of the new firm broke on the front page of the Sunday edition of the New York *Times.* The new partners were not ready, but the story—inevitably, I suppose—had leaked. Two weeks later I left Random House.

The years at Random House provided in many ways a most satisfying publishing experience. I remember with respect and affection the partners—and now I most definitely include Robert Haas, although he sold his holdings a little over a year after I came, and kept, in semiretirement, only a small office thereafter.

Bob, as I have already indicated, was that rare and temporarily outmoded figure, a gentleman. Quiet, urbane, always faintly amused, and well weathered by his six and a half decades, he was a constant source of joy to me. He was one of those men who had inherited a vast fortune, wore it with grace and modesty, and gave not only in money but in unremitting energy to many good works.

Nothing more distressed him than showiness, pretentiousness. I shall never forget the time he came into my office and, closing the door behind him, almost whispered, "Come to my office. To see is to believe."

I went. There was John O'Hara, whom I had not met before, and whose swaggering manner was not much to my taste. There also was a vast, glittering plaque, studded with shining emblems. Bob gravely explained to me that this preposterous object was Mr. O'Hara's Christmas gift from his wife, and that each of the emblems on the plaque represented a club to which Mr. O'Hara belonged.

With an irony invisible to O'Hara, Bob went over the entire board, now and then pausing to make a further inquiry about this one or that. I managed to maintain sobriety by saying only "Oh" and "I see."

Later I asked myself whether on the whole I hadn't been actually uncomfortable, whether this hadn't really been a "mean" thing to do. As though reading my mind, Bob reappeared in my office and commented on the scene with glee. It was not malice; it bore a resemblance to that statement of George Meredith's about what happens whenever someone waxes bombastic, overblown, fatuous—that then, *then,* a volley of silvery laughter is heard: the laughter of the Comic Spirit. Bob was gleeful—and that was the word—over one more demonstration of "man, proud man, drest in a little brief authority." He did not look down on such antics; it soon became evident to me that he also believed that "every true man's apparel fits your thief." He had no exalted opinion of himself; he seemed rather to believe that we are all a sorry lot, and it is more salutary to laugh than to weep.

There were deep roots, I learned, behind his philosophy. His one son had been killed in World War II. He talked to me about him only after we had known each other several years. Bob's life had been lived in two acts: the first took place while the boy was alive; the second was the long after.

Bob had his own place in the triumvirate at Random House;

he was pre-eminently the businessman, the man who understood money. Once again I wondered, perhaps foolishly, over the discrepancy between the apparent and the substantial. In my opinion Bennett had the best editorial hunches of the three. Yet a casual acquaintance would suggest the reverse—that the quieter, at least seemingly deeper natures of Haas and Klopfer would qualify them better for this function.

At any rate, the three complemented one another admirably, as did the two before and after Bob Haas's partnership. They provided strong evidence that my rather simple slide-rule generalization about publishers makes some sense. Very rarely could one man alone build and sustain a successful and distinguished publishing house. Aside from the fact that few men possess all the requisite diverse skills and knowledge, almost everyone needs a sounding board.

Two is perhaps the ideal marriage; not even the most radical scoffer at the "monogamous" institution of matrimony has proposed as solution the substitution of three participants for two. Three is notoriously a risky number in human relations. In the very first year at Atheneum, I visited in Baltimore Harry Parois-sian, the American representative for Penguin, whose books we were then distributing. After dinner, over brandy in his yard, Harry mused, "Three of you. Hmm. I wonder who will be out five years from now."

"Three" worked for Random House, but it did not constitute a fully equal partnership. Bob was the outsider. Liked and well treated, he still could not, of course, share the intimacy that with Klopfer and Cerf had begun when they were very young men working at Liveright. But among trios, this one was outstandingly successful.

Not, I hope, to press the obvious too far: a happy couple, not only in publishing, means a meshing of complements. Each of the two has his genuinely fulfilling role, one that satisfies himself and his partner. One will surely be dominant, if only in a psychological sense. Crown had Wartels, Random House Cerf. But dominance in neither case meant tyranny—however tyrannical Nat may have been to employees. Indeed, in these combinations, a good argument could be advanced that the ultimately stronger partners were Bob Simon and Donald Klopfer. The more aggressive nature might be the "president"; this hardly told the whole story. . . .

Random House in my time was an outstanding publishing house in almost every respect. It had a strong trade department, in books for both adults and children. Its college department was growing, and the *American College Dictionary* was beginning to provide that stable, "money-in-the-bank," ongoing item of sustained financial security that every publishing house needs if it is not to sacrifice consistent quality for big-selling, inferior books. And although the partners were certainly concerned about making a substantial profit, they were also very jealous of the Random House imprint and published few shoddy books.

Finally, they ran an organization in which all their employees were really thought to be—and treated as though they were—human beings. In terms both of financial participation in the firm's growth and of simple human dignity, we employees were, I believe, among the most fortunate of all those working in publishing.

To the best of my reckoning,* the Atheneum affair began one day on a commuter train between Westport and New York—probably late in 1957 or early in 1958—in a conversation with Pat Knopf. Pat (Alfred A. Knopf, Jr.) and I had become friendly riding the 8:48—or was it the 8:52? He got on at Southport, and spread his newspapers over two adjacent seats in the coveted car with the "best" ones, for my friend, neighbor and lawyer, David Marks (I shall remember him as the lawyer who convinced me that law and justice were more than kissing cousins), and me. We climbed on at the Greens Farms station.

The pecking order of that commuter society still amuses me. It was, I suppose, to some degree an extension of the hierarchies established in colleges—with senior honorary societies, fraternities, classes, offices held in extracurricular activities. Games: competitive–co-operative, ritualistic games.

The first car on that morning train, and its opposite number in the evening, the 5:25 (or was it the 5:42?), was limited to those who paid a higher fare for the privilege of having parlor-car seats. These we sometimes called the Tycoons: they were

* Written before the Senate select committee's Watergate hearings.

thought to be men of vast means. But the regulars in our car at least professed scorn for them, on the grounds that we didn't have to pay extra for having a more enjoyable time. And there was a good sort of camaraderie in our section. Ken Loomis, with whom I had gone to Amherst long before, held with grace the office of car jester, good for at least two or three resounding sallies a morning. I recall him with inordinate affection.

This group did not share a similar homecoming car because of differences in business schedules, but usually two or three of us were in whichever bar car together. It would require a separate chapter to do full justice to the frenetic atmosphere of those bar cars. They, again, were fitted out with the most comfortable chairs. But woe to him who entered for comfort and didn't buy a drink. He was ejected promptly, to hoots and jeers.

I solved this problem technically, although I don't suppose I would have gotten away with my solution had I not been an ancient commuter. I would board the train early, get a drink from the bartender (those men deserve at least a full-length article), and claim my favorite chair in one corner. The value of this position was that it was comparatively sheltered. (The car was always jammed, with as many standing as sitting, and since there was heavy traffic involved in securing second or third drinks, not a little trampling and elbowing took place.) Settled in, I would finish the drink and go to sleep. Despite the din, I rarely awoke before the end of the trip. . . .

In those days, Pat was in frequent distress over the state of things in his father's firm. Harding Lemay has written at length of that absolute monarchy, and the machinations of its cabinet, from firsthand experience, and I know only what Pat told me. But the occasion to which I referred at the beginning of the chapter was at the point when Pat's position and state of mind were at a melancholy low.

This must have been before he and David Marks and I became a regular threesome, because he opened up with that completeness that is always reserved for a single listener. He did not believe, he said, that he was ever going to get anywhere at Knopf. He said that his father and mother had no confidence in him, that others in the firm had it in for him, and that he was often tempted to leave. He mentioned in passing that his friend

Dick Ernst, who had once worked at Knopf and who had access to considerable money, had offered to stake him to some capital to start a venture of his own. But, Pat concluded, there wouldn't be enough, and anyway he hated the thought of leaving the house that bore his own name.

I don't remember that I had anything very wise to say, but it seemed helpful to Pat to be able to talk about his troubles. And from time to time we returned to the subject, as the turn of the wheel made him now more optimistic, now less again.

Then came a brief time of jubilation. His father and mother had unexpectedly informed him that they were thinking of retiring before long and turning the business over to him! But his publishing experience was lean on the editorial side, and they advised him to start the search for an editor of some stature who might buy into the business and become his partner.

A few days later he returned to the subject and wanted to know who my candidate would be. I told him, of course, that it was only *his* candidate that mattered—only an editor in whose judgment he had an ultimate confidence, and whom he would find congenial. He pressed me, saying that of course he must make the decision himself but he'd feel better if I'd give him my opinion.

I said that he must already be aware of my choice because I had had no trouble deciding to whom I would send the manuscript of my new novel. That was Simon Michael Bessie, of Harper. Pat said that Bessie was his choice, too.

Mike and I had been friends since sometime in 1945 or '46. He and his wife Connie (the daughter of the flamboyant lawyer Morris Ernst, of Greenbaum, Wolf and Ernst, and a cousin of Pat's friend Dick) had moved into the Sullivan-MacDougal Street Gardens, between Bleecker and Houston streets in the Village, several years after we had. In fact, they had bought the house at 178 Sullivan Street shortly before we moved out of it across the Garden to a duplex on the MacDougal side.

We saw a lot of the Bessies. Connie, a dark beautiful gypsy one, who had inherited her father's voice box (husky, deep), was a leader in our little Garden community. Vital, generous and outgoing, she had enough energy for a dozen people.

Mike was much less active "locally," but I saw him fairly

often in the evenings and occasionally at lunch. Then, when we left the Garden for Connecticut, the Bessies invited me to spend my nights in town (once a week I taught a late class at the New School) in a room on their third floor, and thereafter I saw a great deal of them.

I'd arrive about ten-thirty or eleven, and we'd sit around the kitchen for hours, trading anecdotes, talking shop and laughing inordinately. There was always laughter.

I liked and respected Mike a lot. He was very witty, had traveled a great deal in Europe, with resultant stories, and was an ardent Francophile, with a fluency and a perfection of accent in French that was almost preternatural. Our styles and points of view on many matters differed sharply but amiably. He was very quick, impatient with slowness, especially of mind, and an indefatigable talker who strove for the epigram, the sharp turn of phrase and, in debate, the *coup de grâce*—and often achieved them.

He was also a dandy, and there was a fine sheen to his manner that many people disliked. But it disappeared in even casual intimacy. And we went beyond that. As a weekly member of their household, I shared to some extent in their griefs and joys—the death of Mike's father, Mike's progress at Harper, their ordeal with the agency through which they were trying to adopt a boy (I was one of their sponsors, or references), Mike's eventual forcing of the issue at Harper (would he or Evan Thomas become the chief editor?) and his defeat.

Friends of mine expressed their bewilderment over my loyalty to Mike. They found him a "runner," an arrogant and avidly ambitious man who was incapable of the sort of friendship I seemed to think we had. Other charges were that he was a name dropper, an insistent parvenu on the make for fortune, fame and the *haut monde*. (I replied that whenever a person whose name he had "dropped" showed up, it was evident that they were very good friends.) The kindest word any of them had for him was that he was "amusing."

I battled back. The Bessies' (Connie was never included in these charges) hospitality was generous, our talks spirited and full of affectionate candor and rowdy gossip. They were good to me. I remember the night that I had a Niagara of a nosebleed during class; it was Mike who found me a nearby doctor and galloped to his office to bring me home. And when they were away during the summer, they insisted upon my using their apartment as though it were my own.

On the other hand, I was able to be of assistance to Mike in a number of ways—several times in matters of which he is still not aware. And eventually, when Bennett Cerf wanted one more top-line editor, I recommended Mike and was empowered to try to persuade him to come to Random. But Evan Thomas had not yet been given precedence over him, and he decided to stay at Harper.

In the meantime Mary and I were beginning to see a great deal of the younger Knopfs in Westport. There was a large group of writers and publishers there, and we saw Pat and his wife Alice often at their gatherings as well as at our own houses.

We were very fond of them. Pat had an endearing quality somehow reminiscent of Winnie-the-Pooh. He did not care for the allegation, and he once grew furious when I told him that every individual looked like a particular animal, and his was the tapir. He took his pipe out of his mouth and hissed, "Anti-Semite!"

That pipe—it was as though he felt unclothed without it. When absorbed or impatient or angry he would tug on it vigorously, sending out short puffs of smoke in vicious spurts. And he would emphasize key points in his exposition of some opinion by pulling it out of his mouth and jabbing it in the direction of his listener. Then he would bite on the stem throughout the rebuttal. He preferred corncobs.

Despite being built like Babe Ruth (with a brawny torso and thin legs), Pat is a strikingly handsome man. As Mary said of him, "He really looks the way his father thinks _he_ looks." But he would never permit such a statement. "Ridiculous, absurd! Who, me?"—pointing his pipe this time at himself—"I've got Saint Vitus's dance, for God's sake."

In fact, he was never still. His stride was fast, his gestures abrupt. The idiom of his articulation was a staccato bark. Social occasions at his house kept him in perpetual motion. On entering a room filled with the women of our circle, he would rush from one to another, crying, "Mary! Yum! How wonderful you look!

110

. . . Barbara, you look beautiful, yum, yum . . . Hel-en, how great! Oh, yum!"

The yums were little pecking kisses.

Yet I repeat: endearing. Open and blunt, even rude, but at such times, *all there*—to be seen and heard. Yet there were certain unexpected matters about which he would be shy, even secretive. His code in these terms was so highly idiosyncratic that I seldom understood why something I had just said had offended his sense of propriety.

With those powerful parents, he had had a cruel childhood and youth. He told me much about it, not to be repeated here. Many of his uneasinesses and distrusts, much of his lack of confidence in himself, must have derived from that time. His own courage, and the devotion and steady honesty of his wife Alice, had brought him through.

Yet he still fears (or did, when I last saw him, in 1964) intimacy, even though his *nature,* as I see it, is essentially a trusting, even loving one—only badly disillusioned. I remember one incident in the early days when I called him lightly, casually, "my friend." I was set back a few steps when he said fiercely, "Don't talk about friends. I have just two friends, David Herrmann and Nick Katzenbach. The rest are professional acquaintances."

So we come back to the spring of 1958. Pat asked Mike; Mike accepted and began trying to raise money. Then, sometime in April or May, Blanche Knopf returned from a European trip. She had changed her mind.

Pat told me the story as we drove together to the annual meeting of the American Book Publishers Council. He had gone to welcome her home and tell her and his father of his choice of an editor. She had not only changed her mind, but implied that it was absurd for him to have taken a passing comment on what might eventually occur as something definite and imminent. Alfred Sr. remembered their talk the way Pat did, but he was not going to oppose Blanche's wishes. The plan was canceled.

Pat, of course, was shaken, and I was indignant at their treatment of him. As days passed it became apparent that Mike Bessie might suffer as much as if not more than Pat from this capricious reversal. Pat was not the most discreet person in the world, but

Mike was in some ways even less so. It seemed certain that the story must have leaked, and before long two incidents at Random House seemed to confirm that certainty.

The first followed a frantic telephone call from Connie Bessie. She wanted to see me urgently. Mike was in Europe, had been when the bad news broke, and she had to talk to someone who knew about Pat's and Mike's plan.

She was really distraught. She was afraid that the story was known at Harper, and that Mike's already endangered position there would be forfeit. But what had upset her most was that she had talked to Pat about it, and he had seemed almost callously unconcerned. He had, he told her, enough trouble of his own: *sauve qui peut.*

She did learn from Pat that he had repeated to his father (in an effort to show Mike deserving of a partnership) what I had told him of Bennett's asking me to invite Mike to Random House.

The sequel was brief and angry. The following afternoon Bennett summoned me to his office. His voice, on the telephone, conveyed a familiar flaring of temper.

I entered his office and closed the door. There was a miserable Pat, looking a little like a boy who had just been expelled from school.

Bennett demanded that I give Pat the lie. Alfred Sr. had revealed to him what Pat had said about Mike and Random House. Bennett, who had dreamed since infancy of eventually purchasing Knopf, didn't like, wouldn't entertain, this friction with Alfred. (I never understood why their exchange should have caused such irritation, except that Alfred wanted to belittle Bessie.)

I was equally angry. I repeated that of course Bennett had asked me to feel Mike out about coming to Random, and I was not going to call Pat a liar when it was Bennett who was lying. And I said that I was sick of the way the senior Knopfs and Bennett (*in loco* uncle) treated Pat—that he was a man, not a boy or a chattel. Then I left the room, slamming the door behind me.

Bennett came to my office later, and with that unfailing honesty of his apologized and said what I had done was right.

Pat wrote me that he would never forget my "fierce loyalty." . . .

It was not until November that there was any further development in the Bessie-Knopf case. On the afternoon before Thanksgiving Pat and I rode home on the train together, and he opened up again about his miseries at Knopf. Shortly before we reached Westport, I reminded him of Dick Ernst's offer, and suggested that now might be the time to accept it. Surely he could raise other money, too.

Later, Pat said several times that that was the decisive moment for him. I saw little of him during the next month; he was busy. But just before Christmas Mike Bessie called me, and made a date to meet me at the Harvard Club a day or two after Christmas.

We met in the afternoon. Mike was in no hurry to get to the point, and was further delayed by a long interruption caused by a famous friend of his. When he finally came out with his proposition, he did so, I thought, rather warily.

He and Pat were going ahead together, were going to start a new publishing house. (This much Pat had at least hinted at.) They were for the present telling no one else, but they hoped to find other backers to come in with Dick Ernst. They believed that the combination of Bessie and Knopf would appeal to authors and would impress the publishing world. But they also thought that the strength of the new house would be greatly enhanced if the combination could be Bessie, Haydn and Knopf.

I told him I was flattered, and I was. But I also said that I couldn't consider it. I was about ten years older than the older of them; I had one of the most coveted editorial spots in the business; I was making more money than ever before, and had a large family to consider. It would be folly for me to take such a gamble, whereas it made good sense, unhappy as they were in their present positions, for them to do it. But I pledged any help that I could give them. Mike accepted my point of view, had anticipated it—but urged me to stay open about the whole thing. Perhaps they would be able to offer me greater inducements than I thought possible.

I was almost sure that I would not be interested in whatever inducement. My only quiver of doubt was the thought of starting a new enterprise, of being my own boss. But there were too many ifs. For one thing, it occurred to me on the train going home, wasn't this venture being built on a rather shaky foundation, entirely aside from the question of money? I was remembering Connie Bessie's story about Pat. After that incident, whether or not Connie's emotions had overcolored Pat's "callousness," how could the two men come together again so quickly to plan a lifetime association? And if that could happen, how much could I count on their assurances to me?

There was also the manner in which they had chosen to ask me to join them. In the last year, partly because Pat had told me so much about his problems, I had felt much closer to him than to Mike. It was not a question of my changing my opinion of Mike, but we had had far less opportunity to see each other than in the days of those weekly evenings. Why had Pat not talked to me directly?

I asked him later that week. Seeming flustered, he mumbled something about "not being any good at that sort of thing." But he did urge me to reconsider. He argued that it was absurd, at this point in my life, with all the writing I wanted to do, to be forced to go in to New York every day and carry my large editorial load. With the new firm I should be able to limit my time in New York to two or three days a week, and thus live on a much relaxed schedule.

This did appeal to me. But there were too many obstacles, and I told him that there was, had to be, very little possibility that I could do it.

I believe that it was in mid-January that I had a date for lunch in New York with Marc Friedlaender. I had first met him when I taught in the same department of English in North Carolina in 1942–44. He had stayed on; I had gone back to New York to the Phi Beta Kappa job. But his friendship meant so much to me that I wouldn't permit us to lose touch. I believe that it meant a good deal to Marc, too, but he was not much of a letter writer.

At any rate, in the academic year 1958–59 he was visiting professor at Vassar, and this gave us an opportunity to see more of each other. At lunch he told me that he had about decided to give up teaching. He had greatly enjoyed it (he was perhaps the best teacher I have ever observed—genuinely Socratic), but he had had his fill. He had been thinking about a new direction, and had come to the decision that he would like to find his way into publishing.

He assured me that he had no illusion that he would seem a very attractive prospect to an established house. Without publishing experience, and now in his early fifties, he could hardly expect to be received with a ticker-tape parade. But, as I must remember, he had money "of his own," and he was hoping that I might know of some new enterprise that would need capital, in exchange for which he would like an appropriate job. He suggested a sum the equivalent of what Dick Ernst had offered Pat.

The coincidence staggered me. Without revealing names, I told him about Pat's and Mike's plans, and about their proposal to me, and my refusal. I was thinking about the joy of having him and that delectable woman from New Orleans, Clara May Friedlaender, nearby—to see from day to day.

He listened with interest, and said he would like to meet them. He also said that if they worked matters out satisfactorily, he hoped I'd change my mind and "come in."

I was suddenly in love with the whole idea. Gone my apprehensiveness. I don't know if I can convey, soberly and yet convincingly, the importance of Marc Friedlaender to me. I think I had best turn to a better man's words.

> . . . *thou hast been*
> *As one, in suffering all, that suffers nothing;*
> *A man that Fortune's buffets and rewards*
> *Hast ta'en with equal thanks; and blest are those*
> *Whose blood and judgment are so well commingled*
> *That they are not a pipe for Fortune's finger*
> *To sound what stop she please. Give me that man*
> *That is not passion's slave, and I will wear him*
> *In my heart's core, ay, in my heart of heart,*
> *As I do thee.*

That is not excessive in speaking of that round, wise, gentle man. Buddha in a business suit, I have sometimes thought.

I went back to my office, called Pat and Mike. We set up a

meeting at my house with Marc, for the next weekend, which he confirmed.

The meeting went well and was followed by another at Dick Ernst's home in Darien. I had not yet committed myself, but I was weakening perceptibly. Even my wife, who was totally opposed to the whole venture from the beginning, viewed it as a little less like a disaster if Marc was to be part of it.

Progress seemed slow, but as I look back on the period now, it was incredibly fast. Pat was alternately hopeful and despairing as I still dragged my feet; he took to leaving notes in my mail box telling me what it would mean to him if I joined them. One of them told me the story of how important winning his wings in the Air Corps in 1942 had been to him. He went on to say that having me come in with Mike and him meant even more to him. He felt that he and Mike hadn't a great deal to offer me beyond their devotion—except a chance to be my own boss and to leave something substantial to my family. He ended by saying that he would work his ass off for me.

The advent of Marc Friedlaender made me think of other friends. I wrote a long letter to William M. Roth of San Francisco, asking if he would be interested in investing, and received a reply suggesting I meet him for breakfast at the Saint Regis the following week. By the time I saw him again, on Saint Patrick's Day, he was sufficiently interested to agree to send a family representative before long to go over all our plans and financing in detail.

This, too, had a strong impact on me. Roth had inherited considerable means, including ownership in the Matson steamship line. His family also held a major position in the Honolulu Oil Company. Later he became assistant to Christian Herter as our representative in Geneva in connection with Common Market negotiations, then succeeded him as special representative for trade negotiations, in which role he distinguished himself by effecting the first genuine economic rapport we had had with the Common Market nations. He has also been very active in the Democratic party in California and, as the chairman of Roth Enterprises, given extensive funds to many worthy people and projects. As I write, he has entered the state Democratic gubernatorial primaries.

Such a man could be of inestimable value on a board of directors. But there were other ways in which he could be of real help. He had been a publisher himself. After a rather dismal apprenticeship at Prentice-Hall he had founded the Colt Press as an adjunct of the famed Grabhorn Press in San Francisco, and published a fine list of books.

Finally, he is a man of great and genuine charm, one who seems never to have been deflected from his true nature by either his wealth or his participation in world affairs. He is another of those whose expansive career has never "gone to his head"—neither hardened nor corrupted him. He is tough, in the good sense, but never callous or indifferent. Mary and I are deeply fond of him and that bewitching sprite, his wife Joan.

In February I told Donald Klopfer of my intention to leave Random. Of that, and Bennett Cerf's reaction, I have already written. By early March, although no formal papers had been drawn up, Pat and Mike and I were orally committed. Dick Ernst and Marc Friedlaender were, also, and Rupe (a name acquired in Burma, during World War II; in poker games, he invariably bet a rupee) Roth was at the threshold. Our lawyers were communicating with one another, but we were far from ready to announce our plans.

Then, on Sunday, March 15, with very little warning, the story broke on the front page of the New York *Times*.

The night before I had had a telephone conversation with each of my potential partners. Mike, as the only one living in the city, had received several telephone calls from the *Times*, and reported that although he had not talked carelessly, it was evident that our plans were now known by other publishers and there would probably be a story in the Sunday paper.

The scope of the story was what astonished us. So far as anyone could remember there had never before been a publishing house story on the front page. And it was continued at some length on an inside page. An unidentified publisher said that it was as though the presidents of General Motors, Ford and Chrysler had resigned their posts to found a new company. A rather extravagant comparison.

Morris Ernst engineered a conference call, the first of my parochial life, and it was agreed that Mike would come out to

Westport to my house, where Pat would join us, because *Time* magazine was sending out a photographer. All day the telephone kept ringing. I had two lengthy conversations with people at *Time*. The other calls were mostly personal ones of congratulation.

One refreshingly abrasive note was struck. An old friend, Louis Hausman, said, "You're a jerk. You had it made, and you've thrown it away. Are you crazy?"

The photographer took a picture of us sitting at a table.

He asked, "Who's going to be president? I want him in the middle."

I think it was Pat who replied, "Who looks like a president?" and installed me.

It was only an hour or so later that I abdicated, although I did not know it at the time.

For there came still another call from *Time*. Wearily I asked Mike if he wouldn't take this. He did, with glee and gusto.

Five years later, after our break had become final, I asked Pat if it wasn't true that that was the moment he changed his mind about me, deciding that I wasn't a true leader. He looked startled and said, "How did you know?"

I had known for a long time. Only a few weeks after that first Sunday, Pat "announced" that we would draw straws to decide who would be the first president. It was to be a rotating presidency—each partner in turn for a year, then repeat the three-year cycle. I asked what had become of the original decision, and he said he had reconsidered it. He appealed to Mike, who agreed with courteous and careful circumlocution.

Irony attended the drawing. I drew the longest straw, Pat the second longest.

Pat's feverish comment pronounced us lucky. I would be the first president, which would make the right impression on "the outside world." He, as the second, would have the least important year. Then Mike, the fighter, would be in charge during the year when we shifted to our permanent corporate structure, the year when the chips would be down. This he said right out in his peculiar style of simply thinking aloud about those present.

We soon began a round of visits to all the literary agents. At the inception of each meeting Pat would intone, "Mike is our spokesman." And Mike would begin a highly colorful account of our program. After the first hour the eyes of the agent would begin to glaze, but Pat never seemed to notice. Mike's theory was clear: if twenty words were adequate, then two hundred must be splendid.

These incidents, it seems to me now, should have made it abundantly clear that I was not going to be treated as promised. But I was too neurotically proud to complain—for a while, even to myself.

It was equally evident that Pat was playing kingmaker, but he kept insisting that he knew he was the weak link in the chain of command, that he had no ambition to run things. Finally exasperated at this reiteration, I told him that he was just as ambitious as any of us, only he chose to run forward back-assward.

I wrote "playing kingmaker," but I think I understand Pat's motivation better now. In that marvelously funny record, *The 2,000-Year-Old Man,* Carl Reiner asks Mel Brooks what the usual means of locomotion were in his early days. Brooks promptly replies, "Fear. Yes, I think fear was our main propulsion."

Pat's fear was of failure. He had made that heroic break. It was his assertion of manhood, of freedom from the tyrannical father. It became his *life.* He was fiercely dedicated to making Atheneum a success. The firm, its preservation and profitable establishment, became his mistress—indeed came to mean more to him than friendships or individual loyalties. There is ample evidence to prove this. Yet I am inclined to believe that, although eventually he sought full open domination, and got it, it was only after he became convinced that nobody else was equipped or willing to take over-all charge effectively and leave him to run his own "department"—sales, promotion, advertising, the business side.

At the time, his frequent abrupt reversals were bewildering. For, with his obsessive drive for success, he was often crude, occasionally downright offensive. Yet there were balancing times when he worked together, in good harness, with the rest of us. And he and I still drove in to New York together at least once a week, so we continued to have sessions during which we talked directly and openly.

119

As I now see it, little by little Pat's original image of me gave way to a more realistic appraisal, which he then, in turn, came to exaggerate. But he preferred the original image; it better suited his needs and Atheneum's, as he saw them. From the beginning of our talks he had thought of me, as he finally said, as like Donald Klopfer: "quiet, steady, thoughtful, a good decision maker." Such a description won Pat no medal for psychological insight. He was describing some of Donald's qualities, but overlooking the fact that Donald's was not usually the decisive voice at Random House—even that Donald was "human," like the rest of us, and his steadiness was hard-won. Passions shook him; defeats and rejections hurt him; he was Donald Klopfer, not Pat's dream father.

Which mantle, I believe, was now, in the pre- and early Atheneum days, wrapped around my rather stupid shoulders. Stupid, because I should have understood that, and what it meant. That I didn't, I now think, was due to my then condition: I was infatuated with myself. I had made my way, often with the help of friends, but substantially alone, from the obscurity of a third-grade teacher's desk in a boys' country day school, to this (as I saw it) prominent position in publishing. Moreover, with almost overwhelming financial difficulties, finally at the age of forty-one I had paid off all the considerable family debts. Now, eleven years later, I reviewed my achievement rather solemnly.

Hence I did, from time to time, feel outraged at my partners, particularly Pat—for either he had never meant his original picture of my place at Atheneum, or he was failing increasingly to remember and honor the pledge it had implied. What had become of the "more relaxed pace" that had been dangled before me? He—and Mike, too, to some extent—grumbled over my schedule, which had me coming in to New York on Tuesday morning and returning to Westport Thursday evening. They needed me on the spot constantly, they felt; in a beginning venture, decisions came daily. But I held out for a year or so, insisting on their keeping the original agreement intact, and pointing out that they could always reach me by phone with minimal effort, and that I always responded.

This situation became aggravated by the fact that I was at the time "in" psychoanalysis. Two or three times a week I would spend my lunch hour in a visit to the analyst. That fifty-minute hour, plus twenty minutes in a cab each way, seemed to them an exorbitant absence, despite the fact that Mike, at least, seldom had a lunch shorter than three hours.

When I told them, in 1963, that I had given up the analysis, they greeted the statement with more enthusiasm than they had shown me in a year. When I asked if their reaction wasn't rather out of proportion, Pat replied, "Well, we think the time comes when a man has to take care of himself."

I did some foolish things, to their justifiable concern. At one session of negotiation with a prominent British publisher, I became enraged over what seemed to me his breach of faith, and went at him pretty heavily, to the dismay of my partners.

But perhaps what most horrified Pat was the fire I started at Atheneum. On the top floor of our building we had a bedroom, for the use of the Knopfs or Haydns. One night when I was alone there, I committed that ultimate stupidity, smoking in bed, and fell asleep holding a lighted cigarette.

When I awoke, the flames were about a foot and a half high. With the extinguisher, I reduced them to a smolder. Then I dragged the mattress down three flights of stairs, pausing at each landing to apply the extinguisher again, and blacking the walls. Finally, I carried it out the front door and dumped it in the gutter, where it smoldered all night.

But our disagreements, which sometimes extended to open wrangling, constituted only a small part of our irresponsibilities in those days. As I look back now, it seems to me that we were, with one or two exceptions, a bucket of boys.

"Scratch a man and find a boy." When I think of some of the goings on in the early Atheneum days I believe their best epitaph would have been:

> *Man, proud man,*
> *Drest in a little brief authority,*
> *Most ignorant of what he's most assur'd*
> *(His glassy essence), like an angry ape,*
> *Plays such fantastic tricks before high heaven*
> *As make the angels weep. . . .*

Several attendant lawyers made similar observations in somewhat less poetic language after a full meeting devoted largely to finding a name for the new house.* Mike Bessie, for instance, was only partly joking when he proposed Chutzpah House.

Our early weekly meetings, attended by the principals and by Dick Ernst, who lived in town, had a certain adolescent flavor. Dick, a very likable man, nevertheless seems to me the only practicing cheerleader over forty years old whom I have met. He would come bounding up the stairs, his face shining with anticipation. He kept assuring us that we were wonderful and that everything we did was wonderful.

At a dinner party about this time, Dick sat next to my wife. Aware of her skepticism about the Atheneum project, he assured her that he personally would see to it that none of us suffered any financial harm. He would take care of us. Dick's expansiveness may someday get him into trouble.

Every so often we had a big family party, at which we would play such fantastic tricks as bestow letters (the sports variety) on each other for outstanding performances. This practice began when Alice Knopf, at Pat's request, sewed a large *A* on a tee shirt, for Pat to present to Mike for his acquisition of our first big best seller, *The Making of the President* by Theodore H. White. But we all had our turns, as I remember it.†

At the time, I enjoyed it hugely. With naïve insouciance, I would explain to anyone who asked, and to some who didn't, that we were not just a publishing house, but also "a society of friends." It never occurred to me that Pat and Mike had sought me more for the alleged prestige I brought to the house than for our friendship and my ability. If anything, I was rather vain over

* The name Atheneum came to me when Loren Eiseley called me to tell me that he had won the Athenaeum Award in Philadelphia. Bennett Cerf promptly converted it to Half-Atheneum.

† Yet to be accepted by Pat, the stunt had to be in his idiom, and to symbolize in some way success. Before the introduction of athletic awards, Mary had made a centerpiece for the table at one of our get-togethers. She had filled a bird's nest with a big *A* and four hard-boiled eggs. On each she had painted a vividly faithful caricature of one of us: Pat, Mike, Marc and Hiram. Of this Pat took a dim view. Whether he considered "egghead" derogatory, or his sense of seemliness was offended by the inclusion of Marc, who was not a partner, we were not sure.

the local joke that I was the firm's "Golden Goy." It was my wife who suggested that, for all the laughter, they meant it. Some years later, when Tom Wilson went to Atheneum, she remarked, "They have a new Golden Goy."

If I was guilty of infatuation with myself, Mike Bessie's attitude came closer to self-idolatry. Neither of us carried his new eminence very well. Mike would spread his hands in self-depreciation and say, "I am the only one who came alone." But he never seemed to doubt that the rest of us found him so valuable that his "aloneness" seemed a virtue.

His remark implied two points. By then our "initial" capital was one million dollars. Pat, with Dick Ernst, had accounted for a quarter of that amount; I, with Friedlaender and Roth, had brought in a half. The fourth investor, Trumbull Huntington of Middletown, Connecticut, a leading bookseller in Hartford, represented the final fourth. Both Pat and I had known Trum, but it was I who "found" him through his brother-in-law, my friend and college roommate at Amherst, Herbert P. Catlin. And I also closed the negotiation with Trum.

Further capital was forthcoming later from Roth and Ernst. So, of an eventual million and a half, Mike had raised none.

The second meaning of "alone" referred to personnel. Pat had brought with him, or shortly afterward, Dave Herrmann as our treasurer, Harry Ford as art and production director, Nat Zecher as sales manager and Gloria Karmin as his own secretary. I was responsible for the signing of Dorothy Parker and Herman Ziegner as editors, Lillian Brahms as my secretary, and eventually Pat Ullman as director of publicity. No one had "come with" Mike, although later Cornelia Schaefer joined us. . . .

At any rate, Mike was always on stage. His entrances were spectacular, though repetitious. He would literally stomp his way up the stairs to the second floor of the graystone house we occupied. He seemed to feel that going clump-clump-clump not only expressed fatigue and determination, but was also, in some esoteric way, the epitome of charm.

His monologues at our meetings, his anecdotes, his French quotations usually contained wit and point, but always seemed interminable and often modestly self-congratulatory. But he was hardest to take when he made a candid confession. He was so

123

insistent about looking you in the eye that, embarrassed for him, you had to look away. But you could not escape the synthetic sincerity of the voice.

What then of our friendship, of my earlier and frequent support and defense of him? As I have often been told by my own family, it is one thing to see a person fairly often; it is another to live with him. I am sure, if Pat and Mike read this, they will be remembering their "before and after" experience with *me*.

But what must seem bewildering to the neutral reader at this point is that Atheneum survived. Not at all. We were, and are, all able. If the wide favorable attention we received when we opened our establishment went to our heads, it nevertheless helped to bring us many fine authors. Our announcement ad, naming these authors, made an impressive list. And Mike Bessie kept scooping up still more. All our early best sellers were his.

Furthermore, Pat, Marc Friedlaender, David Herrmann and others were very sober workers at our financial status. When we secured the fine paper-book deals with Harvard, Princeton and Stanford (an operation Marc ran) and a good editor of children's books, we rounded out a balanced program.

Our first list (summer–fall 1960) was distinguished. Among the leading titles were Jan de Hartog's *The Inspector*, Wright Morris's fine novel *Ceremony at Lone Tree*, Loren Eiseley's *The Firmament of Time*, Henry Beetle Hough's *Lament for a City*, William Goldman's *Soldier in the Rain*, Ignazio Silone's *Fontamara* (a new version), Giorgio Bassani's *The Gold-Rimmed Spectacles*, *Touch Wood* by Morris Ernst, and André Schwarz-Bart's superb *The Last of the Just*. Pat became a daemonically effective man at getting high prices for paper-book leases, and in our second year Theodore White's *The Making of the President* brought us much money and more renown. This, as well as *The Last of the Just*, was Mike's book; I didn't have a best seller until Frederic Morton's *The Rothschilds*. On the other hand, I was responsible for the prize winners: Randall Jarrell's *A Sad Heart at the Supermarket* won the National Book Award for poetry, and Joan Williams's *The Morning and the Evening*, the John P. Marquand Award for the best first novel of the year. But eventually our bread and butter were to come from Marc's paperbook list and Jean Karl's books for children. . . .

During the first couple of years, we were also very indulgent toward each other about the acceptance of manuscripts. I don't know how many times Pat said to me, "If it's good enough for you, it's good enough for me." And Mike and I seldom read the same scripts—rather, we congratulated each other on whichever new acquisition.

At any rate, we came to 1963, huffing and puffing. Our original agreement was that Mike should go to Europe two years of every three, and I one. This made sense, because of his larger contacts, language facility, etc. But so far he had been over in '59, '60, '61 and '62. It was certainly my turn.

Pat objected bitterly. By now, he had his own map of everything: Mike was the man for Europe, I for straight American practice and young authors. I pressed; he yielded ungraciously. The day I was setting out, he came to my office to say good-by.

"Have a ball," he said emphatically. "Just have a big fat happy vacation."

I went. I came back in August. In late October, we had scheduled a directors' meeting. I remember asking to have a session of the three partners first, to catch up on exactly where we "were"—especially financially. Pat said it would be impossible; it would take him until the meeting to do all the figuring required.

The first order of that meeting was the proposal that each of three employees, Ford, Herrmann and Zecher, should be awarded two per cent of the stock, with each partner giving up two per cent of his. Up to that point, each of us owned twenty per cent, the directors the remaining forty per cent. This arrangement, with each principal having been enabled to purchase his shares at an absurdly low price, was shocking to the lawyers representing the four investors. They considered it pure and simple philanthropy. But the members of my "society of friends" were ready to have it that way.

I didn't hesitate to vote for the surrendering of our two per cents. All three men were working devotedly and well for the house, and I didn't have the faintest idea what was coming next.

What did happen could be called Pat's Wailing at the Wall.

He presented a dismal, even frightening picture of our financial plight. He was full of figures—present and projected. He prophesied doom. He proclaimed an ascetic regime. He said we were going to have to cut to the bone, and that meant *everybody*—no exceptions.

It was a glum occasion. One of the directors—I think it was Roth—said that obviously they could hardly comment intelligently on the vast array of facts, figures and projections that they were only now presented with, let alone take constructive action on them. He suggested, with what seemed to me amazing composure, that hereafter all directors be provided the material to be discussed at least a week before each meeting. The others were largely silent.

I left the meeting badly shaken. Alone, I reviewed the past few days—remembered the expression on Pat's face, the sense of something withheld, concealed, as he proposed the yielding of our two per cents to the three employees; remembered that this very morning I had seen him coming out of Mike's office with a great sheaf of papers in his hand.

The next morning I dictated the following letter to him, with copies for all directors.

October 31st, 1963

Mr. Alfred A. Knopf, Jr.
Atheneum Publishers
162 East 38th Street
New York 16, New York

Dear Pat:

We all left yesterday's meeting quite sobered, I think. It was certainly clear that everyone was ready to go on to war rations, but I was sobered for another reason as well.

History, it seems, repeats itself. Several years ago at a Fall directors' meeting you came, full of bad news that you had not in advance communicated to your partners—at least, for this letter is all my own—to me. In advance of yesterday I had heard only two details of what you had to say: on Monday you told Mike and me that by January 1964 we would need to call half of the further money pledged by Dick and Rupe. On Tuesday I heard the new figures of our loss for 1963, although not from you. No more than these two things.

You and I have talked before about my feeling that I cannot be a full partner in any real sense of the word if I am not informed about what is going on. Certainly I was aware during these months since my return from Europe that things were not going as well for us this year as we had anticipated, but I was not informed in advance of that meeting of any of the particulars of the stringent new program that you proposed. I hope that you understand that I am not challenging the realism of your description of the situation or of your proposals for remedies. What I am mostly concerned with is in pointing out that you cannot expect a meeting to be really fruitful when grave and crucial matters must be discussed but no one except the one or two people you choose to consult in advance has had any real warning of what the situation is.

I would not resort to this sort of open letter had this experience not been repeated again and again since Atheneum was founded in 1959. I am sure you remember that I have often protested to you about this way of handling our affairs. What you cannot know is how many other times I have remained silent in the interests of what at least seemed to me to be harmony. Nor am I now writing this letter for any other reason than to make it as clear as possible that with Atheneum in real difficulty it seems to me of crucial importance that we should all be kept fully and immediately aware of all details pertinent to the situation.

I have no opinion about or very much interest in *why* you continue to conduct our business in this unilateral fashion. I do think that it is harmful to Atheneum's best interests and an irritant—at least to me—that distracts from the main business at hand. I have found both the writing of this letter and the lonely business of deciding to write it painful—the more so because of all the misunderstandings that have preceded it and our attempt in September to come to a better understanding. But I feel now driven to it, I at least think, for the good of us all, which means for the good of Atheneum. Surely, while the world thinks we're great and while we know we have these very serious problems to settle, we must communicate—we must communicate to each other—not just at our rare formal meetings, but every day.

Yours,
Hiram Haydn

HH/aw

cc: Simon Michael Bessie
    Harry Ford
    David U. Herrmann
    Marc Friedlaender
    Trumbull Huntington
    Richard Ernst
    William M. Roth

It was Friday. I mailed the letters that afternoon, then called Pat up in the evening. I told him that I wanted him to have advance notice that the letter was coming, and that copies had been mailed to the homes of all concerned.

He was noncommittal, but Sunday evening Mike called me up. He sounded vastly amused. "I can't say that I share your feelings," he said, "but I certainly admire your courage." Or was it "guts"? Or "chutzpah"?

Monday was the third of November. I remember, because that is my birthday. Pat asked for a meeting of the partners in the afternoon. He came straight to the point.

"I've lost faith in your judgment," he said to me.

I replied that I'd lost faith in him. He answered that if I meant by that his *character*, the kind of person he was, that didn't matter to him. It was business, not character, that was the issue. He cited the many books I'd accepted that hadn't sold, my pigheaded insistence on going to Europe, but especially my breach of faith. We had in effect signed in blood an implicit contract to stick together and not act singly, especially in relation to our backers.

I pleaded guilty to the first charge, saying rather nastily that everyone couldn't be a procurer of Mike's sort. But Mike's *amour-propre* enabled him to misinterpret my words. Getting up and pacing the floor, with difficulty controlling a smile of self-satisfaction, he said modestly that he just didn't understand it himself. He supposed he'd just have to face the fact that he was for some reason awfully good at securing best sellers.

I repeated my stand on the European trip, and as for breaching faith, wanted to know what Pat considered his own unilateral actions. Since he had repeatedly violated our agreement, I no longer considered myself bound by it. We had other responsibilities, too, and mine included what happened to the money expended by Friedlaender, Roth and Huntington.

Eventually it was Mike's turn. He was circumlocutory, cautious in what he said, but he clearly stood with Pat. I asked Mike whether Pat had shared advance information with him. He indicated, "Well, once in a while." After all, *he* was always available.

They seemed, hesitantly, to be moving toward a proposal that

I no longer work full time, but serve in an advisory capacity. I inquired why, if they no longer trusted my judgment, they wanted my advice.

And then I broke it off myself, saying that I had no desire to stay where I wasn't wanted, and that I'd get out when I was able to make new arrangements. I left, and went across the hall to the office I shared with Marc Friedlaender.

I told him about the meeting. He was badly distressed, the more so because his unflagging honesty made him feel that he must say that he was not excusing them, but he, too, thought some of our trouble was my fault.

"You've been too self-indulgent," he said, "in terms of time, leadership and the books you've selected."

That's what I mean about Marc. It's like moving into another world—that largely inaccessible region in which people mean what they say and say what they mean; their eyes are clear and honest, and you are not hurt when they tell you *no* because they can be critical and loving at the same time.

Even then, I could face that: that I had been fat and complacent. But I still bitterly resented what seemed to me the duplicity of my partners. I counted fingers. That six per cent for the key employees made the difference, if our struggle was to be put to a vote, because all three men were Pat's. Some fifty-sixth birthday . . .

The investors of course wanted to hear the full story. Trum Huntington had a session with Pat and Mike, then one with me. When I finished my story, he told me that he was sure that I had been the only one to be totally honest with him, but he guessed that he would have to string along with the house—that his investment was important to him and he believed he would recover in the end. I understood his feeling; the rest of his family thought he had been foolish to enter so quixotic a venture.

Roth asked me whether I wanted to fight, pointing out that in corporate matters so thin a margin in votes was not conclusive. I said no, that after such a struggle the house could not continue to function effectively. Then he tried to effect a compromise, an arrangement whereby I would have a free hand with a certain limited number of books. But neither Pat and Mike, nor I, cared for the idea. I kept remembering the story Cass Canfield had told me about negotiating with that outstanding nonman of Penguin, Allen Lane. The day before the signing of an agreement between Harper & Row and Penguin, Lane had called him and told him the deal was off. This despite an initialed memorandum confirming it. When asked why he didn't insist on the strength of that document, Cass said, "How could I work with a man like that?"

Only a little over a month after our climactic meeting, Roth sent a memorandum regarding the call of his and Dick Ernst's notes—a memorandum that echoed, in a new context and more graciously, my earlier complaint.

Washington, D.C.
December 12, 1963

Memorandum to: Hiram Haydn
                     Simon Michael Bessie
                     Marc Friedlaender
                     Alfred Knopf, Jr.

I hope you will pardon a brief memorandum that is addressed to my four associates most concerned, and not to the Board itself. I did, however, want to get off a quick reaction to Hi's formal letter* notifying me of the call in January of Dick Ernst's and my notes. This memorandum does not relate to the other problems of which Hi has also informed me and which I would be delighted to discuss at another time.

What did disturb me greatly is that a considerable commitment was called without any accompanying or prior justification or explanation. Certainly, there is no legal obligation to explain to an investor the need for such additional financing at this time. On the other hand, it seemed to me highly desirable—not only from Dick's and my point of view, but also your own, that a carefully thought out plan of action accompany any such request.

It has certainly been clear from the sales record that Atheneum might be facing a deficit at year end. On the other hand, the deficit indicated does not necessarily justify financing of the scope contemplated. It seemed to me, therefore, that there must be other plans; or, if there are no other plans, there should be—spelling out fairly carefully where the money is to be spent and for what reason.

Publishing is a marginal business and it is particularly difficult to build up an entity that has any real dollar value and therefore an assurance of future existence. I have been concerned ever since Atheneum

---

* Mine, because it was my turn in the rotation.

began that rather than living from best-seller to best-seller it would be necessary somehow to build up a continuum of income that would give the company value and stability as a "going concern." What disturbs me is that although attempts have been made in this direction, i.e., paperbacks and children's books, I have still not seen anything on paper which indicates planning for anything other than a hand-to-mouth existence. Will the financing requested only keep Atheneum alive for another year or so without any real indication that our basic economic problem is being licked? How does Atheneum expect to live more than another year or two unless we are fortunate enough to have several bestsellers? Under the circumstances, a successful season does not insure anything more than that the bills are paid that season. What are your plans? How will you achieve them?

I feel that enough has been invested in Atheneum and in your joint abilities to make these serious and important questions. Frankly, I see no point in prolonging the future of the company for a year or two if no plans—and *workable* plans—have been laid to insure a permanent corporate existence. I am sure you have this all well in mind, so I raise these questions only for my own information.

William M. Roth

The period from November 1963 to August 1964 was one of those wastelands that occur in the lives of many people—when they go through familiar motions that have lost their meaning. The real decisions were not going to be made before me, so the weekly meetings were necessarily empty. Yet some strained moments did occur, particularly because Pat had for some time been trying to make a scapegoat out of Marc. He was impatient with the progress of the paper-book line, and disapproved of many of Marc's selections.

In this matter, Pat was really wrong. The list eventually proved a triumph. But at the time he was continually heckling and bullying Marc, and this enraged me and led to more battles. As it turned out, Marc didn't need my defense. He took the needling as long as he could, then finally told Pat off. I wish I could remember what he said: it was strong, lucid, finely tempered, and ended, "And you will never speak that way to me again."

Marc left the firm several weeks after I did. He is now one of the chief architects of *The Adams Papers,* Harvard's distinguished publishing project.

Mary said that I was like an enraged old bull in those months, snorting and shaking my head. There was a long delay before any communication between the firm's corporate lawyer, Sidney Winton, and mine, David Marks. David pointed out that the action must be initiated by the firm, and perhaps their dilatory tactics were intended to evoke anxiety in me. At any rate, we finally met in late spring or early summer.

Sidney Winton is the most chilling of men; his body temperature I would estimate at eight degrees Fahrenheit. The offer for my stock was equally low. At this stage his attitude was "take it or leave it," and he said that Pat and Mike wanted me out as soon as possible. I was in good form that day; afterward David told me that he had let me do most of the talking because I was saying all the right things more forcefully and picturesquely than he, as a lawyer, could.

David managed to get me better terms eventually, but they were still pretty low. Roth, with his power as one of the two principal investors, was the person who could have swung an improvement, but he was out of the country—for which he later (for no sensible reason) severely blamed himself. So David and I were forced to settle for what we could.

The irony of the situation was capsuled in my final meeting with Pat. I was to leave in August, and he spent all of August on the Cape. On the last working day of July, he came into my office. The burden of his message was that he would have thought I would value my stock at more than what I was settling for!

Sad, what we do to one another. I have come to believe that Pat was feeling considerable ambivalence about the way things had turned out, and that this was his way of saying that he was sorry, perhaps even feeling a little guilt. And I think it is true, if strange, that I feel comparatively little resentment toward him. Partly, I suppose, because he always was serious about the firm, dedicated to our job, whereas I think that Mike and I were often frivolously extravagant. Yet in Pat, as I see it, that dedication hardened into a process of reifying everyone connected with the enterprise. Like Machiavelli, he humanized and personified the "state," and in so doing reduced its citizens to objects, "good" or "bad" in accordance with their functional value to Atheneum—

and, ultimately, to his own ambition. I was not the last "friend" to go down in the path of the juggernaut.

Pat's way of dealing in retrospect with his callous acts is to seize them by the forelock, hold them before whichever interlocutor, and say, "This was a rotten thing I did," thereby forestalling accusation, and thereafter usually washing his hands (and mind) of the whole matter.

Mike Bessie's approach to the same problem is to ignore it— to act as though it never happened. I think nothing else during my last painful months at Atheneum more infuriated me than his pretending to take it for granted that we were still good friends, even after I had made it clear that I felt he had withheld any hint that he had been "going along" with Pat for a long time, and in so acting, had treated me shabbily.

He simply ignored my hostility, continued to greet me cheerily every day, at functions introduced me as "my partner, Hiram Haydn," in a tone that implied he was proud of our connection, and tried to draw me into the discussion at our meetings as though avid for my opinion.

I think he must have had some secret code or model of behavior that he had adopted because he didn't have a natural one, wasn't in touch with himself. It was, perhaps, some concept of magnanimity, but it didn't affect me that way.

I felt that he was always buzzing attention at me. After eluding his invitations for weeks, I finally desperately agreed to have lunch with him. Halfway through the meal, he looked at me affectionately (that's what I wrote) and said, "You don't feel resentment toward me any longer, do you?"

I told him that there were times when the thought of him filled my head with blood. No effect. He smiled. Then I learned why he'd wanted this lunch. He was intensely curious about my plans. Where was I going? What was I going to do?

And so it went. On my last day in the office he called me up from Nantucket to wish me cheerfully all good fortune. Feeling claustrophobic, I stammered something about why couldn't he leave me alone? Didn't he understand *anything*?

And even months later, when I was attending the international publishers' meeting in Washington, I stood at the head of an escalator and watched Mike being carried up, a glad smile on his face, and his hand extended! And I had to take it, because Connie was with him, and I continued to be fond of her.

But I remember other, poignant moments—rare ones, when he became open and direct, and told me of things he had done that now distressed him. At such times I felt that I had been grossly intolerant and unfair, and warmed to him.

One day during the first season at Atheneum, he flew into a rage at Harry Ford for having completed some arrangements with an English publisher without consulting him. I stepped in, reminding him that the book in question was mine and that Harry had acted in consultation with me. I then added that I thought he was getting too big for his britches, that he was incorrigibly ambitious and seemed determined to be top dog. He sprang at me, fists doubled, though I am about twice his size. There was something symbolic in his act. In the early days I had dubbed him "the bantamweight champ," and now I caught a fleeting montage of what must have been a long sequence of struggles.

We both sank into chairs, belatedly mindful of the others present, and he said almost despairingly, "Yes, I suppose it's true. It's probably true of me."

I couldn't think of much to say, but on impulse reached over and ruffled his hair.

He said fiercely, "Yes, that's what I need—affection."

So? I don't know. There's too much to unravel.

One thing I really found hard to forgive was his attitude toward Herman Ziegner. I first knew Herman when he was working in Indianapolis for Bobbs-Merrill, as I have already written. He was a personable, able and highly imaginative young man, great on close editorial work. He and his wife Lou became family friends; our children were devoted to them.

During Atheneum's first year we needed a chief copy editor, who could take charge of that department and farm out the actual copy editing and proofreading to free-lancers. Herman had left Bobbs-Merrill and was now with a New York firm where he was not very happy. He was delighted to take the job with us, hoping eventually to become a full-time regular editor.

Herman did fine work, but he was very meticulous and

consequently slow. Staccato Bessie was impatient with him, but restrained himself—until my final months at Atheneum. By this time Herman's old association with me was no boon to him, and in several editorial meetings Mike attacked him pretty brutally. Herman became very anxious about his job, and I tried to find him another one.

When you add all this to Herman's sudden tragic death a few weeks later, at the age of forty-eight, you have I think some sense of the nightmare these months seemed and still in retrospect seem.

Soon after the final separation papers were signed, I was faced with the necessity of finding a new job. The demoralizing effect of the situation on me I could trace back to an unusual element in my career: I had never sought a job. From my first teaching position on, the jobs had come to me; I had never had to look for one. I believe that only someone else with an identical record could understand fully the dread I felt facing this new experience so late in the mortal game.

I pored over the *Literary Market Place,* looking at the listing of one after another publisher. Finally I decided that two old associations would furnish the best starting place: those with Scribner's and Viking. I saw Charlie Scribner; he was most considerate, but he was directing his house toward a different emphasis, away from fiction and general nonfiction toward special books whose markets were more predictable. He and I agreed that my strengths did not apply to this new program.

I then went to see Tom Guinzburg, who had succeeded his father as president of the Viking Press. I asked him if his father had ever told him of the several times he had tried to bring me to Viking, and he answered that he had. My acquaintance with Tom had come through Bill Styron, and the hunch that took me to him now had something to do with his apparently affectionate name for me: Big H.

He seemed very courteous and friendly, and said the idea appealed to him very much, but he wanted to think about it overnight. He would call me the next day.

Before telling my story, on both visits, I had explained that my errand was confidential. I asked each of these two men to promise to honor the confidence, and not even to disclose its nature to colleagues without first getting my permission. Each agreed, promptly and firmly.

But the next morning, I learned that Tom Guinzburg had immediately called Pat and told him all about our conversation. Big T . . .

One stable comfort to me during these unhappy months was a man named Melville Cane. Soon after I went to Bobbs-Merrill, Ross Baker asked me to accompany him to lunch with our lawyers, Pincus Berner and Melville Cane. He explained that "Pinkie" and he were great friends, and he hoped that I would hit it off with Cane, who was "a little literary" for Ross.

I owe Ross one of the great joys of my life. For more than twenty years, Melville has been my counselor, guide and friend. Terse, witty, gifted, with a penchant for wry understatement and priceless "throwaways," Melville has practiced a double career, as lawyer and poet, for more than sixty years. Today, at ninety-four, he has retired neither from the law nor from poetry.

And what an extraordinary poet he is! His range is from light verse, at which he is a master, all the way to superb lyrics and philosophical poems. As I have written elsewhere, I believe that the best of his lyrics, especially several about snow, belong on the shelf with those of Emily Dickinson and A. E. Housman.

Why, then, has he received so little recognition? And even that only in these last years, leaving some question as to whether the poet or the nonagenarian was being honored. I think there are two basic reasons. One is that his prominence as a writer of light verse, in the days when his work appeared regularly in FPA's column and frequently in *The New Yorker*, did him a disservice as the other sort of poet. No—did his reputation as a poet that disservice. To the ponderous mind that enjoys cataloguing everything, Cane is a light-verse man; ergo, he cannot write serious poetry.

To me, the very opposite is true. The technical dexterity, the nimble virtuosity required for first-rate light verse, stand the poet in excellent stead. Cane's poems are hard to match in the assured craftsmanship with which he employs assonance and internal rhymes. Indeed, he is a master of rhyme, making it perform the subtle musical magic that is its (presently neglected) function.

The second reason for his comparative neglect, I believe, is his career in law. If I am right, the same shabby reasoning is at work: how can a lawyer be a poet?*

Well, to answer that rhetorical question: he can be if he has it in him. A more sensible question is: how can a poet be a lawyer? There's the rub. But the answer in this case is that he'd better be a literary lawyer—that is, deal with writers and publishers.

This Melville Cane has done. He was Sinclair Lewis's lawyer, advised Thomas Wolfe, drew up the incorporation papers for Alfred Harcourt and Donald Brace (who were undergraduates at Columbia when he was at law school) and remains one of the firm's main attorneys. He is still a director of Harcourt Brace Jovanovich.

He has survived two partners and a host of friends. I asked him at one of our frequent lunches if he could explain not just his longevity, but his amazing vitality. He jested a little, as is his wont, then looked directly into my eyes with his extraordinary clear blue ones.

"You're really asking?" he said gently. "Well, then, I've lived with my pain. Now let's talk about something else."

I shall not forget that.

Perhaps yet another reason for his relative neglect. Capable of great tenderness and lyric felicity, he still is in some ways an eighteenth-century poet, a child of the Enlightenment, with a grave respect for reason, for order and discipline. Hardly our characteristics today.

But the quiet order of his days, and of his mind, may well also have contributed to his unusual life span. And his splendid constitution: one day we met for lunch just after he had had his annual physical checkup.

"What did he say?" I asked.

Melville looked solemn.

"He said—" and now he broke into imitation, characterization: his voice slowed, deepened—" 'Mr. Cane, you will never die. We shall have to kill you.' "

There is a small unincorporated Cane Club at HBJ. Bill

---

* To be sure, William Carlos Williams was a physician, and Wallace Stevens an executive in an insurance company. But exceptions are few.

Jovanovich, Helen Wolff, Hilda Lindley and I belong, and take turns giving his birthday luncheons. Together with his partner, Paul Gitlin, we meet at a club or restaurant. Of late I have been the self-appointed laureate of the group. Each year I select one of Melville's poems and rewrite it in his honor, retaining his rhymes, meter and all the other technical devices I can manage.

The first time I tried this, I used his poem about Gertrude Stein's obscurities, recasting it around his own longevity. At that lunch I read it aloud. When I finished, he looked at me with that inscrutable gravity of his and said, "Haydn, I've underestimated you."

To say that he has a long, mournful face that turns utterly gleeful when he smiles; to say that he is only five foot six; to describe his physical presence—is to give no hint of the richness of that presence.

> *We that are young*
> *Shall never see so much, nor live so long.*

I close this section about Melville Cane with the toast I offered on his eighty-eighth birthday: "To the Commander-in-Chief of the Forces of Light!"

During those last months at Atheneum I saw Melville quite often. Indeed, at one point, David Marks, having had little experience in legal matters involving publishing, sought him out and asked his advice. Melville knew all about the situation, and when I finally told him that I was about to seek a new place, he asked my permission to talk to Bill Jovanovich about the possibility of my joining Harcourt. I agreed, but thought it an unlikely possibility; I knew Bill only slightly, and we had not hit it off particularly well.

But I was wrong again. On a Saturday Melville called me at home, a rare elation in his voice: "When I asked him, he said, 'Hiram Haydn is the only publisher to whom I would make an offer.'"

As it turned out, Bill was to offer me the role of "copublisher" or "associate to the president." The only people to whom these exalted designations had been attached were Kurt and

Helen Wolff, the distinguished German publishers who were the leaders in founding Pantheon in this country in 1941. They retired to Switzerland when they were forced out of Pantheon, and, on Melville's introduction, Bill wrote them, asking if they were interested in "publishing with me."

I quote the phrase from Bill's description of his invitation to the Wolffs because, as he has also said, they "noted the distinction immediately," and consequently expressed an interest they would not have had in becoming customary editors for Harcourt, Brace & World. (In two visits to Switzerland, Bill completed arrangements with them.)

The concept of copublishing, at least in the contemporary era, originated with Bill. As he propounded it to me, its most distinctive features were first, that I would deal only with the company's chief executive officer, himself, and second, that I would receive a nonreturnable annual advance against a commission on sales and a percentage of all "other income." In addition, I received my expenses and some other financial considerations. It has the advantage of giving to the copublisher his editorial independence without expecting him to enter into sales, promotion and accounting responsibilities. It is, in short, a partnership that does not depend upon a close cost accounting. On the other hand, the pooling of earnings gives the company the chance of recouping all the advances over the years.

Melville Cane, a good friend of the Wolffs, had participated in that negotiation with close interest, and now talked with Bill about his making a similar arrangement with me. Since then, several other such associations (I know nothing about the *terms*) have been set up by other publishers, notably between Harper & Row and Cass Canfield, and between Dell and Seymour Lawrence. . . .

Melville asked me to call Bill to arrange a meeting. I went to his office several days later.

I was immediately impressed by his directness and his courtesy. In fact, after some recent experiences, I found these qualities almost inhibiting.

He began by saying that he had no intention of hurrying me, but he wanted me to know immediately that he was making me a definite offer, to which he would remain committed, however long it might take me to reach my decision. Then he proposed terms in some detail. I replied that, if I were to come to Harcourt, I would need certain adjustments in those terms. He immediately agreed to the changes I asked for.

His approach to dealing with a badly troubled man was healing. The magnanimity of imagination that grasped what I most needed—a sense of security, of being respected and wanted —and then implemented that understanding with the courtesy of interpreting his action in terms only of his own eagerness—that magnanimity still overwhelms me in memory.

At the time I was too shaken to appreciate fully Bill's thoughtfulness. He has told me since that he was much concerned at my condition, that I found it difficult to finish sentences, seemed choked, and stammered in speaking of Atheneum. He has also told me that when I had entered his office carrying a briefcase, he had thought, "Oh, God, he's going to show me a lot of stuff, to impress me with his work." (I simply carry that briefcase everywhere.)

Followed the visits to Scribner's and Viking. The memory of my talk with Bill sustained me, and soon I saw him again and accepted his offer.

It was late August when we signed the contract. I was commuting weekends to Martha's Vineyard. When I arrived that Friday night, there was a message to call Bill, no matter how late. He told me that the news had leaked and, to beat Atheneum to the gun, he had issued a press release, which he would read to me, not wanting me to encounter it in the paper without any warning. He hoped that I would approve of the wording.

It seemed fine to me, but a day or two later Mike Bessie let me know that he thought it had been Atheneum's place to make the announcement! He also didn't care for the implications in Bill's final sentence, as quoted—that he and I were going to work together to build a list of high quality.

When I left Random House, there had been only one telephone call expressing the conviction that I had made an unwise decision. This time there were many. Bill's spectacular and rapid rise to the presidency of what was then Harcourt, Brace and Company had convinced many people in publishing that he was ruthless, and various rows with people in the trade editorial department, with subsequent firings, had persuaded them that he was also tyrannical, an arrogant monarch.

About two weeks after I began work at HBW, Bill suggested that we lunch at the Brussels, at that time a favorite restaurant among publishers.

"I want us to be seen together," he said. "I want to size up reactions."

So we ate at a conspicuous table. And we were inevitably noticed. Bill is an extraordinarily fine looking man, with an assurance and decisiveness of manner that command attention. For that matter, everybody in publishing knows him.

He suddenly asked me what I was thinking.

We were seated side by side. I replied, "I was thinking how glad I am that I am exactly your height. I wouldn't like to be shorter than you, and I'd be afraid to be taller."

He was much amused. Then he asked me what people were saying to me about my coming to Harcourt.

"Most of them are telling me that you will swallow me alive."

His keen eyes studied me.

"And what do you reply?"

I laughed.

"I tell them that I would rather be swallowed alive than nibbled to death."

There was quite a bit of sparring in those early days of our acquaintance. Bill used to enjoy playing games with people, testing them with all sorts of sudden challenges. His play with the rapier was often glittering, at times frightening in its deadly accuracy, its merciless persistence. And at times he was not beyond using the flat of the broadsword to batter someone into submission. He never treated me in this way, but we did have some few difficulties.

But he has kept his weapons sheathed for years now, at least in my presence and experience. His brilliant gifts as an entrepreneur, an administrator, the builder of a business empire, had matured over the preceding fifteen years. Perhaps by the time I came to know him well, the long and solitary struggle for achievement, for power and recognition, had reached fulfillment, to allow the public man to turn inward more often, to pause and evaluate, discover unexplored resources of patience, understanding and tolerance. Perhaps the several months that he was hospitalized in 1967–68 brought him, as such sobering intimations of mortality have many of us, to a strengthened sense of fellow-humanness.

I say perhaps. I do not know. I cannot know. I once heard René Dubos discourse lucidly on the small percentage of our genetic equipment that all of us, even the most fulfilled and successful, use. Therein, I thought, must lie the radical meaning of change in human lives. A shift in environment, a turn in either the inner or outer weather, may uncover for effective use capacities until then largely dormant.

However, it would be presumptuous of me simply to assume that Bill Jovanovich really has undergone such a change. On my very first visit to his office, the largeness of his nature was evident in his imaginative insight into my condition. Is it not more probable, then, that this "change" is rather the multiplying of my opportunities to know him, as our collaboration deepened into friendship?

But I must let history interrupt these conjectures. William Jovanovich was born in a coal camp near the small mining town of Louisville, Colorado, not far from Boulder. His father was a coal miner, a Montenegrin immigrant, his mother a Polish immigrant at the age of fourteen. They were proud poor people, of whom Bill is fiercely proud. He often refers to the highlander strain.

In 1967, shortly before my heart attack, I was at the Rocky Mountain Writers Conference in Boulder, mostly, as I remember it, because that noble team of writers about science, Lorus and Margery Milne of New Hampshire, had recommended me. One day Mary and I drove to Louisville and had a meal there.

Afterward, I asked the proprietor if I might take along the menu as a souvenir. He said, "Of course," but why did I want it? I said I wanted to send it to a friend who had been born in the town. That interested him: who? Jovanovich. But, he said, Mrs. Jovanovich lived in Denver. Did I mean to send it to her? No, to a son, William.

That crazy wild boy? What was he doing now? They hadn't heard about him for a long time.

I told him. He raced to the kitchen, yelling, "Hey, Ma! What d'you know? That Sonny Jovanovich is a big shot in New York now! Imagine that!"

Bill was graduated from the University of Colorado with distinction, and won a fellowship in English literature at Harvard, where he worked under Howard Mumford Jones. After the war, in which he was a naval officer, he entered Columbia, with only his dissertation to complete, and then he ran out of funds. Already married and with a child, he needed a job and secured one in 1947 as college traveler for Harcourt, Brace at fifty dollars a week. Within six years, he was the head of the school department. In 1954 he was made president of the company.

Among the unimaginative, the bald record has created the legend of a brilliant, single-minded achiever. The truth is that the first promotion was simply earned by extraordinary ability, the second through a catastrophic split in the management of the firm. Alfred Harcourt and Donald Brace fell into dispute over nepotism in 1940, and they remained at odds until they acted together in 1953 to oust two officers. In 1954 the management was caught anew in turmoil. Neither Mr. Brace nor the Harcourts—Alfred Harcourt died in the summer of that year and his holdings were then voted by his son—could agree to the accession of the other, and they agreed, in the end, to take a chance on a man who was the youngest officer and manager in the company. At this time Bill owned no stock in the company, and until 1960, when it "went public" and its shares were traded on the New York Stock Exchange, his aim was, he said, to create a "neutral" and professional management.

And in the years of Bill's presidency and chairmanship, the firm has gone from a privately owned corporation of about $8,000,000 in sales to a publicly owned company of about $180,000,000.

In 1964 Bill predicted to me the forthcoming domination of the book business by giant conglomerates. His response was to become a conglomerate himself. He has bought an educational-film house, farm magazines, business periodicals, a school-supply

143

house and a graphics manufacturing company, scholarly journals, medical and scientific book and textbook and test publishing houses, and insurance companies. In terms of profit, the multiple tail may wag the dog, but the dog is free of a leash—there is no alien in control, demanding profit regardless of standards. Bennett Cerf once told me that Bill Jovanovich is the one certain genius in American book publishing.

To work closely with such a man is, obviously, stimulating. And work closely we have. Despite the heavy demands of his many enterprises, he has found time to read almost every manuscript I have brought to him as a possibility for our joint list, and almost every one submitted by an author already on that list—usually within two weeks!

Our publication record is, I believe, a good one. We have had only a few best sellers, but have consistently published good books, many of which have had more than one printing. My old enthusiasm for new writers has not waned, but Bill has been more successful in curbing its excesses than have other associates.

The success of our collaboration has owed much, I think, to our editorial sympathies. I choose the word in preference to "tastes," for our tastes often differ. What we share, I believe, is a hard-won ability to transcend personal idiosyncrasies in selecting books—to see and respect that ultimate vitality that is central to any good book, even when its content or tone is alien to one or the other of us. Once, when I came to his office to discuss an unusually large number of manuscripts submitted to us, he turned a sheet of paper face-down on the table.

"There," he said. "I've written down my opinions. Now give me yours, and then I'll show you mine."

A game. But an instructive one. It turned out that we both thought "no" about two of them. One other I liked and wanted; he didn't like it, but thought we should take it. Another reversed this process exactly. The fifth I said we must take; opposite its title he had written, "A must." This was Jack Matthews's beautiful novel about a boy who told the truth, *Hanger Stout, Awake!*

I have, then, found my copublishing experience a satisfying

one. But that does not mean that it has been an arrangement without any difficult aspects—for me or for my editorial colleagues in the trade department. I refer to Julian Muller, the editor in chief,* and to the senior editors, Ed Barber, Bill Goodman and Dan Wickenden. I have often thought, during my nine years with the firm, how I would have felt in the circumstances, had I been one of them. The special privileges granted the copublisher: the close working relationship with the head of the house, the reduced office schedule (at first two days a week, then two days every other week, and finally, after much illness, a wholly irregular attendance), the personal colophon in the books on his list—these privileges, I believe, would have made me resentful. Yet none of them has shown me any discourtesy; all have been friendly and helpful. And that has been equally true of others, whose own work has sometimes been inconvenienced by my absence: Roberta Leighton, Hilda Lindley, Pat McEldon, Margaret Mary McQuillan, Rose Martini, Helen Mills, Denise O'Toole, Mildred Salivar, Gertrude Sauer, Rita and Jerry Vaughan, Priscilla Colt, George Vay, Gene Gordon and others. Ed Hodge, who retired recently as head of the trade department, was always a joy to work with.

These are not the pious statements of an after-dinner speech. This is not an advertisement for HBJ. Nor am I writing character testimonials. But in a book about people, it is surely not inappropriate to salute those who have generously and graciously accepted one's shortcomings and offered comradeship and help.

Bill Jovanovich is outsized in his complexity, as well as in all else. In a single visit of an hour or two, he may be (or seem to me) mercurial, quiet, confident, conscience-ridden, forceful, wistful, elegant, corny (I know he won't like that one), insistent, gentle.

We are utterly different, he and I. Yet we share a stubborn romantic dissatisfaction with the *status quo,* establishmentarianism, routine, moderation. Our idioms and idiosyncrasies are unalike, but there is some common dissenting maggot that gnaws at us: a kind of metaphysical ache that wants to force life to be more exciting, beautiful, dramatic—even simply to be *more.*

* Since become the director of the trade department.

In Bill's case, I suspect that the origins of this yearning are to be found in his Montenegrin heritage. I recently read a passage from Milovan Djilas's *Njegoš: Poet, Prince, Bishop* that may be apposite.

It was among the men of Katuni, more than anywhere else, that heroism was bound to become the highest virtue. Njegoš's cult of heroism was not fabricated, but borrowed . . . though refined and idealized. It is of a special kind—not only bravery in battle, but also humaneness and resistance to all evil . . . : to kill without torture, to raise weapons only against those who bear weapons, to take but not to steal, to forgive but never to ask for mercy. Marko Miljanov called it *manliness* . . . but Gesemann, being unable to translate it, called it *humanitas heroica*.

To combine a translation of this *spirit* into contemporary American terms with a working conviction of the validity of the Protestant ethic is to grasp at the elusive complexity of William Jovanovich. But it gives little sense of the excitement of being with him—of the heightened vitality of talking with him. I have never gone to an appointment in his office without a sharp and heady anticipation of the next hour or two.

One man who doesn't like either of us has described us as resembling a rare species of parasitic life (I forget the name) in which two parasites feed on and destroy self and other. That is not my experience of our friendship, which I have found sustaining through trials and troubles.

It began, that friendship (as distinct from our association), abruptly when I sent him a letter from the hospital in Santa Fe in August 1967, shortly after my heart attack. Whether my sojourn in the suburbs of death inspired it, I suddenly wrote to him an intimate letter about himself, one in a completely different key from those we had previously exchanged. He promptly responded in kind.

Since then, we have written in this vein from time to time—letters rarely about business, always largely about our various preoccupations, convictions, hopes, disappointments. There may be long intervals in which neither writes. Then will come a flurry of letters, as urgent as though there had never been a pause in our exchange.

I know no better way to convey the quality of this man, his

restless, probing, unsatisfied mind, than to quote (with his permission) from a few of these letters.

August 30, 1967

Your letter was touching in a way you probably cannot know. I've been quite at loose ends the past month, wondering whether I had not cheated myself out of the merest rewards of being simply alive, but to have a friend like you makes me know it can't be wholly true. You are quite right in saying that I've devoted myself to being a public person, and this seems curious because I truly do not seek publicity or réclame. Maybe it is because I've not dared to be a private person, which is harder to do and riskier on the nerves, I think. It's not that I avoid exposing my innermost feelings because they might, thereby, be bruised: it may be that I am fearful these feelings are trivial. One thing does bother me, perhaps, and that is the notion that as a private person I have no subject matter, as it were. Does this sound strange? We must talk at leisure some day, and I'll explain what I mean.

October 31, 1967

Your letter in red ink—the graphics of which I took as a sign of life, not depletion—I have read several times, each time being moved by the affection and understanding that underlies it and as well plainly informs it. I know the feeling you describe whilst you were undergoing the attack and immediately following it. Did I ever tell you about the strange circumstance when I was stricken by a coronary in 1953? I was in great pain even before I left New York for the suburbs and on arriving home called the doctor, who quickly diagnosed my situation and called for an ambulance. He was an old man, one-legged, with a great craggy, sorrowful face. Somehow he seemed to understand me in the moment, for he immediately told me what I was undergoing. The ambulance came, attended by two rather spindly men who were assigned to carry me from the second floor to the street. One of them dropped his end of the stretcher going down the stairs and I remember laughing at this inwardly, realizing that one can be killed by kindness. It was night-time, and Martha had gone outside to round up the children so that they would not see me taken to the ambulance—they were quite young then—and so I was inserted into the ambulance in the dark, alone. As the ambulance made its way down the streets, I had a relapse of some sort, with the pain now so great that I could not speak. I looked up at the nurse who was sitting next to the stretcher and fixed her with a look that, for all my dumbness, must have appeared strange to her. I kept wishing that she would, this unknown, worn, and unhandsome woman, reach down and kiss me. Then, suddenly, I thought to myself: by heavens, that is what Nelson meant when he asked "Hardy, kiss me"—he wanted a sign, some last sign of human connection, benediction. The minute that I realized that I was clarifying an historical, literary allusion, I felt better and somehow knew that I would live, for my mind was active, curious, and probing something, no matter how trivial. . . .

Your letter, read again and again, has helped me to face myself. It has been, in its own way, the human connection.

Stefan [his elder son] wrote me from Vietnam to say that he thought I was like Dr. Johnson, "abstemious but not moderate." Of course he is right, and I am sure you, of all people, will know how he is right. I have always been a Puritan whose rage to extend himself never allowed for a lessening of the constrictions of conscience. I have always wanted myself—and others—*to do right and to do more,* and while I have been sympathetic, and not unkindly, to those who lack talent or resources, I have never been satisfied with them. This is what, perhaps, leads to the boredom in me that you speak of. When I become bored, I become enraged (as you say) with myself and sharp with others. . . . Although I was born and brought up in poverty, and lived the life of the poor, I cannot be sentimental about it, probably because my instinct is that no circumstance cannot be bettered. The rich I do not care for, and indeed do not think about, for they have no place to go and nothing to do with their resources, which inevitably turn about the *fact* of money, the very presence of it. Yet, too, the middle class is alien to me in so many ways because it is so frightened of life: its commitment is to property, to propriety, to holding on. All of this is too ready a generalization, I know, but what I am trying to express is the feeling of aloneness I have always suffered, for I do not identify myself by groups of people, by conventional manners and ambitions characteristic of various groups. I am an intellectual but I have rarely met an intellectual I like. I am very strongly, perhaps ridiculously so, an American, yet I am offended by the manner of my countrymen. And beyond feeling alone, I feel a certain waste—Hegel said waste was the essence of tragedy—in myself. I know that I am capable of larger things than running Harcourt, Brace & World, yet I don't seek other enterprises and other roles. (It was, laughably, a relief to turn down, within a minute literally, the job offer of $600,000 a year and $2,000,000 cash, that I received three months ago. That sort of thing is not what I mean by "larger.")

Yet, there are ways out for me, and people like me, and I intend to find those ways. I've been shaken by my illness—it was a "close run thing," as Wellington said—and I know that I don't have too many chances left. I shall try to understand more, and perhaps *do* less, and I shall try to observe the human circumstance and write about it well. You see, my writing, which so many people have told me is "reasonable" and "rational in the eighteenth century manner" is not at all reflective of the rage (and the constriction) I feel in my daily life. Somehow, I have to bring into proportion what I feel and what I do with what I think. That's obscure, maybe, but I rather think you will understand it.

All of the foregoing is brought on by your expression of a compassion in your letter. I think you care about me, Hiram, in a way that few people will comprehend. I think you want something for me: a resolution of my sometimes pointless angst, a fulfillment of my life. And I thank you deeply for that, for nothing is more unselfish than to want for others.

February 16, 1970

Like you, I've written and discarded. In fact, I wrote a reply to your first letter, and the second; neither was sent. I suppose I can't now really answer those particular letters, for what I had to say now seems rather insignificant. Let me, instead, just tell you a few things that ought to be said at any time and should not wait on occasion.

You are not a burden to me or to anyone else. It is quite painful for me to think that you may be worrying over this. I should know the truth: I do. Our friendship is dear to me and enriching. Your relationship to me as a publisher and to Harcourt, Brace is valuable both in an intellectually critical sense and in financial terms. I need say no more.

I have an idea what you wrote in the long "down to earth" letter you didn't send. Going on hunch, or more probably guilt, I'd suppose that you were wondering aloud why I don't make more of my "personal" life and why I don't reveal more of myself to the people I trust and love. If that is what you are wondering, then let me say that I wonder also.

For two years I have been confounded. I am confounded because I have spent most of the days of my life living for the future. Once we talked of this. I commented that creative people are said to live only in the present and that I envy them this habit or instinct or discipline, whichever it is. Frustrated people live only in the past or future: either they mull over earlier failures or they fret over the prospect of failure. One can go on endlessly making up categories of this kind, most of which may be untrue, and I shan't dwell here upon it further except to describe my own condition as I know it to be. Erich Remarque once said of his wife Paulette Goddard that she's gone through life slamming the doors of her past behind her. I do that, too, and I do it not because I choose to forget any crimes I have committed against myself or others but because I rarely find the past to be useful. (I don't know why Paulette slams doors. She once said to me that she was a train of consciousness going into the unknown and that she felt I was so sensitive to her that I, too, was on this train. "I'm getting off your train," I told her. "I just pushed you off," she rejoined.)

Should the past be useful? I've lived by the pragmatical principle that leads me to urge everyone, most directly myself, to do right and pretend to nothing. This is not to be mistaken for raw ambition, which settles its bills too late, or indeed for plain Calvinism, which holds that belief in virtue is itself a virtue—something no right-thinking pragmatist would accept. Adhering to the pragmatical principle means this: one looks ahead; one works hard to alter circumstance so that future events will be salutary in one way or another, recognizing always that events and circumstances can be wholly arbitrary; one works hard because action creates circumstance, favorable or unfavorable. It's obvious that if one looks ahead constantly and if one always works hard, he is left with little sense of the present.

It's perhaps not unexpected that I have changed, Hiram. I am possessed by self, quite the opposite of self-possessed. I am not withdrawn or bitter or scornful, as you yourself can attest. But I am distracted at times. I am greatly surprised by that distraction, for I'm not used to the condition of thinking to no end. If at times I seem to shake myself and look up at you—"being there" for you, as you say—it is simply that gesture of a man who has been away, looking at his life, and is embarrassed by his own presence.

March 21, 1970

Your "book" letter means a great deal to me, for you reply to what is at the heart of darkness, the fearful cry, "did I tell them that I cared, that I loved, that I could forget myself?" We'll talk more—maybe by letter—of this. In the meanwhile, I *do* think I caused you anguish. It could not be helped, but I can regret it, for my best part is to bring ease, not grief.

July 15, 1971

Well, you're right, of course. I am scared. I have no fear of pain, of crippling, of dying—and I take no pride in saying it, I think. I am fearful that it was and is what we talked about before: there is no end for which life is lived, and the means and the ends are the same. I used to think that if you produced something worthwhile in your life, a book or sonata or a sheaf of verses, then the travail of it all was paid off and you ended ahead of the game. But I don't think these things anymore. There are percepts and there are concepts. You see things (wind ravaging the trees) and feel good. You need then to make a concept out of what has happened—i.e., you need to if you are a Western Judaic-Christian man— and so you devise a religious or esthetic or scientific concept. To make a concept you have to use all you know, and so memory is called. René Dubos says that "genius is childhood recaptured," and Robert Lowell says that "genius is memory." You see how quickly one leaves the moment, and the sensations of the moment! It is hard for Western man to feed his memory so that he can make sense out of what is happening to him. That's it, you see, Hiram: sense (common) and sensibility is what we are after, not sensation. Western man has been taught to live for *something*. Since he rarely can make much sense out of what is happening at the moment, he is forever recapturing the past, which can be fashioned into pleasing concepts, intricate and beautiful ideas and art forms. "Copping out" is a metaphor that can only mean that you forget childhood as children live it (under authority, according to rules) and choose childhood as you imagine it (quite falsely, I think), a childhood in which everything is fresh and new and different because you have no past and no memory to weigh you down, keep you straight. So, you ask, why not live differently? I don't know how to live differently from the way I do, maybe, or more probably, I'm afraid to live by other means, other devices and stratagems. I'm a Western man, remembering, remembering; but now I begin to think that I've forgotten why I am putting together concepts, why I am working hard to create things (books, films, jobs for other people), why I seem to believe that there is a reason for all this, an end toward which the work is aimed, an end that is different from the means.

No, this isn't very clear, I guess. It isn't clear, maybe, only maybe, because I do not understand how Time works. The Western notion is that one is allotted so much time (three score and ten, and all that) and that one ought to use it well. Hedonists say live well; religionists say do well; existentialists say be well. What do I say? I say that time is running out for me, for my world (a concept, naturally), and that I feel cheated because I don't enjoy my memories and don't see much use for them in living out the time that remains. Genius isn't memory. Genius is not missing something. My trouble, among other things, is that I haven't forgotten the old maxims that governed my conduct as a child, youth, and middling man, and I have lost—missed—great occasions. If I feel cheated, I don't feel resentful. Nobody ever promised me anything—never. And a great many people have given to me. You say you don't know what to suggest to me. I agree that if one knew what next to do that was really different from the cycles in which we move, then he'd have it made. He'd find a different means, and that itself is good enough, I guess, because I don't believe the end is discernible or even conceivable except in art, which is not life.

August 17, 1971

I have read and reread your letter of the 20th of July instant, and I choose this campy usage because your letter is immediate in its motivation and ministration. Yes, I shall think on Bergson, and the Flux. It's all a matter of change, this feeling that you are somehow fitted out for the future. I think I've never seen anyone as willing as you are to abandon the prejudices, and even the passions, of your past, when you can seize the day better without them. I cannot do this now. Whether I can do it later is really the question, isn't it? You say that your letter was made possible only by my letter. I thank you for your letter most of all, Hiram, because it made me know that somebody is out there.

Yours, as always,
Bill

I find these extraordinary letters, which could come only from an extraordinary human being. I am unceasingly grateful that I am his friend.

Part Two

Irita van Doren, like a rosy poppy, full of grace and sweetness . . . Christian Gauss, his lined, gnostic face like Ovid's under invisible laurel . . . Harlow Shapley, broad round face under a square brow, chattering gleefully about the Red Shift, Henry Wallace and the Dead Sea Scrolls . . . Irwin Edman, on leave from *The Crock of Gold,* pale head cocked to one side, bubbling as blithely as Mozart . . . Jacques Barzun, shattering his own elegant gravity with a dreadful pun and an expression of mock horror.

John K. Galbraith, towering over the table, his great hatchet head from Easter Island thrust forward, his sardonic grin punctuating briefly the torrent of his words . . . Margaret Mead, incongruous wren, topping everyone else with a sally at once shocking, serious and ironic . . . Erik Erikson, massive white-maned Viking, speaking only through his complexion: the red stain celebrating emotion—otherwise, pallor and silence.

Reinhold Niebuhr, as urbane as Talleyrand, hiding his passionate metaphysical ache under an almost suave civility . . . Arthur Schlesinger, Jr., his crab-apple face twisted in fury, so that he looked like a twelve-year-old boy who was either going to strike or cry . . . Jerome Frank, spectacles pushed high up on his sallow forehead, a disenchanted bombardier* watching with kindly scorn . . . Sumner Welles, all weary elegance in gray flannel, drinking his dinner.

* Stolen from Richard Chase, on T. S. Eliot.

Paul Robeson, overpowering Othello, a courteous gentleman . . . Hannah Arendt, her sharp plain face blossoming into beauty as she expounded polyphonic measures about the political scene . . . William Allan Neilson, that unlikely Pan moonlighting as an educator . . . David Riesman's kind and sensitive eyes over a heavy sensual mouth . . . Max Lerner, with the beauty of small square ugly men, facile, prolix, profligate and profound—insatiable and generous, cocky and thoughtful.

Vann Woodward, president of an unannounced establishment of not-so-young Turks: Bell, Heckscher, Hofstadter, Hughes, Kazin and Rovere. President—for the rest did defer to him. And the rest? Augie Heckscher, the White Rabbit, replete with wit and vision . . . Stuart Hughes, debonair Lord Weary in appearance, sharp and earnest activist in life . . . Dan Bell, solemn in seriousness, profound in lightness . . . Dick Rovere, deceptive satyr, wreathed in cigarette smoke and cynical tenderness . . . Dick Hofstadter accepting reverence painfully—some inner substance gnawing at his vitality . . . Alfred Kazin, for all his well-merited distinction, coming on at times as hard as Muhammad Ali, his rabbinic face flushed, his voice swollen.

Ralph Ellison, smoky, troubled man of some ambiguous midregion between ethnic *ambiances*—cryptically silent, then violently articulate, holding at bay some twelve colleagues for an hour and a half, while he inveighed against everything we did and were . . . And then Alain Locke, fastidious pilgrim, never raising his voice, infinitely tolerant, sadly wise . . .

Van Wyck Brooks, of the purest face, falling asleep at a dinner meeting over his coffee cup, to rise, uncorrupted, to meet Schlesinger's snide question, with, "Well, yes and no. You must be more precise."

Saunders Redding, aristocrat sans portfolio, favorite comrade, always knowing, seldom saying, enduring, true as true steel . . . R. L. Duffus, modest, tempered, game, quiet and learned . . . Henry Allen Moe, a round man, soft-spoken, alert, merry at times, but before the congressional committee investigating tax-exempt foundations, strong, ironic, impregnable . . . Paul B. Sears, the father of ecology, with a black mustache under silver hair, so softly plausible (like a "bad man" in a Western) that you could not guess the integrity that triggered him.

Louis Kronenberger, eighteenth-century dandy, elegant of mind and person, arbiter of taste . . . Elmer Davis, looking like a male impersonator of a female impersonator, with a cigar-and-whisky-hoarsened voice, but the bravest man in the McCarthy era . . . Crane Brinton, a sandy-colored gentleman and, I suspect, as just as Vann Woodward . . . Marston Bates, wiry, convivial zoologist, a magus who served insect hors d'oeuvres with an anticipatory smile . . . Senator Paul Douglas, vast polar bear who remained silent at his first *American Scholar* editorial board meeting until the end, when he said reverently, "My God, you all mean what you say, don't you?"

Joseph Wood Krutch, critic of Samuel Johnson, Eugene O'Neill, the desert and the state of the republic; prickly, honorable and unreconstructed humanist, the champion of quivering life . . . Guy Stanton Ford, intransigent elf of the enduring values . . . Randall Jarrell, saturnine and epicene monk of American letters . . . Loren Eiseley, lonely traveler of the night spaces, incredible combination of the Poet and the Provost . . . Perry Miller, gout-ridden nineteenth-century squire of the rubicund phiz . . . Phyllis McGinley, who remained a Westchester housewife while writing poetry that Alexander Pope would have applauded or envied . . . Robert Penn Warren, that frostbitten, grainy and prophetic man who sings of the wastes of loneliness.

We come to the Wizard of the North: Henry A. Murray. My beloved guru, the buccaneer of the Galactic Wastes, who will not receive fame, "that last infirmity of noble mind." And Philip Hallie, the redeemer of Cro-Magnon man, who has brought guilt to a new nobility through his savage and intransigent assault on his own "rottenness." An irresistibly lovable man . . . Those two likable but to me impenetrable men, Walter Gellhorn and John Hersey. Who can put his dowsing rod *down there* to find out? . . . Or Gerald Holton, so obviously, as the commentator on Einstein, a sensitive, *feeling,* knowing man?

Then there is Rupe Roth—William Matson Roth—the San Francisco champion who has frustrated Governor Reagan, terrified (through his driving) the streets of San Francisco, and survived with honor the jousts of the Common Market in Geneva . . . Robert Coles, the champion of the undiscriminated underprivileged . . . And, appropriately, Pat Moynihan, the cham-

pion of the underprivileged undiscriminating . . . Richard
Ellmann, with his gentle amusement and sympathy . . . Robert
Motherwell, voluptuary of the imagination, lovable curious
savant.

But here we are in the present, and Renata Adler, Peter Gay,
William Jovanovich, John A. Wheeler, William Styron, Kenneth
B. Clark, René Dubos, John Hope Franklin, Lillian Hellman
and Kenneth Keniston have lately joined us. For I have been
invoking the mythic faces of memory, the figures seated around
that long table, whether in the Phi Beta Kappa building in
Washington or the Hotel Biltmore or the Century Club in New
York—that long table of the meetings of the editorial board of
The American Scholar, the table of thirty years.

I have described how Marjorie Hope Nicolson gave me the
opportunity to become secretary of Phi Beta Kappa and editor of
the *Scholar,* and how, after coming to know Edmund Fuller, I
resigned the one office and retained the other. What I have not
told is the story of those first months on the job.

Shortly after I learned from Miss Nicolson that my appointment had been confirmed, I received a visit in North Carolina
from William A. Shimer, who had not long before held the joint
post I had just accepted.

He came to offer his condolences. He warned me against Miss
Nicolson, Christian Gauss and Will D. Howe. These three, he
said, ran the show; he seemed to be implying that they were
arbitrary and capricious. I was in for a hard time. He also gave
me the impression that he found me naïve and bookish, easy prey
for such movers and shakers. He exuded condescending pity.

I was not upset. He made me uneasy only for the duration of
his stay. I knew Miss Nicolson well, respected and admired her.
And when, soon after, I met Christian Gauss, any lingering hint
of a doubt dissolved.

Dissolved in five or ten minutes. Many tributes have been
paid Christian Gauss, teacher, scholar, dean—above all, man.
Perhaps the most impressive was the portrait by Edmund Wilson
in the summer 1952 issue of *The American Scholar.* But to me, in
retrospect, the most extraordinary thing about Dean Gauss was
the immediacy of his quiet impact.

His quality shone from him. Those steady eyes, alternately

thoughtful, amused, resolute, looked out upon the world, its inhabitants, and saw. I trusted him instantly, and continued to throughout the nine years I was privileged to know him. That day, when I left after a session of several hours, I took the train back to New York with an exultation so strong that I was forced to examine it.

I had spent those hours with a man I revered. Perhaps he was a great man—certainly a great teacher. But more important to me at the time was my deep conviction that he was a good man.

What did I, do I, mean? No hero, no exemplar of ideal courage, honesty, kindness, probity. Rather, a deeply lived person who had been racked by conflicts, been often tempted and tried, had known failure, dissatisfaction with (perhaps even contempt for) self, disappointment, grief. But also a man who had never relinquished his standards in dismay at the discrepancy he found between the ideal and the actual, between profession and practice. However much he disappointed himself—and I was to learn that that was often—he knew the good, *his* good, and he continued to test himself against it.

The richness of his mind and tastes, the alacrity of his wit, the patience of his forbearance, yet the vigor of his actions—knowledge of these was to come later. But on the train that day it was his goodness, as defined, that filled me. And the exultation I felt came from my sure knowledge that he had accepted me—that he liked and trusted me.

The confirmation of oneself that comes from those one respects and is drawn to is one of the liveliest catalysts to self-respect and to constructive change in one's personality. Christian Gauss was second in a line of older men who have so affected me; Melville Cane and Henry A. Murray were the others.

Christian was, in 1944, not only active in the affairs of *The American Scholar,* but also a member of the Executive Committee of the United Chapters of Phi Beta Kappa and in line to succeed Miss Nicolson as president of the Society, which he did in 1946.

In the spring of '44, as executive secretary, I brought to that committee a full report of the current upheaval at the University of Texas, whose board of regents had dismissed its president,

Homer Rainey, on a set of antediluvian charges. It was agreed at that committee meeting that an investigation was in order, and that Gauss, the only one present who also served on the Committee on Qualifications (which investigated colleges and universities seeking Phi Beta Kappa chapters, and also those chapters on campuses where academic freedom or intellectual caliber seemed threatened), should be one of the investigators.

The Executive Committee held interim powers for the Senate, which convened only once a year, on the date of the founding of Phi Beta Kappa, December 5. Hence the report on the University of Texas by the Committee on Qualifications, and the resultant decision, could be made only in the next December.

I went to Princeton for this meeting, my first and only as secretary, much concerned about the Texas fracas and the outcome of our investigation. I arrived early, to meet alone at dinner with the chairman of the Committee on Qualifications and hear about these matters.

The chairman, also the president of a Southern college, confirmed our fears about Texas. The regents had indeed exceeded their authority, and acted upon a radically reactionary set of principles. Some of Rainey's "offenses" were even laughable—such as permitting John Dos Passos's *USA* on the library's shelves.

Faculty and students were largely behind the president, the chairman reported. As he went on, I relaxed, satisfied that we would act decisively and suspend the Texas chapter. But my confidence was premature.

"Now all this is true," the chairman concluded, "but our committee is not going to recommend suspension. We believe that such an action would cause more harm than good."

He noted my patent bewilderment, and proceeded to explain that one had to understand the South to recognize the appropriateness of such a course. "Evolution, not revolution." Things had quieted down under an acting president; the university would clearly take no further action on the Rainey case, and it was up to the American Association of University Professors or the American Civil Liberties Union to carry on the fight, if anyone did. For Phi Beta Kappa to punish the regents by suspending the chapter would be a carpetbaggerlike action that would be deeply resented by all the other Southern chapters.

I protested only a little, because I was stunned, and probably also because I was new at the job and dealing with a stranger. I excused myself.

"Now, remember," he said in conclusion, "I told you all this because, as executive officer of the Society, you are entitled to this full knowledge. But I warn you, young man, that should you repeat my story, I shall be compelled to give you the lie."

After leaving him, I reeled to the telephone to call Christian Gauss. His vital, cordial voice made it easier to tell my story. When I finished, he sighed and said, "Try not to worry. I was afraid it would be like that. Well, I'll have to deal with it tomorrow. And don't be upset at any action of mine that surprises you."

I repeated that last sentence to myself several times. Did he mean that he, too, would compromise? No, not after that heavy sigh. By this time I had come to know its significance: it represented the decision to undertake some difficult or unpleasant task. It was the reluctant acceptance of responsibility.

The next morning, the Committee on Qualifications met. I was present, ex officio. The chairman gave a markedly different report from his informal one of the previous night, then called on two colleagues who corroborated his findings. It seemed clear that Phi Beta Kappa should take no action.

And still Christian Gauss was silent. Finally, with deference and some uneasiness, the chairman asked him if he was in accord with the rest of the committee.

That heavy sigh. "No," he said. "But before we go further, into full executive session, you might say, I suggest that we free Mr. Haydn. This may be a long discussion, and he has many responsibilities."

I left, a little mortified until I remembered his final words of the previous night: "Don't be upset . . ."

The meeting did last two more hours; when I saw Christian at a distance, he gave me an impish grin, but there was no opportunity to talk. Nor was there later. I came to the full Senate meeting the next morning still ignorant of the outcome of that two-hour discussion, and waited impatiently for the committee reports.

At last Miss Nicolson called on the chairman of the Committee on Qualifications. When one of the other committee members rose, I suddenly realized that the chairman was not present.

"Madame President, Senator ———— sends his regrets. He was called home on some rather urgent business, and I am serving as acting chairman. The Committee on Qualifications has no majority report."

Miss Nicolson raised her articulate eyebrows, gestured with a small lacy handkerchief she always carried.

"Indeed. Is the chair to infer that there is a *minority* report?"

"There is, Madame President. Senator Gauss will present it."

Christian rose, adjusted his famous pince-nez, and in a cool voice read a list of the charges of which he found the regents of the University of Texas guilty. In conclusion: "Therefore, Madame President, I move the suspension of the chapter of the University of Texas for an indefinite period."

The motion was carried unanimously, with two abstentions.

I finally understood. The sheer moral weight that Christian Gauss carried had stood off the other three men during those hours. I learned later that the chairman in a fury had resigned and gone home, and the others, not wanting to risk open conflict with Gauss in the Senate meeting, yet cherishing their Southern solidarity, came up with no report and no vote. I realized, too, that Christian had not wanted to implicate me, young and new in office, in the struggle he foresaw—lest I incur some lasting grudges. . . .

This was not to be the only time I was to see Christian embattled. Yet he was not by nature a fighter or even an activist. He was a great scholar of European literature, though—again like my father—the rare sort of scholar who subordinates publication to teaching. Edmund Wilson's is only one of the many testimonials to the artistry of his teaching.

Christian was also a passionate lover of sports; he followed the fortunes of the Princeton football team with ferocious enthusiasm. Of middle height and slight frame, he was one of the many intellectuals who participate in sports vicariously only, but with intensity. He had, I believe, excelled in tennis, but that was before I knew him.

A sandy, freckled man, he was something of a dandy, fond of greenish and tan tweeds, and sported a walking stick. But he was also bald, with a heavily lined face, and there was an antique cast to his appearance (I think of the busts of Greek or Roman thinkers and poets).

He also loved good food and drink, and I remember happily our lunches at the Nassau Inn and the Century Club. He was a great talker, shifting from anecdotes to speculation, whether philosophical or psychological, then suddenly to sports or domestic matters or *Scholar* business.

Christian was said to have a formidable temper, but I never encountered it. His tone, his style, was gentle, subtle and ironic, his wit mellow. When the final sad day came and I, a pallbearer, was delayed so long in heavy traffic difficulties on the New Jersey Turnpike that I arrived to see the other pallbearers carry the coffin out of the church, my only consolation was the thought of the merriment with which Christian would have told the Tale of the Dilatory Pallbearer.

His sensitiveness to the emotions of others was acute; he often had a clear perception of what was troubling me before I was sure myself, and was very deft at pointing the way unobtrusively. I remember vividly an incident after one of the Princeton meetings, while he was driving me to a tea in honor of Albert Einstein. Suddenly Christian pointed ahead and said, "Why, there are Einstein and Eisenstaedt! Let's pick them up."

Two figures walking slowly on the road, one with a great shock of white hair, a turtle-neck sweater, and baggy Chaplinesque pants. (Has no one else noticed the physical similarities between Einstein, Chaplin—as made up for the screen—and Toscanini? For me, Chaplin's is the middle face, the one blending the elements of the other two.)

We stopped beside the two men, and I got out of the car, to fold up the seat on which I had been sitting. I looked directly over the top of the car into the face of Albert Einstein. It is no secret that he sprouted whiskers, as do other men. Yet it struck me forcibly that there was light coming out of his face—that light grew there, as hairs do on the faces of all men. It seemed to me that this was not a man in the ordinary sense, that this face belonged to another, a different species.

And then he smiled at me. This act constituted the most profound religious experience of my life. At the tea that followed I did not participate at all; I sat alone in a corner, shaken by that meeting. Others came over and urged me to come up and meet Einstein. I said that I had met him, offered various vague excuses.

When Christian had driven me back to the inn, he detained me briefly with his hand on my arm. "Such moments," he said without preamble, "tear a rent in ordinary perception, cut a hole in the fabric of things, through which we see new visions of reality."

So far I am sure of the words. What more he said I now understand to have been his way of letting me discover for myself why I had not needed to stay alone in that corner. Its burden was that at such times there is no need to turn away for fear of being unworthy. The insight would not occur to one who is not worthy. Nor could more familiar contact tarnish the first experience.

Such was the man with whom I was to work closely during my first years with *The American Scholar*. Coming to know him before I attended my first meeting of the editorial board was of crucial importance to me, for I was really frightened at its prospect. Frightened at the thought of conducting a meeting of such distinguished people, mostly much older than I.

At that time the board was composed of Ruth Benedict, Henry Steele Commager, Irwin Edman, Christian Gauss, Henry Hazlitt, Will D. Howe, James M. Landis, Burton Livingston, John W. Nason, William Allan Neilson, Harlow Shapley and Irita Van Doren. Miss Benedict and Mr. Landis were not present at my first meeting: I never did meet them. But the others were articulately, vigorously present.

The talk! Marjorie Nicolson thought of those days as a return to the Mermaid Tavern. Perhaps, though to me it was of another order, closer to the Socratic dialogues, yet more mundane, with talk about elections and conservation and megatons as well as essences and light years.

At this initial meeting I made another new friend in Irita

Van Doren, who was our first lady until her death in 1966. Irita comes close to defying description. Her graciousness was unmistakably innate, not simply bred. It came from some well of sweetness (that is the word Jacques Barzun stressed, in his tribute to her in the summer issue of 1967, dissociating it completely from its saccharine substitute) deep within her. She bloomed rosily with affection, was our belle as well as our hostess. The gallant older men of my original board attended her like Castiglione's courtiers. Neilson and Gauss were her then favorites, and I remember the night, after his third or fourth meeting, when Guy Stanton Ford (historian and former president of the University of Minnesota) approached her in a courtly fashion and asked whether he was too new a member to be kissed good night, as were those other two. (And that was only twenty-five years ago!)

Irita was also our peacemaker. It much disturbed her that Jacques Barzun and I regularly addressed a few tart words to each other at our gatherings; she would chide us gently, and she was obviously happy when, as we grew older, we came to a better understanding of each other. I remember, too, that when a disaffection developed between Miss Nicolson and me, Irita had us both to dinner in a vain attempt to heal the breach.

In 1946, when Miss Nicolson yielded the presidency of the Society to Gauss, we elected her back to *The American Scholar* as a regular member of the editorial board. But eight of that earlier board were gone by now, and she did not find the new members as congenial. She accused me "of selling out and going downtown," by which she meant balancing the members in academic life with others from "the other world." For her the Mermaid Tavern had been replaced by an inferior alehouse. When I replied by pointing to men like Barzun and Irwin Edman, she waved my argument aside. "They're not real scholars," she said scornfully; "they write for the outside world."

So Irita brought us together for another try, but Miss Nicolson remained unmoved. I can, in retrospect, see her point of view more clearly. Although in Hazlitt, Howe and Landis the earlier board had journalists and men of affairs, it was heavily weighted with people in academic life—scholars and administrators. I was young, new to New York, and excited by the "great world"; I was also and (at thirty-six) belatedly an active liberal, joining some of the organizations of the time and seeking for "my" magazine a more vigorous liberal position. For me "her" board was too much like the Phi Beta Kappa senators; for her, "mine" was composed of unscholarly downtown elements.

At the Senate meeting of 1944, the terms of four "old" members expired, and I nominated, to replace them, R. L. Duffus of the New York *Times,* Max Lerner, Paul Robeson and Sumner Welles. After the nominations were duly, if warily, approved by the Senate, Will Howe said to me with a glee that did not come from his political convictions, "Wow, four new members. Two Communists and two fellow travelers! The party will take over Phi Beta Kappa."

Perhaps his elation was of the order of, "Oh, boy, now are we going to have trouble!" At any rate, it was neither a sober nor accurate statement. Max Lerner was never a Communist; Duffus was a moderate liberal whose tutelary deity was Veblen, not Marx; and Sumner Welles was a career diplomat of Rooseveltian persuasion, recently retired as under secretary of state. Robeson alone was Communist, at that point not yet embittered about America. This was the time of the alliance with the Soviet; the prevailing winds were favorable to cohabitation, or at least mutual tolerance.

Yet there was quite a stir at the appearance of Robeson's name on our masthead. During the three years of his term on the board, I received hundreds of indignant letters, many demanding his removal. Most of these came from members of Phi Beta Kappa in the politically conservative regions of the country. They alarmed Miss Nicolson, but when Christian Gauss became president I felt I had firm support. "He was duly nominated by the *Scholar* and elected by the Senate of Phi Beta Kappa. We have nothing to be ashamed of or afraid of. Just ride it out."

An ironic aspect of the situation was that Robeson never attended a meeting of the board. He wrote one editorial and read several manuscripts; these were his total contribution. I did have one long talk with him, during which he promised to come to meetings, but he was too involved in politics and civil rights to keep the promise. I shall never, however, forget that one encounter. He seemed to me as big a person as he was a physical being: open "to a fault," generous, passionate and courteous. I had seen him in *Othello* only a few weeks before; I was struck by the appropriateness of the role for him.

Paul Robeson was a member of Phi Beta Kappa, but some of the new members of the next few years were not. When I first came to the national office, one of the odd things I discovered concerned the constituency of the Senate. At that time all senators were, of course, members of the Society, as were the members of the *Scholar's* board. But of the twenty-eight current senators only six had been elected in undergraduate days; all the others had become *honorary* members later!

I used these figures as part of my plea to permit the election to the board of people who were not affiliated with Phi Beta Kappa at all; as a clincher, I pointed to the fact that under the existing rules, a man like Reinhold Niebuhr could not be elected to the board! My amendment carried, and before long we didn't even know which of our members were also Phi Beta Kappas. . . .

At my first board meeting I was, I suppose, most impressed by William Allan Neilson, the president of Smith College. He was a new kind of president to me: courtly, crisp, handsome, a mellow scholar as well as a successful administrator. I was downright awed.

But of all those new to me, the one who became most closely a friend was Irwin Edman. A small, bowed man who was an albino and could barely read through the most magnifying lenses, who sometimes needed a guiding hand across New York streets, he was the most consistently cheerful man I've ever known. Blithe as a nightingale, he wore his genuine profundity so lightly that the unimaginative never discerned it. A student of philosophy, he had achieved, despite his handicap, a doctorate at Columbia in two years, side by side with that other brilliant young man, John Herman Randall, Jr. A philosopher himself, Edman belonged to the order of Montaigne and Voltaire rather than that of Kant and Hegel, and was known widely for his delightful *Philosopher's Holiday* and other books of wit, urbanity and style.

He was perfectly capable of systematic philosophy, but his true métier was the informal essay—full of charming anecdote, shrewd observation and fresh and penetrating speculation. I proposed to him that he contribute a regular column to the *Scholar*.

He accepted. The first installment ran in the spring 1945 number, and the department—which he named, in honor of his beloved Santayana, "Under Whatever Sky"—continued until his death in 1954. Two books resulted from it, too.

Irwin was also the only man of my acquaintance who could carry on a monologue for half an hour and still keep a rapt audience. Perhaps in some sort of natural compensation, he had a fabulous memory. He could literally read just once some essay in which he was interested, and have it "by heart." There was one dialogue of Plato's that he also knew by heart—I forget which. Added to his other qualities, this made him an outstanding teacher and an unmatched raconteur—for his memory held equally well for anecdotes and long complex conversations. "When you can only see a little, you must really *look* at that little," he said.

Irwin had countless admirers, even worshipers, but there was a small circle of friends, chief among them Ben Huebsch, whom he cherished. I am proud to have been one of those friends, though it was a relation in which, it seemed to me, the giving was one-sided.

As I have said before, these were years of heavy financial responsibility for me. I don't believe I talked much about it, but somehow Irwin was aware of it and helped, always insisting that it was simply a matter of something needing doing, and my being the right person to do it.

His brother-in-law, Lester Markel, the editor of the Sunday magazine of the New York *Times,* needed an article on the plight of the college president. Through Irwin, I got the assignment. College-department editors in publishing houses were always plaguing Irwin to edit this or that anthology for new programs, whether the suddenly fashionable humanities courses or ones in American civilization. With his eye problem, all time for reading and writing was precious to him; these offers were of no real interest. Yet when he learned that I was trying to get such an assignment he volunteered to go into it with me. He knew, of course, that his name as coeditor would insure the successful negotiation of the contract. Fortunately, I found another way to recoup.

Edman was one of John Dewey's favorite students, and when I founded at Bobbs-Merrill what we called the American Tradition series, I persuaded him to do the book on Dewey. This, a labor of love, was the last book he completed. He died at the end of the summer in 1954, only a month after finishing it. I wrote a short tribute to him for the *Scholar*, which I want to reproduce here.

When a true voice is stilled, one little relishes chirping in its place—even in tribute. And so, wanting somehow to express here our sense of loss and our thanks to Irwin Edman, I turned to his own words, written a few short weeks before his death and printed in this issue in the department called *Under Whatever Sky*, which has been his in every number since its inception in the Spring of 1945.

And there I found (as you will find), to my surprise, intimations of what has happened. Nothing could be more inappropriate, in writing of that dry, bubbling intelligence, spring of wit and irony and true sensibility, than to attribute to it sentimental forebodings, mystical or intuitive apprehensions of a morbid kind. Nor do I mean anything of the sort—but rather simply that in these pages you will find allusions and references to death that suggest, at the least, that he had turned his face in that direction and fixed there his clear, perceptive gaze.

He writes of first things and last, first times and last, and says how seldom one realizes at such occasions their significance: "Nor, as a matter of fact, with respect to either personal or public events, does one often remotely know that this is the end. One leaves a friend in perfect health and the next day one hears he is dead." And a little further on in his column, he quotes Edna St. Vincent Millay's address to Persephone over a friend who has just died:

> *Say to her, "My dear, my dear,*
> *It is not so dreadful here."*

When I turn back to the very first column he wrote for THE AMERICAN SCHOLAR, I read his endorsement of the feeling that "serenity can come only from seeing events in that light of eternity which is commonly called philosophy." It is my simple conviction that Irwin Edman thought and lived in that light.

He was "a master of the ready word"; he loved and practiced the intellectual quip, the ironic twist, the epigram, the gay and charming turn of phrase. An apt parodist, with an extraordinary memory and the gift of the raconteur, he could often make a half-hour's monologue delightful. Yet, as he once wrote, "The true master can in a few words speak volumes"—and the quick but courteous retort, the brief gay sally, were equally characteristic of him.

Still, for some curious reason, many people assume that such a man, such a mind, may not be profound. I have heard professional philosophers and others drag in this tired comment, "Edman is light and popular; he is not a serious philosopher or scholar." This is a facile and, I think, foolish judgment. But a sour puritanical dislike of the light-hearted is a part (thank God, not a decisive part) of the Anglo-American heritage.

Only those who, like Irita Van Doren, have known him long and cherished him have the true measure, I believe. She writes, "He had the most extraordinary gift for making difficult and abstruse matters clear and simple to the layman." His writing, his teaching, his conversation—all illustrate this gift.

No true friend of Irwin Edman's can blink at the fact that he was not, in the conventional sense, a devout or pious man. Yet I think of him as a genuinely religious man of a humanistic faith, and one who stood courageously by this faith in the face of whatever disapproval, opposition or danger.

Moreover, in this last installment of *Under Whatever Sky*, he concludes his account of first and last times with these words: "I have good authority for believing that in larger matters it is simply world without end." And therefore I feel, as it were, his amused blessing when I say that I am sure he will not need Persephone to comfort him. For fourteen years he sat among us, dispensing challenge, cheer and wisdom; and I more than half-believe that he sits now at a higher board, with Socrates and Voltaire and Montaigne, perhaps with his old loved masters, Santayana and Dewey. I think I can see them rise as he comes, and they are saying, "Welcome."

In time, I came to realize that the most extraordinary man of the whole group was Harlow Shapley, the Harvard astronomer. It was Shapley whose *Studies Based on the Colors and Magnitudes in Stellar Clusters*, singlehanded, changed the position of our sun. To put it accurately, until the publication (1915–21) of this series of nineteen papers, astronomers were in general agreement that our sun was a star close to the center of our Milky Way system. Working with the great telescopes of Mount Wilson Observatory, Shapley, still a young man, was able to convince all colleagues that our sun was at a distance of thirty thousand light years or more from the galactic center. And later, at Harvard, Shapley and his associates did valuable work in the study of variable stars and the distribution of the galaxies.

Possessed of enormous energy, Harlow did not find these activities sufficient to fill his time and mind. Religion had always fascinated him—and troubled him. He scornfully rejected the limited sectarian variety, but the Holy Ghost haunted him. Although he was given to speak of God as "Nature with a capital N," I do not believe that this definition was capable of the exorcism he wanted it to perform. In later life he was always on the search for some reconciliation between science and religion, and even much earlier, in the forties, he would frequently suggest for an article a topic involving some aspect of religion.

A memorable incident related to this preoccupation occurred at a *Scholar* board meeting held in '48 or '49. Early on, during cocktails, Harlow and Reinhold Niebuhr debated hotly the question of whether there was such a thing as Truth, or only truths. This conversation began casually, gained intensity as we went in to dinner, and continued throughout, and after, the meal. The rest of us realized that we were present at one of the great confrontations and were silent. Only Max Lerner dared to interrupt, and he only once. Plato and Aristotle, Arnold and Huxley, Niebuhr and Shapley.

Would that we had a tape recording of that encounter: two rapierlike minds, passionately but courteously dueling. At last, spent, they faced each other in silence; there was on each face an expression of understanding and affection. It came to me that each, in the manner of Yeats's Hic and Ille, had been opposing his other self throughout: Niebuhr, his keen intellectual skepticism; Shapley, his yearning for a tenable mystical faith.

I adjourned the meeting; we had never discussed the affairs of the magazine. . . .

Harlow Shapley did have a religious mission, however: to bring sanity and scientific analysis and method to the national and international scene, in the interests of peace and opportunity for all people in all lands. He was as great an impresario of science as Francis Bacon. In the forties, despite the claims the Harvard Observatory had on him, he took time to commute over the nation, speaking, organizing, exhorting. His wit and scientific training kept him from the usual weaknesses of evangelism. He preached sanity, equality, conservation and brotherhood.

In time, the Joe McCarthy time, this got him into trouble. McCarthy labeled him one of "the Communists in the State Department," and he was eventually subpoenaed to appear before the Congressional Committee on Un-American Activities to confront the rancor of Representative Rankin. But no one who really knew him would ever permit the tar to stay on him. He was no Communist; he was a Utopian. Moreover, he was preternaturally impatient. He moved, he thought, he spoke in a continual presto. I often thought, at board meetings, as proposals for articles on conservation, archeology, cybernetics, parapsychology, monopolies, astrophysics and advances in medicine poured from him in the staccato manner of a machine gun, that his mind was triggered at a pace that sometimes had the rest of our distinguished group panting to keep their reception of his ideas no more than, say, thirty seconds behind his delivery of them.

This impatience made him indifferent to the coloration of those with whom he worked in the political arena. Anyone who saw the inequities and follies and needs of the world as he did was accepted as a fellow worker. He was not interested in party affiliations; his slogan was "Let's get on with it."

When I first met him, I was much impressed with his mind, his vigor, his friendliness. That such a man, with such a schedule, should find time to sit and talk with me about the parochial problems of our magazine, amazed and delighted me. And it was through him, for example, that I secured the services of William and Eleanor James of New Haven as advertising agents. A magazine published by a nonprofit organization needs every bit of income it can find, and the work of the Jameses greatly improved our annual balance sheet.

This association with Harlow also nudged me into action on the political and social front. Faced with his dedicated activism, I felt ashamed of my some fifteen years of nonparticipation. He proposed that I join the National Council of the Arts, Sciences and Professions, of which he was president. It was an organization primarily devoted to keeping Franklin Roosevelt in office (this was the election year of 1944), and it was, in the fashion of the day, a coalition of idealists, artists, liberals, Socialists, Communists and fellow travelers.

I accepted, and Harlow appointed me to several committees. Before long, I began to lose some of my naïveté about political convictions, tactics and strategies. It became clear to me that there were two languages employed in these groups: one that depended for communication on a vocabulary standardized and defined by some invisible book of rules, and the other the familiar one of individuals speaking each for himself, in an idiom of his own, with the familiar resulting difficulty in being sure one knew exactly what another was saying.

The first of these two languages was very efficient to anyone versed in it; even when metaphor was intended, there was unmistakably a central American-Marxist clearinghouse of terms to which the informed could refer. The second was ragged, individualistic, quite inefficient—and had all my loyalty.

Roosevelt re-elected, the NCASP slowly slipped from public view, many of its members re-forming their patterns in new groups with ostensible other goals. I say "ostensible" because in time it became clear to me that there was a central "establishment," Communist-oriented, which might have no formal structure, but whose members initiated or infiltrated each new liberal cause. And these—all but one, Harlow Shapley—spoke the first of my two languages.

Let me illustrate the point with two experiences. Still zealous, however wary, I joined a new group called the New York Society to Win the Peace. I was impressed with its listing of affiliated organizations, endorsing its general goal. They ranged from the American Association of University Women to the Communist Party, U.S.A. This, I reasoned, was the way it should be—open and honest. This group would not be dominated by the party, since it was only one of many "backers." On the other hand, the inclusion of the C.P. was right in the struggle for peace: it represented in microcosm the United States' relation to Soviet Russia.

The executive secretary of the New York Society was an attractive young man whose real name, I learned later, was not Dan Wells. Big, blond, amiable, he looked ripe for a *Saturday Evening Post* cover—like the outstanding football player he had actually been. We got along very well, and when he proposed to me that I accept the chairmanship of the group, I agreed. I did say that I was willing to do so only with the understanding that the Society was not secretly Communist-dominated, that the actual operation was what its "face" proclaimed it to be. He laughed good-naturedly and reassured me.

My two not very arduous duties as chairman were to conduct our meetings and sign the press releases sent out following actions resolved at those meetings. What continued to make me uneasy was that all these resolutions condemned various actions of the American government or some other American organization. In most cases I believed our charges justified; but, as I once pointed out, the Soviet was doing or saying some of the same things we objected to on the part of our own country. The rejoinder was that it was our job to straighten out our own problems first.

Then came a motion to censure some action of Secretary of State James Byrnes's. The resultant story in the New York *Times* upset me. I had read our news release and signed it. But the article excerpted our statement in such a way as to make me, quoted as chairman, appear to be supporting a straight party line.

Naïve, I was shocked that the great *Times* would so distort a news story. Inexperienced, I was afraid not only that I was getting myself into trouble for a cause that was different in actuality from its profession and from my own convictions, but that this trouble might include the *Scholar* and hence Phi Beta Kappa. In short, I felt that impulse had led me into irresponsibility. I needed seasoned advice.

I remember dismissing instantly the thought of going to Harlow Shapley. I was sure he would chide me and urge me to continue as chairman. So I turned to Irita Van Doren, who, beginning with my first board meeting, had befriended me, guided me, supported me. Her interest and kindness were extraordinary, and this remained true through the years. And her judgment matched her generosity.

"Do this, Hi," she said. "At the next meeting, yield the chair and move the censure of some recent Soviet action. That will be a real test."

174

I followed her counsel, not without some apprehensiveness. I stepped down from the chair; I made the motion. After an awesome silence, the substitute chairman asked for a second. Only silence.

I resumed the chair, asked if there was any further business, waited, called for adjournment.

Dan Wells and I faced each other, knowing it was all over. He said defensively that it was not Communist domination when there was a consensus of sincere opinion. I resigned.

That was it, I thought. No more do-gooder organizations. But several years later Harlow Shapley invited me to join the Committee of One Hundred. Its goal was in essence the defeat of Joe McCarthy and all he represented. An executive committee of five or six was being formed to select ninety-four or -five others. Members so far were himself, Archibald MacLeish, Van Wyck Brooks, Olin Downes and perhaps one other—if so I have forgotten who. I was flattered at the company I would keep, but I hesitated, then told Harlow about my experience with the New York Society.

"Not the same thing at all," he said with some impatience. "This is totally nonpartisan in nature. We're trying to develop a real grass-roots movement against the new kind of fascism that's cropping up everywhere and threatening intellectual freedom and civil rights. And we want you on your own terms; so come and see for yourself."

That was certainly fair enough. And the first several meetings were earnest and constructive. It was the first time I had met Van Wyck Brooks, and I was much impressed with the simplicity and purity of his face and ideas. I also found MacLeish congenial. We met in Olin Downes's apartment, over the Metropolitan Opera House—a handsome Victorian set of rooms, spacious and high-ceilinged. Downes, the music critic of the New York *Times*, was a sophisticated and genial host.

The plan was to establish connections all over the country with leaders chosen chiefly from education, the arts, sciences and professions—people respected locally, who would take the initiative in organizing groups to oppose the loyalty oaths then infiltrating university and college campuses, the smearing and firing of liberal individuals who had the courage to speak up

175

against the curtailing of honest dissent, and other manifestations of creeping McCarthyism. The movement was to cut across all lines of classification: sexual, ethnic or racial, religious, political, economic. Especially, we were—or seemed to be—in agreement in our emphasis that the group must be totally free of any partisan political connection if it was to be effective and appeal widely. In short, I felt that at last I was just where I belonged, in active support of a cause I cherished.

It was agreed that at our next meeting we would spend the entire time selecting a chairman and the members of the Committee of One Hundred. This done, we would dissolve our committee and become, ourselves, simply five of the one hundred original sponsors.

At this meeting, Harlow Shapley walked in with guests, Lillian Hellman and Jo Davidson, the sculptor. I had met both of them during the NCASP days. Davidson, a hearty, vital man, I liked but really knew only slightly. I had seen more of Miss Hellman, had found her cold, strong, somewhat intimidating. (*Had* is the right tense, for since that time I have come to know her much better, to like and admire her intensely, and to feel her warmth and generosity of spirit.)

Perhaps Harlow had telephoned Olin Downes in advance, but I am sure that the rest of us were not prepared for guests. To be sure, all of us were acquainted, but their appearance seemed, at least to MacLeish and me, an intrusion.

At any rate, the meeting proceeded, but in a wholly new direction. Shapley, backed by his guests, who seemed to be self-elected members of the committee, was pressing now for a lobby in Washington, and presented names of people to consider for a professional staff. (I recognized unhappily several from NCASP days.) It was only in Washington that we could exert direct influence on legislators, he said. He was not abandoning our grass-roots program, but strengthening it in a realistic way.

A recurring experience of mine, and I suppose of many people's, is what I call "no transition." In its most virulent form, a position completely incompatible with that previously held is presented, without the slightest acknowledgment that an about-face has been performed. It is an infuriating experience to anyone trying honestly to grapple with issues and problems of whatever sort. Infuriating—in several ways: the abandonment of logic and coherence, the inevitable implication that much has been going on behind the scene, and the sheer impudence of trying to bluff one's way, with confidence that others will be so taken aback that they will accept the change without comment.

Harlow's reversal was not of that variety; he acknowledged our previous direction, but urged us to complement it with another. Yet the new proposal was completely at odds with our agreement about partisan politics: no lobby (at least at that time) could wholly avoid political alignment.

Brooks, MacLeish and I objected on several scores; Harlow and his guests responded with various arguments. At last Downes persuaded us to table the lobby question and move on to the original agenda. Let the Committee of One Hundred decide strategy; our task was to organize *it*.

We proceeded to the consideration of a chairman. I don't remember the others suggested, but shortly I proposed John Dewey for at least honorary chairman, pointing out the confidence his name would inspire throughout the country, the conviction it would bring that we were genuinely nonpartisan.

I shall never forget Lillian Hellman's expression of delighted amusement. I can only guess, of course, but I think her delight had to do with the amateur asking the unaskable question, as a small boy may confound a sophisticated audience.

At any rate, Mr. Dewey was not chosen, and the meeting broke up without decisive action. MacLeish and I descended the great staircase in silence, then faced each other on the pavement.

"I'd like to talk to you," I said.

"I would welcome that. Could you come to my apartment tomorrow afternoon?"

I went, and learned that our experiences had been close to identical. I think that we framed a *joint* letter of resignation, but I am not sure of that. What I am sure of is that I welcomed the chance to know better this distinguished reticent man who, frequently tortured by doubts and conflicts, spoke out courageously and eloquently against the mounting pressure of conformity and coercion. More about that later.

Harlow's and my friendship inevitably cooled off, but after

the '48 election we had a long talk that much surprised me. I had been sure he was a Wallace supporter, but he told me then that he had voted for Truman.

"Occasional streaks of realism in me," he said with the old beguiling grin.

This was after a board meeting. Some of the members and the staff always got together after meetings for an informal talk over drinks. Increasingly, as the years went on, Harlow and I would linger, and I would prompt him to talk—sometimes about the galaxies, sometimes conservation, and once poetry. I learned that before he had turned to science, he had wanted to be a poet. Suddenly, he broke into Tennyson's "Maud." He recited the whole long poem, face flushed with pleasure, eyes bright and insistent. He loved the melodious lines, and he especially revered Tennyson as the only Victorian poet who had understood and written of Darwin's theories and other new scientific concepts.

In the later years, very little politics. But he missed it; he was saddened by the conviction that he was no longer "working for the world." At one of the last board meetings he attended, he beckoned to me.

"Look," he said, the paper trembling in his hand.

It was a clipping from the heyday of the fight over civil rights, the freedom to dissent. It mentioned him and a speech he had given.

"All gone," he said. "Gone. Receded."

As I write, he is living with a son in Colorado.* Now well into his eighties, he has only flashes of the old spirit, his son tells me. He was happy, I learned, that we had a "celebration of Harlow Shapley" section in a recent issue, one in which Bart J. Bok wrote:

Shapley's name will be forever listed with the names of the great scientific philosophers, from Aristotle and Ptolemy through Copernicus, Galileo and Newton, to Hubble and Einstein. These are the names that, centuries hence, will figure in all introductory texts on the history of astronomy.

* He has since died, in the fall of 1972.

The struggle of the late forties and early fifties had its resonances at our board meetings, and twice I was the focus of attention. The manner in which the members of the board handled several attacks on me and one on Christian Gauss is interesting, I suspect almost unique.

The first of these incidents involved Sidney Hook. In the summer of 1948 I invited him to write a portrait of John Dewey for our series of *American Scholar* portraits. Superficially they resembled *The New Yorker*'s "Profiles." Their format involved "getting at" the man within, the scholar or thinker—taking cognizance of his work but concentrating on his character, personality. We had had one on Neilson by Marjorie Hope Nicolson, one on Whitehead by Theodore Spencer, and one on Einstein by Leopold Infeld.

Hook questioned me on the details, agreed to write the portrait. When it came in, I read the first part with much pleasure, but became increasingly dismayed over the length at which he treated the famous Dewey-Trotsky episode in Mexico. He quickly moved on from the incident itself into a long harangue about Communism that must have consumed from one-fourth to one-third of the whole article. John Dewey all but disappeared from sight throughout this polemic.

I asked him to trim this part down, reminding him of the emphasis *on the man* that we had agreed to. He objected sharply, claiming this part was essential to any full study of Dewey, but, as I remember, finally grudgingly consented to some cutting. Our contact then broke off, abruptly and not too pleasantly.

Came the annual autumn meeting of the board. After I had called it to order, Jacques Barzun asked for the floor.

"Mr. Chairman," he said, "a letter has recently been received by everyone in this room except you. Since it concerns you, I propose to read it aloud and then ask our colleagues to consider the charge it makes."

My bewilderment soon changed to anger and dread. The letter was from Sidney Hook to all the board members, giving his (to me, very distorted) version of our exchange over his piece on Dewey, in effect suggesting that I was pro-Communist and recommending that they censure me or take an even stronger action.

Anger, obviously. But dread? As I look back now I realize, as

I did not then, how insecure I still felt in that company of the elect that we had brought to that table. I knew that there was no truth in the allegation, that I had in no way betrayed the responsibility of my post, yet it must fleetingly have crossed my mind that now surely I would be drummed out of the order, become again the dismissed outsider I had been as a boy.

But only fleetingly. For Jacques, in his most elegant manner, turned to me and said, "What I propose is that we do not honor this charge, so palpably unjustified, with any credence, and that my colleagues and I unanimously express a renewed vote of confidence in our editor, and gratitude to him for the splendid work he has done with the *Scholar*."

Irita beaming, Christian beaming, everyone rising and voting "aye." A moment that it is hard not to be sentimental about.

It was Christian who was next attacked at one of our dinners. Each year the newly elected members come to their first meeting in January. In 1949 the newcomers were Alain Locke, a distinguished philosopher (and the first black man ever to win a Rhodes Scholarship), and the equally distinguished (though much younger) historian, Arthur M. Schlesinger, Jr.

Through the first part of the evening Christian had been telling several of us his experiences of a year or two earlier, when he and two others had initiated a Russian-American conference at the Waldorf. He and his colleagues had gone to Poland and met with several Soviet artists and scientists to promote a meeting of the intellectuals, artists and scientists of both nations.

The conference was finally held, Shostakovich being one of the Soviet delegation. But it was something of a fiasco. There was picketing, widespread heckling; Sidney Hook and Arthur Schlesinger set up a rival anti-Soviet meeting at a nearby hotel, and when Harlow Shapley went over to try to effect a reconciliation he was summarily thrown out of the room. The Soviet guests went home, whatever illusions they had arrived with thoroughly shattered.

All this Christian was telling in his wry way when Schlesinger sprang to his feet and denounced him. His face contorted, he looked like a preadolescent boy in such a fury that he would either attack the nearest person or burst into tears of frustration. He did neither; he launched a flow of vituperation, condemning

Gauss as a fellow traveler, a traitor, the very worst kind of American intellectual, undermining our national integrity. It was quite a debut.

When he stopped, to stand there trembling and staring malevolently at Christian, there was a stunned silence. Such an outburst might have had this effect in any case, but when its object was our beloved Christian we were literally paralyzed. All but Judge Jerome Frank, Schlesinger's associate in the Americans for Democratic Action. He pushed those memorable eyeglasses high on his head and looked grimly at Schlesinger. "Arthur," he said, "sit down and shut up."

He did, but two years later he rose again. In the autumn 1951 issue, we published an article by Howard Mumford Jones, entitled "Do You Know the Nature of an Oath?" It was about the loyalty oaths then being required of the faculty of many state universities, with special reference to current troubles at the University of California at Los Angeles. I have forgotten whether Schlesinger first read the piece in manuscript form, or whether we had actually published it before he read it. In either case he sent me a letter, angrily protesting its publication. He called Jones "an emissary from the Kremlin" and attacked me as either an accomplice or too naïve to be an editor. He added that he was sending a copy of the letter to all board members, demanding that the matter be thrashed out at our next meeting, scheduled within two weeks.

Usually I, as host, was the first to arrive. But this time I found some five or six board members already in our meeting room. They had obviously been there for some time. Irita drew me aside and explained that she had called the meeting to discuss Schlesinger's letter. They were all, she said, behind me, and they had decided that the best way to handle the situation was to go into the room where we dined early, and leave Guy Stanton Ford to reprimand Schlesinger in privacy—Ford, because as a fellow historian and editor of *The American Historical Review,* he knew him best. Moreover, as the then president of the United Chapters, he had the authority to speak for the publisher, Phi Beta Kappa.

Probably no one but Schlesinger himself knows what Ford said to him, but when they finally entered the dining room it was evident that Ford had achieved his purpose. There was no reference to either the Jones article or the Schlesinger letter during the entire evening. Once again I was reminded of my exceptional good fortune in the composition of the board.

Those were angry years, rife with tumult and controversy. The scenes at our meetings were instinct with the issues and altercations of the larger scene. I look back with some pride at the part the *Scholar* took in the struggle for intellectual and academic freedom. Except for avowedly partisan journals of politics like *The Nation* and *The New Republic,* I know of no other magazine that so consistently invoked freedom of thought and conscience, the right to dissent.

That we could maintain such a policy was due in large part to the courage of the presidents of the Society, as ex officio consulting editors. Christian Gauss, Guy Stanton Ford, Goodrich C. White and William T. Hastings were all staunch and fearless in their stands for academic freedom, and had the controversy continued longer in full force, the next two presidents, Laurence M. Gould and William C. De Vane, would have carried on the tradition with equal vigor. Without their support, I could never have followed the course I did.

From my very first issue, autumn '44, when a new department, called "The Forum," was introduced, we became a clearinghouse for debate. That Forum, "The Function of the Liberal Arts College in a Democratic Society," contained six essays presenting variant views. Among the contributors were John Dewey and Alexander Meiklejohn.

In the winter number, Henry Hazlitt and Max Lerner debated "The Coming Economic World Pattern"; a year later, there were four contributors to a discussion of "The Future of Religion"—among them Paul Tillich and Sidney Hook. The Forum for spring '46 was called "Life with the Atom." In the next year or two, other titles were "Overseas Report" (a symposium of veterans), "Science and Militarism," "Education under the G.I. Bill of Rights" and "World Federation" with Mark Van Doren and Walter Lippmann.

It was in the summer '49 issue that we tackled "Communism and Academic Freedom." In the following winter number, we had an article on the banning of *The Nation* from public-school libraries, a year later Elmer Davis's "The Scholar in a Time of Peril," and in spring '51 Lawrence Sears on "Security and Liberty."

One of our board members, signing his editorial Hippocrates, Jr., wrote a sardonic "Loyalty Oath for Scholars" for the summer '51 issue, and in autumn we published Mark Van Doren's "If Anybody Wants to Know," on the removal of his books from the library shelves of Jersey City Junior College. In the next several issues came Helen Lynd's "Realism and the Intellectual in a Time of Crisis," Jones's "Do You Know the Nature of an Oath?" Julian Boyd's "The Fear of Ideas," "A Modest Proposal for the Care and Use of Subversives" by Alan Valentine, and Archibald MacLeish's "Loyalty and Freedom."

MacLeish's essay was a bold and ringing attack on the accelerating use of loyalty oaths, and an eloquent appeal for defiant dissent. I thought it so important and controversial that, for the only time in my editorship, I sent a copy to every member of the board prior to our winter '53 meeting and opened the meeting with a discussion of the piece.

The two new board members were Louis Kronenberger and David Riesman, and Riesman made a debut as spectacular, though not so unpleasant, as that of Schlesinger. He heatedy denounced the MacLeish article as rhetoric, blowing out of all proportion the danger to academic freedom. He found it typical of Rooseveltian liberalism.

A number of members disagreed with him, defending stoutly both the piece and the validity of the issue. Whereupon Riesman turned an angry broadside on the entire board, the editor and the magazine, stating that what he had just said about MacLeish applied equally well to us and to it. He rang the bell for us, saying, "You are a defeated nation."

Pandemonium. A long altercation, then a vote. We published the MacLeish piece in autumn '53, and followed it up in the winter number with "Some Observations on Intellectual Freedom" by David Riesman, to which MacLeish replied briefly. It happened that in the spring '54 issue, we published a well-reasoned letter, correcting Riesman on a number of points, by Peter Gay, who, seventeen years later, became a member of the board.

David Riesman never exploded like that again. As I came to know Dave better, and to become very fond of him, I often wondered whether this hadn't been part of what I came to think of as "the first-time jinx." Two reactions seemed to predominate in first appearances at our meetings: a tendency to be very shy, sometimes totally silent (Erikson, Eiseley, Ellison, for example), or to dominate the conversation (Galbraith, Kazin, Riesman). I have come to no profound conclusion about this matter, but I suspect that it has to do with the basic insecurity most of us share. No matter how distinguished a person may be, to encounter a formidable group composed of equally distinguished people in other fields is a little intimidating.

Yet the only other time that a single board member held the floor almost literally against his colleagues was at the *last* meeting Ralph Ellison attended, in October 1968. He had come to the end of his term, which had been one of the pleasantest associations we had had. He attended regularly, and spoke soundly in a most useful way in the give-and-take of our discussions.

I admired him greatly—still do—as a fine writer, a courteous and cultivated gentleman, and a charming raconteur, who salted his anecdotes with irony and peppered his viewpoint with passion. But this one night his passion got the better of him—and us.

Early in the business part of the gathering I was answering questions concerning articles accepted but not yet published, which some of those present had not read. It was, and still is, our editorial procedure to have most of the pieces under serious consideration read and voted upon by at least two board members, once the managing editor and I read them. The first two votes to go either way settled the case. Although I had the authority to accept on my own, I used it only when exigencies of time or a conviction of the article's urgent importance made it seem the appropriate course. Otherwise I preferred to have various opinions, even when they led to my own being overruled.

At any rate, Ralph singled out a piece by Kenneth Keniston, "Heads and Seekers," about the use of drugs on campuses, and asked rather curtly why he hadn't been given it to read. The roots of the whole drug problem, he said, lay historically in the advent of jazz and hence in the black culture. He was an authority on the subject, and it was absurd for me to accept this piece without consulting him.

I replied that I had not known of his special interest in the subject, and that in any case, this article was not historical, but dealt exclusively with the current campus scene.

He did not accept my answer, found it irrelevant, and wanted to know who had read it. I replied, "Henry Murray and Robert Coles." He doubted their authority. Then he plunged into an attack as vague as it was angry, at the general tendency not to recognize accurately people's qualifications. He made so many sweeping generalizations, spoke with so much forcefulness, went so far afield from his starting point that it was difficult to follow him. It was impossible to quiet him.

I tried, Harry Murray tried, Jacques Barzun, I believe, and Gerald Holton, in attendance for the first and last (small wonder!) time. Nothing would stop him. He continued his tirade for at least an hour and a half. Hannah Arendt said good night and left, telling me that she was too upset to stay.

It was a strange experience: a group of some fifteen men and women sitting still for so long a period, with only three or four attempts at interruption, while a fiercely angry man harangued them. I think that our silence was in part dictated by the pain and outrage that were pouring out and our certainty that Ralph Ellison would later feel very bad.

I don't know, but I suspect that this was one manifestation of the lonely burden that certain black men of a transitional generation have carried. Disclaimed by the new militants, yet too genuinely liberal for black conservatives, widely accepted by the white community, yet always aware of that *one* difference, these aristocrats of the mind and spirit have often achieved greatly in our society, yet have belonged really to no community except the small one of their peers. The strain of this isolation must eventually tell on anyone, and I believe that October evening was one time when the load was too great.

I pause to ask myself: why have I told these stories? My answer is simple, but I hope true. This is a book of experiences—happy, sad, depressing, exhilarating, painful, pleasant. A book of experiences—and of people, those who participated in the experiences. I look back and I first see faces, first hear voices. Not great events, not weighty issues, not principles, plans and programs, but people. And that is because individual human beings are what matter to me. People in comradeship, in confrontation, in consultation, in action, in enmity, in friendship.

My desultory progress, learned from Montaigne, though obviously not practiced with his grace and profundity, is intentional. I listen to hear, look to see what will come next in my return journey through the three decades with *The American Scholar*. Hence, in these recent pages, the memory of one altercation or crisis has led to another.

But I have come to the end of that road. I remember no other outbursts of the sort I have described. I do, though, remember meetings, on an average of one every two or three years, when complaint after complaint has been offered by the members of the board. Say that four or five or six consecutive meetings have been models of constructive discussion, producing a wide range of topics proposed for future issues, and people suggested to write on them. (I have sometimes left our meetings with as many as thirty really first-rate ideas to work on.)

Comes the dark. One board member is tired of a certain regular columnist. A second one doesn't mind him, rather likes him in fact, but urges us to get rid of a different one. A third, ignoring the specific context, wants to know why, when we're doing so well, we don't pay larger fees to our contributors. A fourth thinks that our reprint fees are too small. A fifth feels that the most recent issue was mediocre, although he didn't speak up when I asked earlier for opinions about it. A sixth returns to the assault on the second columnist. Then the person who started the whole discussion points out that the cover design is really old hat; we need sprucing up.

At times it is overwhelming, this epidemic of censure, and the staff and I leave the meeting feeling downcast. But throughout, I try to find consolation in the early advice of Marjorie Nicolson: "Let them talk all they want to. People who get together this way only three or four times a year feel that they must express opinions, to show that they're actively interested. And it's much easier to blame than praise. So let them ventilate all they want to. But never let them vote."

Enough of negatives. Throughout the years, this group of distinguished men and women, combining continuity with new blood, has contributed the most amazing service that I can conceive of a magazine's enjoying. The play of minds, the wit and wisdom, the lively informal disagreements and the thoughtful contribution of topics and writers would be very difficult to match. Most of what's good in the magazine is owed to them.

And the gatherings after the formal meetings have been delightful. The camaraderie of those sessions, often prolonged past midnight, is a happy memory. Those who were too shy or too busy to stay on missed an essential part of our association.

The selection of new board members, when I first came to the job, was largely up to me. The three-year terms of two, three or four might have expired, and I would recommend which of them should be nominated for re-election, and which replaced by new nominees. As time has passed, I have retained the recommendation privileges on renominations, but given up that about new candidates to the board. At each October meeting we vote on all the people whom board members have cited for consideration. The final approval of the slate rests with the Phi Beta Kappa Senate, but the senators have never exercised their veto.

At the December '44 meeting of the Senate, the terms of Ruth Benedict, Henry Hazlitt, Burton Livingston and James M. Landis expired, and I replaced them, as I've already said, with Duffus, Lerner, Robeson and Welles. The next year Commager, Neilson and Nason went out, and Barzun and Donald Stauffer of Princeton came in. The third "new" member was Miss Nicolson, brought back to the board when her turn as president of the Society had ended. In 1946 Van Wyck Brooks, Jerome Frank and George Whicher of Amherst, one of the best teachers I ever studied with, were elected; Welles, Will D. Howe and Christian Gauss retired. Christian, of course, now president, stayed on as consulting editor. The following year, we decided to enlarge the board. No one left, but Walton Hamilton, the distinguished legal authority, and Reinhold Niebuhr joined us. Finally, in 1948, Miss Nicolson and Donald Stauffer left. That was when Alain Locke and Schlesinger became members.

I say finally, because by that time most of the original cast had gone. It was definitely not a purge, but I do confess to having wanted avidly the most distinguished group I could find, and to believing that many of these new people greatly strengthened us. Of the original group, I considered Edman, Gauss, Shapley and Irita Van Doren immortals. Soon Barzun joined their company.

Since then, the majority of those elected have been re-elected once and retired after a six-year stay; then, sometimes, after an interim of a year or two, they have been newly elected. There have been a few exceptions, who have either left (for various reasons) after the initial term of three years, or served an extra three.

Among the new friendships that came to me through this association were those with Max Lerner and Van Wyck Brooks. It would be hard to find any other two men more dissimilar. Max had become something of a hero to me before I met him. I was enormously impressed with his bold and vigorous column in the New York *Post*. Here was a genuinely independent liberal, in some ways even radical, who said what he believed, directing his fire impartially to right and to left (if the Communist party *was* left of him). My own rather feeble attempts to maintain such a stand in political activities in New York made me admire him the more. Above all, it was his sureness, his strength and certainty that I respected and envied.

These qualities turned out to be abundantly evident in his person. A short, stocky man who exuded a confidence many people considered unpleasant cockiness, and a pungent sexual magnetism, he had made a brilliant academic career, been associated with and much influenced by Alvin Johnson, married twice and fathered a large brood, and only recently left the Williams College faculty to enter journalism.

We hit it off well. My somewhat idolatrous attitude insured that, I suppose, but I felt that he really liked me, too. His wife Edna was a lovely woman, and the four of us saw quite a bit of each other. Through them Mary and I came to know the Maxwell Geismars, Saul Padover and many other people we liked. I remember best a party the Lerners gave for Marc Chagall, at which the great painter held forth with a gusto that exceeded even Max's. Artists, politicians, journalists, celebrities of all sorts came to the Lerners' parties. This was heady stuff for me, and I must confess I enjoyed it enormously.

But I had the best times with Max alone, at lunch. He was, of course, an exciting conversationalist, one whose range of topics seemed inexhaustible. His story about how the Communists had wooed him particularly fascinated me. He did, I suppose, swagger a bit; certainly his ego was fully developed. But he was aware of this, too, and often laughed at it. With all the uncertainties I knew at the time, I especially envied the pleasure he took in himself.

There are many people who don't like him, find (and have found) his column flashy and superficial, and especially have not given proper credit to his great book, *America as a Civilization*. It belongs, in my opinion, on the shelf beside Parrington, and I believe it will survive the ebbing and rising of fashions.

I also associate Max with a strange alignment that developed briefly in the board along about 1945–46. At several consecutive meetings, I noticed that all the "academic" people sat along one side of the table and the "downtowners" along the other. The one side seemed to stress elegance, the other vitality. I thought of them as the Greeks and the barbarians, and found myself wishing I were a genuine barbarian. Max, of course, was in the center of their ranks.

Then changes in membership occurred, and these alignments vanished. Among the new members in 1946 was Van Wyck Brooks, a man I devoutly loved. We were never intimate, but there developed a strong tie despite our relatively infrequent meetings. I had first met him at those gatherings at Olin Downes's apartment, but there we exchanged only a pleasant word or two. By the time he joined the board, we were fairly well acquainted, and that association brought us closer.

Brooks enjoyed reuniting at the meetings with his old friend R. L. Duffus. They invariably sat side by side at dinner. Used to country hours, Van Wyck had a tendency to nod late in the evening, which led to the exchange with Schlesinger that I have mentioned. But he contributed many good suggestions. An old-time Socialist of the Randolph Bourne variety, he shared one thing with Lerner: independence of opinion.

He was a striking-looking man, with short black bristly hair and a snow-white mustache. But it was his face, the expression in his eyes, that was most impressive. There was a kind of purity, of innocence, that somehow suggested rebirth to me. I knew that he had been through a serious psychic ordeal when young, that I at least imagined was reflected by the pain I also found in his eyes. Why then the innocence? To me it meant that he had lived with his pain, gone through some rare sort of purification. My father, in his last years, was the only other man I have known of whom I would say this with confidence.

Van Wyck was, by temperament or necessity, something of a recluse. But his wife Gladys, a charming aristocrat several of whose books I had the privilege of publishing, would not permit him to spend all his time working, and on occasion he could be social to the point of conviviality.

He had also a marvelous way of dealing with those who would try to take advantage of his apparent simplicity and other-worldliness. I remember with great amusement the rather obsequious waiter at the Biltmore, who, having helped Van Wyck off with his coat, asked him if he would have a drink.

BROOKS: Certainly.

WAITER: What kind, sir?

BROOKS: Manhattan, please.

Waiter brings drink. Brooks tosses it off in one gulp.

WAITER (eagerly): Another, sir?

BROOKS: Certainly.

Waiter brings second drink, watching Brooks with an anticipatory eye. Again Brooks drains the glass.

WAITER (wet-lipped and shiny-eyed at his discovery of a lush): May I get you another drink, sir?

BROOKS: Certainly not.

Curtain.

A much more significant version occurred when one of the big networks sent a television crew to the Brookses' house in Bridgewater, Connecticut. They were doing a series of half-hour interviews with the senior statesmen of the American literary scene, each of whom could choose his interviewer. I was pleased, warmed, that Van Wyck chose me—and then shocked when he thanked me, almost tearfully, for accepting. He was in a deep melancholy, feeling a sense of rejection, as do many older literary men when they find younger ones abusing or ignoring them.

Moved, I assured him that I was honored past anything that had happened to me in a long time. Then we both choked and subsided.

Followed the ordeal of a long day in his living room under the hot glare of the camera lights, trussed in our chairs by the microphone cords. Well on in the afternoon, I finally asked Van Wyck a question about his dismissal of Hemingway and Fitzgerald as minor figures in American literature.

"Well," he said tiredly, "it's just that they're really boys. They remind me that we're a nation of boys. In fact, our president is a boy—"

"Cut." The young man directing the show dropped to one persuasive knee at Van Wyck's feet.

"Mr. Brooks," he said reverently, "it's obvious that you're tired. We've had a grueling day, and I called time just now both to give you a rest and because we need to tape only another couple of minutes. When we resume, I'd like Mr. Haydn to ask you a final question or two about those who most influenced you in your early days. I've heard, for instance, that the father of the poet Yeats was someone who meant a great deal to you."

Van Wyck's reply was inaudible, but he nodded his head. I was indignant, finding the suave young man's tactic both transparent and shabby. We were in the Eisenhower years, and Ike was generally idolized. I thought of pointing out to Van Wyck the ruse that was being played on him, but he had leaned his head back and closed his eyes.

After a little, the director announced himself ready, and there followed a series of barks. "Dolly"—I forget the rest.

I had uttered only a single word when Van Wyck said clearly, "As I was saying when we were interrupted, our president is a boy. Out there all afternoon in the yard, playing with a golf club!"

He made it stick. It was never cut.

I watched the show with my family and had a disturbing experience. I have mentioned the purity of Van Wyck's face; it was hauntingly evident on the screen. And in contrast I found myself distasteful. I saw in myself a smoky, masked quality that I disliked. I seemed suave, even false to myself. Sickened, I looked at my family. They seemed normally interested, the children a little restless after ten minutes of Daddy talking. But I could not shake off my reaction. (I am happy to report that long later, in 1972, I saw a preview of a show I was on, and felt much more tolerant of this old, rather cheerful fellow.)

Van Wyck did not recover from his melancholy. His old friends, John Hall Wheelock, Lewis Mumford and others, cheered him briefly. Younger men, like Max Geismar, were devoted to him. But he told me once that that was because they loved him; he couldn't trust their judgment on his work. And that was why he had wanted me to interview him: I had written several reviews (one a long front-page one) on his work before we knew each other well, and the praise I had given was therefore an objective judgment of his books.

He had a long and painful final illness, spending most of the time in bed. During those extended months that noble woman, Gladys Brooks, was with him every day, and read his own work aloud to him to demonstrate its worth. He was greatly cherished, and I believe her tribute was not wasted. . . .

Saunders Redding did not join the board until 1951, but was to stay on for the next twelve years (and came back to us in 1970). I first became aware of him in 1943, when his book *No Day of Triumph* was the first one by a black man ever to win the Mayflower Cup, given annually in North Carolina to the resident in that state who had published the best book in the previous year. In 1943 my friend Winfield H. Rogers, the chairman of the department of English at the Woman's College of the University of North Carolina, was also chairman of the board of judges of the award. I drove down to Raleigh with him and waited outside for three hours while he fought, cajoled, pleaded with his colleagues to give the prize to Redding's clearly outstanding book of the previous year's crop. He finally came out, exhausted but victorious.

A month or so later, the president of some local women's club came to invite me to speak at their annual dinner. I declined, having an engagement that night. Asked to suggest someone else, I proposed J. Saunders Redding, the recent winner of the

Mayflower Cup. She was delighted—had not heard about the award.

I gave her his address at Hampton Institute in Virginia. Later I learned that only after she left me did it occur to her that that was a strange address. He was never invited.

I cannot remember where Saunders Redding and I first met, but I think it was when he was elected, at my urging, to the board. Either that or I wrote to him on behalf of Bobbs-Merrill. At any rate, he signed a contract for *On Being Negro in America,* and it was while we were working on that book that we became friends.

There came the moment when our editorial discussion of an hour or so ended. There was nothing more to be said about the book. But, it seemed, there was something more to be said.

A nervous silence. Finally, at the same instant, each of us said, in his own idiom, how hard it was.

We meant the identical thing: the racial barrier. Jay (as he used to be called by most of us) is a year older than I, and I made much of his birthday, October 13, being the same as my father's. So we definitely belong to the same generation, one in which, if men of good will were to break down that color line, conscious effort was required. Both Jay and I repudiated the difference, yet our rearing made us awkward about dispelling it.

But dispel it we did. I cherish him as a dear friend; indeed, I have a sentimental conviction that he is the brother I never had. He is free to repudiate my conviction that there is something very like about us; I feel proud of it.

The next step in our friendship came when he visited us in Westport. Mary was upstairs, busy with the children's evening bath, when we arrived from New York. I settled Jay in the living room, then went to the kitchen to make him a drink.

Mary and Jonathan, then two and a half, came downstairs and joined Jay. Jon's curiosity overcame his momentary shyness, and soon he was sitting beside Jay, questioning him.

JON: What's dat, man?

JAY (quietly) : That's my skin.

JON (with childish scorn) : No, man, dat's your hand.

And the sound of laughter. When I brought in the drinks, Jon was seated on Jay's drenched knee.

193

We never spoke of this scene, but years later, when Jon was about fourteen, Jay and his wife Esther stopped off for coffee on their way to Brown University, where he was receiving an honorary degree. While we were chatting, the children came in and were introduced. When he could speak to me without being overheard, Jay asked, "Is that the one?"

Meanwhile, I had visited the Reddings in Hampton. My friend Carl Billman drove me down from Washington. On the way I admitted feeling scared.

"How absurd," said Carl. "You're a real liberal. You'll feel right at home."

My convictions, I explained, didn't take care of the malaise I felt over being almost the only white man in a community of some two thousand black people. I was chiefly afraid that through self-consciousness I would commit some stupid gaffe.

But I need not have feared. True gentle folk that they are, Jay and Esther put me completely at ease in the first few minutes. Before long I was sitting in the kitchen, arguing with that fine woman as though I had known her for years. And at the party they gave for me that night I had a marvelous time.

Jay, of course, was one of the lonely generation to which I referred in speaking of Ralph Ellison. For a long time he was the only one of this group whom I knew well, and I used to marvel at his outward composure on evenings when he was the only black person of some ten or twelve present. Close as I feel to him, I shall never know the emotions below the surface at such occasions.

Yet there was one time, in the fall of 1964, when he was visiting writer at Duke University, and I was a fellow at the Center for Advanced Study at Wesleyan. Each of us was alone most of the time, and we had several long telephone conversations. There at Duke he really felt isolated, he said. Whenever he walked downtown in Durham he felt watched, speculated upon. This was a new experience, and he said he was getting paranoid.

Isolated in one very factual sense he had been. As early as 1944, when I was secretary of Phi Beta Kappa, I was trying to persuade various chairmen of departments of English of his quality. They frequently came to my office to ask me to recommend someone, but no matter where the location of their college, when I would ask them to consider Jay, the answer was always, "We're not ready for that yet."

Cornell University finally redeemed the situation a few years ago, but more than two decades is a long time to wait. . . . Meanwhile, wearing a rueful grin, this elegant man has made his way, written his books, and rejoiced the hearts of his friends.

Friends. If I am ever to discourse on the progress of *The American Scholar*, its ins and outs, its ups and downs, however briefly, I must soon stop my account of my friends among the members of the board. But there is one more I must cite.

Henry A. Murray first came to my attention when someone sent me the manuscript of a speech he had given. Its unusual subject was his proposal for a new Bible of the world—a book that would include the myths and the religious and ethical writings of all peoples, but also take into account scientific findings about the nature of man. In short, he was proposing a new ecumenical text as a cohesive force for the world.

This must have been around 1960. I was much impressed with the idea, but in its present form, the script was too long for the *Scholar*, and in his reply, Dr. Murray said that he was disinclined to shorten it. Eventually it appeared in a rather unsatisfactory short version in the *Saturday Review*.

I kept remembering the original, however, and a year or two later I wrote to Dr. Murray, inquiring whether he had any book in progress. He responded by saying that he was shortly to be in New York and suggesting a time he could come to see me.

Our first meeting began inauspiciously. He seemed tired and curt. Being a prickly man, I might have put on my shell and missed one of the great experiences of my life. But something about him challenged me, and I reacted spiritedly. In a few minutes I said something (I don't remember what) that startled and pleased him. He was transformed: his vitality and friendliness shocked me in a pleasant way. Before he left, it was agreed that I would write in advance of my next trip to Cambridge.

I did, and promptly received a wire: STAY WITH ME. The night of my arrival we stayed up until 4:00 A.M., the second night until 3:00.

I have written at length and—I hope—in depth about Harry Murray in the winter '69–'70 issue of the *Scholar*. I shall not repeat here what I said there about this extraordinary man—biochemist who discovered a proactive process in chicken embryos, psychoanalyst, writer, authority on Herman Melville, creator of the famous Thematic Apperception Test among many others, director of the Harvard Psychological Clinic for decades, teacher and sponsor of many distinguished social scientists, and above all, humanistic student of human lives—at eighty still vigorous, curious, alert and challenging. A man who has fled fame as if it were the devil, and courted life as assiduously.

So much for the record. I pause here for a word about friendship. That elusive and magnetic feeling between two people whose every meeting brings hunger for another, who talk and listen incessantly when together, yet never find the chance to say all that there is to say—how can one really define it or trace its elements to their sources? Harry and I fall to instantly whenever we meet; we think often of each other when apart; frequently, when one telephones, the other says truthfully, "I was just thinking of you."

There is an excitement to it analogous to being in love, but it lacks the frenzy, the sweet and riotous madness of that state. (I am not speaking of loving or "having sex" with someone, but of *being in love*.) Nor do I think that a negative statement. Never to have been in love is not to have lived fully; never to have had a friend about whom one feels the way I have described constitutes an equal deprivation of life.

I have suffered many disappointments, many failures, known pain and excruciating shame, grief and misery. But I have been in love and I have had more than my share ("Use every man after his desert . . .") of the richness of friendship. The day one of my sons said, "You've been quite a loner. How many really close friends *do* you have?"—that was the only time I ever counted. Whose were the faces, whose the voices that I was always glad—*glad* to see and hear? I stopped at thirteen, knowing there were more. And I feel an urge to set down their names, to say to them in print, "Look. See what you have done and been, to bring such gladness into another life." But I won't, or the fourteenth, or the seventeenth, would read and miss his name, when all the time I meant him, too. Him too.*

So, with Henry Murray, the usual progression was reversed; he was first my friend, then—in December 1964—became a member of the *Scholar*'s editorial board. And still is, praise be. . . .

I have been tempted to run, without explanation, three pages of names: those who have, during these thirty years, contributed to *The American Scholar*. I have been dissuaded, on sound editorial advice, and chastened my pride in that list. But we have made our way, with an editorial emphasis on diversity in subject matter and in points of view. We have tried to fill the gap between the magazines of special interests, and intellectual cliques, and those of middlebrow, semi-mass-market circulation. If we have failed, it is not the fault of our contributors.

But if circulation is any indication we have not failed. And in our case it must be indicative, for we have had a very small budget for promotion. Yet our number of subscribers has gone from 3,200 in 1944 to about 45,000 in 1972. Immense credit in this respect must go to the ingenuity of Dorothy B. Kerr, who has been in charge of circulation and promotion for some fifteen years. Recently, she has also most competently handled our advertising, succeeding Eleanor James.

I have often been asked, "How can you do it all?" This was usually a reference to my holding down three jobs, most recently as professor of communications at the Annenberg School of Communications, University of Pennsylvania; editor of *The American Scholar;* and copublisher with Harcourt Brace Jovanovich—while doing a good deal of writing on my own. A large part of the answer is "by having the sense and luck to find good collaborators."

* This literally forces me to a footnote about the many *authors* with whom I have worked and for whom I feel great affection, yet who do not appear in these pages. Were such a book written by *my* editor to appear, I would look first in the index, to see if my name was there. And so I want only to say: Jack, Fred, Henrietta, Florence, Sonya, Tom, Helen, Catie, etc., etc., etc., I haven't forgotten. It has been necessary to choose illustrations that related to particular aspects of the substance of the book.

During my administration of the *Scholar* there have been three managing editors. The first two began as editorial assistants and were promoted; the third joined us as managing editor. Lucia Morehead, a thorough, painstaking editor, resigned when Phi Beta Kappa and the *Scholar* moved from New York to Williamsburg, Virginia, in 1952.

I had first met her successor, Betsy Saunders, in 1943, when she was a student in one of my classes in Greensboro. We kept in casual touch, and she was conveniently on the spot in New York when we lost Mrs. Morehead. Betsy became the first self-taught managing editor of whom I have ever heard. I was working full-time in New York, at Bobbs-Merrill, and did all my *Scholar* work evenings and weekends, plus a great deal by long-distance telephone. I paid bimonthly visits to the Williamsburg office, but these were insufficient to give Betsy much help about particulars of her job.

Yet this remarkable young woman made her way with vigor, tact and irrefutable success. She combines, in some extraordinary, even unique way, the outgoingness of the West with the wisdom and serenity of the East. Betsy was at the helm of the staff first at the Williamsburg office and then, finally, the Washington office, for a total of eight rewarding years. The move from Williamsburg was hastened when the original Phi Beta Kappa Hall there was partially destroyed by fire (fortunately with little damage to manuscripts and files). But the decision to move had already been made, and on March 1, 1955, Phi Beta Kappa and *The American Scholar* occupied their present handsome building just off Dupont Circle.

In 1960 Betsy married Robert Turvene and moved to San Francisco. She announced her intention to me on the phone in her customary low-key way and then said cheerily, "And you'll never miss me at the *Scholar*."

I began to protest; she cut me short. "I have my successor all picked out," she said airily.

One short talk with Mary Moore Molony reminded me that Betsy only adopted her "arbitrary" tone when she was completely positive about the matter in hand. It was her peculiar style in teasing me, and no doubt partially a counter to my tendency, when under pressure, to be headstrong and authoritarian.

In any case, I was properly humbled and grateful. I have no intention, ladies, of comparing you: you have both been indispensable.

Mrs. Molony had previously worked extensively as a freelance editor for publishers and writers, and, summer after summer, graced the annual Bread Loaf Writers' Conference as its secretary. She had done some writing herself, as well, and quickly proved herself first-rate at everything from administration to close copy editing. She wielded that copy pencil with such authority that I discovered it still wasn't too late for me to learn.

We worked hand in hand on every issue. We were natural complements; her keen interest in national issues and political matters balanced beautifully my own preference for literature, speculation, the arts.

And she administered our growing staff (now seven or eight) deftly. She established a splendid morale in that group of young women (she and Dorothy Kerr made a fine pair of managers), and when one left to marry, another to travel, etc., she always came up with a good replacement.

Among the outstanding graces of this tiny woman of generous mind and heart were her charm and wit and graciousness at the board meetings. But most of all I owe her a deep debt for her loyalty, her sustaining support. When I had a myocardial infarction in Santa Fe during the summer of 1967, and was out of action for some months, she took over, and carried the whole immense load with skill and great cheerfulness. As my wife said, "You're a very lucky man, to have as a partner someone who can run it all and yet remain wholly loyal to you." It was heavy news when Mary Moore told me, in May 1972, that her husband Charles was retiring from the Federal Reserve and she felt that she must leave the *Scholar*.

I have already spoken of my debt to the various presidents of the Society; I owe even more to its executive secretary. When I left that post in 1945 to work at Crown, there followed an interim administration of several years. Finally Carl Billman,* who became secretary in 1948, came to Phi Beta Kappa from a business job in New York after abandoning graduate work in history at Harvard. Tall, thin, erect, he seemed at first the

* Carl Billman died on January 26, 1974.

epitome of the Ivy League young man. But there was a muted poet in him, and he has rich, cultivated tastes. Few who know him are aware of his informed devotion to Bach, Haydn, Handel, Mozart.

Few, because he rarely speaks of himself. He is reticent, quiet, lonely but full. He has lived alone most of his life; he cultivates his garden (literally and otherwise) with dedication.

Carl has labored strenuously for the Society, though he avoids public attention. At meetings he remains as inconspicuous as possible, partly by taking the minutes himself. He conceives of his job as a service, not as the opportunity to exercise power. But those who have held the presidency—men like Gauss, White, Gould, De Vane, Whitney Oates—have known his worth, and two, Will Hastings of Brown University, that doughty New England combination of academic conservatism and radical politics, and Guy Stanton Ford, have loved him like a son.

Yet it is possible that even most of these have been unaware of the extraordinary logical keenness of his mind. This man could have sat with the great Scholastics (not the latter-day degenerate sort) and met them composedly, word for word, thought for thought. Yet again, I think he would rather not.

Some men are natural magnets of attention. Some achieve attention, recognition, through strenuous effort. Others, having it thrust upon them, endure it when absolutely necessary, but avoid its full glare. Such a man is Carl Billman.

Carl has never been wholly comfortable with the demands of his professional life. He has practiced a modified stoicism in this respect, endured for the sake of his home, his garden, his music. His demands on himself at work are prodigious to the point of perfectionism; he writes out his letters longhand, then revises them before giving them to his secretary. He has been known to make as many as eight drafts of a document that seems to him important. These practices are in part the fault of a parochial demon of exactness that inhabits him, but they are also evidence of a genuinely painful sense of responsibility. He is not just Phi Beta Kappa's executive officer; he is also its conscience.

All these qualities and tendencies I find in this very private person. One of the real pleasures of my life has been to be admitted into that privacy. We have grown old together in our work, and the older we get, the better our sessions together. Laughter, long healing laughter. Whether at lunch or dinner, in a Washington restaurant or in his comfortable house, just over the line in Maryland—stories, memories, laughter. I play the clown, the rowdy companion, shout at his inhibitions, cajole him into indiscretions and irresponsibilities, remind him of the humorous aspects of life at Phi Beta Kappa, whether on East Forty-fourth Street, First Avenue, Williamsburg, or Dupont Circle.

And he responds. Only those who saw him dance barefoot at a party in Williamsburg know the response he is capable of. Then he takes over, tells stories, spills out his life, challenges mine. And I listen, delighted, urging him on. We finally part, weary and happy. To meet again the next time.

I must now bully him into accepting this public appearance. . . .

There is one final variety of associate to mention: our contributing editors—some formally so designated, some not. I refer to those people who have written regular columns or departments in the magazine, for varying periods of time.

Irwin Edman, with his "Under Whatever Sky," was the first. He had many fanatic followers. When he died, in August 1954, it must have seemed to them as though the magazine itself had died with him.

Irwin's column had made it clear that such a feature brought not only continuity but a sense of community. Many readers have told me that they had always a sense of his *talking* to them, telling them of the new wonders he had encountered since last he had spoken. I felt that we needed to continue such conversations, but I also felt both reluctant to think of another such column, to *replace* his, and doubtful that I could find a worthy successor.

Irwin's last installment, with its uncanny but graceful sense of the imminence of death (though almost surely not intended to be prophetic of his own), was published in October 1954. In March 1955 a new department, called "If You Don't Mind My Saying So," appeared. It continued through October 1970.

Before Irwin's death, we had already printed a number of "nature pieces" by Joseph Wood Krutch—essays on the desert, on conservation, etc. A former colleague of Irwin's at Columbia, where he was Brander Matthews Professor of Dramatic Literature for some years, Joe Krutch, plagued by asthma and recurring bouts of pneumonia, decided to seek a quieter life in a more clement setting. He and his wife moved to Tucson, Arizona.

Joe had already a versatile and impressive set of achievements. For a long time he was drama critic for *The Nation*. An eighteenth-century authority, he wrote a definitive biography of Samuel Johnson. In 1929 he published a book entitled *The Modern Temper,* which received wide attention. One of my happier inspirations while working at Bobbs-Merrill was to invite him, several years before the twenty-fifth anniversary of that book's publication, to write a new account of the state of things, looking back on the opinions he had expounded in 1929 and telling us where he stood in 1954.

Settled in Tucson, Joe had acquired a new direction. He had always been a naturalist "on the side"; now he practiced full-time. Hence the series of essays we had been publishing in the *Scholar,* which were eventually to lead to book after beloved book, on the desert, the Sierras, Baja California, etc.

During the winter that followed Irwin's death, it came to me that Joe Krutch was the man to establish a new column. His beautifully written essays on nature had won much attention from subscribers, and there was a sentimental satisfaction in knowing that the new man had been a friend of the other. Finally, although I did not know just what form the difference would take, I was sure the new column would be as distinctive as the old.

Edman had written witty, graceful and sometimes moving comments on recent experiences. He traveled a good deal and took his readers to other climes. I remember, too, a vignette about an airplane trip, in which he discoursed philosophically about the loss of a sense of transition. Each column consisted of from four to eight sections ("and in short measures, life may perfect be") on a variety of subjects. But whether recounting a simple anecdote of daily life, reflecting on the ways to listen to music, or brooding satirically on Hollywood or the Riviera, Irwin's forte was *causerie* of the most elegant sort.

Krutch's column for many years was also divided into unrelated sections, but eventually he narrowed these down to no more than three, and even sometimes wrote a single longer essay. Again there was diversity of subject and treatment, but Joe had two major themes, on which he played dozens of variations. One was, of course, that of conservation, which he brilliantly orchestrated. The other was humanist doctrine. He had long deplored the direction of reductionist behavioral science, with its quantitative measurements and morally neutral judgments.

I remember a confrontation between him and B. F. Skinner when, early in 1952, we held a tape-recorded symposium on "The Application of Scientific Method to the Study of Human Behavior." Others on the panel were Crane Brinton and A. L. Kroeber, the anthropologist, but the battle between Krutch and Skinner was the main event. I can still see Joe, that sandy man, eyes blazing, voice calm but quivering, a latter-day prophet.

Now, in "If You Don't Mind My Saying So," he had his pulpit, and he used it, to lambaste machines, social scientists, materialism and all his other favorite *bêtes noires*. I remember thinking at the time that his attitude toward reductionist behavioral science was obsessional, that he was beating a dead horse. But I later learned that I thought this on insufficient evidence: I had simply been unusually fortunate in those social scientists I had known.

From time to time Joe would write me and ask if people weren't getting tired of his column; I could always answer truthfully that it was the most popular feature of the magazine. When he died and we published his last column in 1970, there was a general mourning. Letter after letter was full of grief.

This time, however, I did not hesitate to find a new columnist. The previous experience had taught me that such a replacement neither was nor even seemed ghoulish. It was not a case of "funeral bak'd meats. . . ." And so I invited René Dubos, the distinguished microbiologist, who had recently turned his lively attention to human ecology.

Dubos hesitated. He had a vast respect for Krutch, and only finally consented if it be understood that he was not trying to wear Joe's mantle—that this was a separate enterprise. It was, of course, an attitude I approved, and he made it explicit in his introductory installment, which he devoted entirely to a tribute to Krutch.

The new department is called "The Despairing Optimist," and it has already found an audience comparable to those of Edman and Krutch. . . .

In the meantime other departments have appeared, with varying degrees of success. The first of these, "The American Scholar Forum," has pursued its erratic but occasionally brilliant course over many years. Sometimes we have had no Forum for as long as three years, but eventually it always reappears. People seem to enjoy its "playscript" form, to imagine the assembled company of people of repute, to be moved by some speeches, irritated by others, to have the opportunity themselves to scold, cheer or "put down" the performers in their own forum, "The Reader Replies."

No other of these Forums attracted such wide attention as one on the New Criticism. Its origin is interesting. Sometime in 1949, Robert Gorham Davis, then of Smith College's English department and later of Columbia's, submitted an article on the fascist roots of the New Criticism, tracing the influence of T. E. Hulme (and through him, Joseph de Maistre) on T. S. Eliot, and Eliot's, in turn, on the other largely American critics and scholars thought of as the New Critics. Hitherto, most references to the so-called New Criticism focused on its methodology in the study of literature, commonly described as *explication de texte*, connoting an exclusive emphasis on the text as the proper subject of study. But in Mr. Davis's persuasively argued essay it was proposed that most of the group shared a common philosophical stance, derived from de Maistre and Hulme, and that this position, extended and applied to social and political matters, could be described accurately as a fascist one.

The article provoked a national uproar. Yvor Winters wired his resignation from Phi Beta Kappa. Scores of poets, critics (whether or not "new") and scholars wrote angry and challenging letters, demanding a retraction, a printed answer, a public apology—everything and anything short of shutting down the magazine.

I think it was Allen Tate who suggested to me that we bring together a small group of critics who were not demonstrably of "either party" to discuss the article and clear the air. Once Mr. Davis had agreed to this arrangement, Allen also helped me to find appropriate participants. So, on Tuesday evening, August 22, 1950, we assembled at my home at 94 MacDougal Street. Present were Mr. Davis, Allen Tate, Kenneth Burke, Malcolm Cowley, William Barrett of the *Partisan Review,* and a male stenotypist. I wish I could remember his name, because he came spectacularly into his own late in the evening.

The first to arrive were Cowley and Tate. These distinguished gentlemen were chattering like schoolboys. When I opened the door, they at once began to lament the sad state of affairs: it was Election Day (primaries) and they had been unable to have a drink, had eaten dinner in sad solemnity.

"And so," said Cowley in a lachrymose voice, "do you—perhaps—"

I led them to the kitchen and provided instant fortification.

Next came the stenotypist, a middle-aged, rather gingerly man with the sanctimonious expression of the prototypical undertaker. Tate and Cowley vastly enjoyed greeting him as Mr. Davis—much to the man's bewilderment.

I describe this opening scene because it somehow set the tone for the evening. No one was drunk, but inhibitions were distinctly missing. Cowley and Tate were, in a gentlemanly way, out to get Davis, not because they disliked him, but because they felt his article false in premise and misleading in effect. Barrett was much more tolerant of the article, inclined to be dispassionate. Kenneth Burke, whom I had never met before, seemed to me (and has ever since) not so much an individual human being as an elemental force. In my experience, only Gilbert Seldes could match him for roaring energy.

I found him enormously lovable, but in the discussion, irritating, distracting, the unintentional artificer of a one-man filibuster. He would talk about the nature of hierarchy. Now it was clear to all of us that this subject was not irrelevant to a discussion of fascism, but Mr. Burke was not interested in making the connection; he was poignantly interested in the *nature* of hierarchy. His discourse became more and more remote from our agenda; after a few early references to the Davis essay, he never mentioned it again.

Mr. Davis and I had the most difficult roles. I thought that he defended himself ably for the most part, although he was constantly interrupted by the others. I was determined, as moderator, to enforce fair play, and while I may have failed, it was not for lack of effort. I have recently reread the record in those old issues of the *Scholar*, and I think my intent is clearly demonstrated, except perhaps toward the end of the discussion when, trying to slow Mr. Burke down and get back to our appointed subject, I talked too much myself.

It was late in the evening, when either Burke or I was holding forth, that I noted Malcolm Cowley, sitting there, rocking in silent mirth. But his amusement was not over our speeches; he was watching the stenotypist.

That unctuous man was *playing* his instrument. Shoulders swaying in appropriate rhythm, he was actually applying his fingers as though to the keyboard of a piano. I thought of it as the Hierarchy Concerto in A Minor.

The record of this meeting was published in two installments: in the winter 1950–51 and the spring 1951 issues.

Another enduring department in the *Scholar* is one we call "Portraits." To date we have printed some twenty of these profiles of outstanding thinkers, scholars and artists, and are currently planning still another.

"Reappraisals" has been devoted to new and fresh studies of the work of seminal thinkers and writers. The chronological reach of subject goes from Plato to Thornton Wilder.

We have also now and then printed short pieces of opinion by members of the board, offering them the opportunity to ventilate some matter of concern in what we named "The Scholar Cornered." "The Scholar's Scratch Pad" has also been available to board members, but its contents have stressed new concepts or developments in a particular field of study. . . .

We did not secure another "single" columnist until 1961, when we inaugurated a section called "An Unprofessional Eye," written by Benjamin DeMott. A novelist and essayist of some distinction, DeMott taught (and still teaches) at Amherst College. Some of his work had been high-grade reportage, and I invited him to continue in this vein for us regularly. His method was to visit some social or political or cultural event, and both describe it and reflect on its significance.

During the next year Ben visited night clubs featuring "sick humor," a demonstration in Washington, a literary party, a convention of gliding enthusiasts—or was it parachutists?—and other phenomena of the American scene. Ben was certainly one of the first "New Journalists"—if not the first.

These were very lively pieces, and I was much disappointed when *Harper's* "stole" him from us in mid-'62. We couldn't find a replacement until recently, when Jerzy Kosinski, the mordant and sensitive novelist, agreed to write a column of opinion on the American scene.

Two other departments were those of Paul A. Zahl, "A Look Around," and of Walter Teller, "The Way It Is." Zahl's ran from 1962 to 1964, Teller's from '64 to '68. Zahl, an editor of the *National Geographic,* drew heavily on material from the many interesting expeditions he took for them. Walter's column was easy, graceful, quiet, dealing with nature, Americana, country living. Unpretentiously philosophical, he wrote like a gentler Thoreau. Many of us miss that department especially.

These have been our formally recorded contributing editors. But the man I think of as our permanent contributing editor is Jacques Barzun.

To me there is something quintessentially right in concluding this section with Jacques. He was elected to membership at the December 1946 meeting and has been with us ever since. Quite simply because we wanted and needed him. He has not been only a permanent member of the inner circle, but a really crucial support of the *Scholar* structure. From the beginning he has always been ready to write for us, to read for us, and to counsel us. He originated such titles as "The Scholar Cornered" and "The Scholar's Scratch Pad." In addition to many signed essays, reviews and editorials, he has written for us under a series of eclectic pseudonyms, in which he took an obvious delight.

At meetings he has invariably been a source of sober strength. During the fracases I have described he has remained cool, rational and humane. Yet he has also been our *arbiter elegantiarum,* witty and precise. I stress precision, because Jacques does. His distaste for sloppiness, his disdain for *approximations,* have led him into numerous skirmishes with the legitimizers of popular and vulgar usage.

Taste, moderation, control, irony, urbanity. A vigorous embodiment of the classical temper.

Jacques's reverence for exactness is sometimes taxing in small matters, but almost always illuminating in large ones. This quality in him has furnished me with a much needed corrective on many occasions. To continue a bit further the questionable practice of tagging personalities, classifying them, I seem to myself a romantic, with a constitutional predilection for the large, the defiant, the individualistic. And this tendency has led me into absurd quixotisms, foolish ventures, excesses of many sorts. Association with Jacques has been steadying, edifying.

I could not have made that statement during our early years together on the board. Almost at once I sensed some kind of polar complementarity. Jacques was born some three weeks after I was, in 1907. Each fall at the board meeting I would take a very good look at this so different contemporary, as though his appearance would give me some sign of the conditions not only of his mortal weather, but of mine as well.

Perhaps this "twinship" stirred in my competitive self a feeling of some ambiguous rivalry. At any rate, in those days we were both prone, as I saw it, to be touchy. I am at least certain that I was. Frequently, at meetings and in the gatherings following them, we engaged in slightly testy exchanges. When this tendency became magnified into an outright quarrel, Irita Van Doren, much distressed, scolded us both. Looking back, I find myself primarily at fault. I was blunt where he was sinewy; I was apt to be literal and explicit while he reveled in subtlety and implicitness. The fighter in me felt outclassed by his boxer, and characteristically, I attacked.

But the years changed that, as the years will. Slowly but progressively I came to appreciate more and more his peculiar strengths, his many courtesies and his thoughtful contributions. At the beginning of each meeting I see him there, across the table, with a deep satisfaction and with affection. . . .

Affection. I look back, with a final affection, to my earliest days with the *Scholar*. My secretary and I were the entire staff. She was Celia Lewis, a spirited, vital young woman who was holding the job while waiting for her husband, Hal, to finish a stretch on the eastern front—in Burma, I believe.

She was a great comrade, and between us we did all the work at first—editorial, advertising, promotion, publicity. We had some amusing experiences with Phi Beta Kappa eccentrics and even some of our contributors. I remember particularly a visit from one of our authors, who was something of a dandy, sporting a Homburg, gloves and a cane. He told me that the only way he could find the time to write a requested article would be to have a secretary to whom he could dictate that coming Saturday. He asked whether my secretary would be willing to work with him.

The following Monday she reported that although they had finished the article, she had spent as much time eluding his "attentions" as she had taking his dictation. The afternoon had ended with a scene straight out of a melodramatic silent movie: his pursuit of her through the various offices. Half laughing, half furious, she told me how she had finally stood him off. He picked the wrong girl, and later completed his melancholy relation with the *Scholar* by never paying for the several hundred reprints of his article that he ordered and received!

I return to 1944 and '45 because the origins are often the most poignant memories. But even as I do, I realize that the zest, the laughter and the satisfaction have never left my association with all these memorable people who have contributed to *The American Scholar*. It has been a vital and rewarding experience.

Part Three

W HY DO YOU WRITE? For all those who have worked either as or with a writer, this seems to become the ultimate question. It is a question that is frequently left unasked; if asked, more often than not unanswered—or answered in so vague, so unsatisfying a way as to be reduced substantially to the equivalent of that perennial reply of children: "Because."

"Because," when you pause to consider it, is really a pretty good answer. Ask "why" and see the child's face, flushed or sad or awkwardly embarrassed or sullen. But look more closely and you also see a flicker across it, in however transitory a passage, a moment's change, a brief stillness that suggests hesitation, doubt, wonder. That is the moment, I think, when the possibility of a definite answer shadows the mind. But how, when so young, to select and isolate, *define* a particular urge out of the bewildering complexity of all that one has become exposed to since encountering the contingency of *other* and the resultant complexity of motivation? And in the end, doesn't "because" come as near as one can to taking account of compulsion, desire, coercion and the illusion of choice?

"I write because I have to" is one decent answer. "I write because I love to" is another. The worst answer, I think, in terms of the living of life, is "I've always wanted to be a writer." True, it is seldom expressed openly and directly. True, it is present to some degree in almost everyone who would give one of the two other answers I have offered—if only in terms of "that last infirmity of noble mind." Yet many lives have been made miserable receptacles of frustration and envy and bitterness because the desire for the recognition accorded a successful writer was never balanced by either the requisite ability or the delight in writing itself—or by both. Obviously a similar pattern will be evident in the lives of those who have dreamed of being outstanding ballerinas, sculptors, composers, actresses, painters, architects, etc., etc.

The evaluations of the writing process that complement writing "because one has to" and "because one loves to" most characteristically conceive of writing (but not necessarily other arts) as (1) a disease and (2) the ultimate manifestation of health, creativity.

I am reminded of the pair of poet-novelists who dominated the British literary scene during the years in which Charles Darwin's discoveries and theories were shocking the general consciousness. To Hardy it was apparent that the universe was wholly neutral, had no purpose, no meaning. If there was a guiding principle, an ultimate meaning, it was either indifferent or sardonically malign. Man was an accident, his consciousness an ironic mishap in a universe that had made no provision for such a phenomenon. To Meredith, on the other hand, evolution was the instrument of a gospel of joy. Here was scientific evidence that there was a genuine progression built into nature (hence evidence of a divine design) that moved not only forward but *upward,* to culminate in the flowering of man, and in man the capacity to reproduce, as it were, the primal act of God: the capacity to create. . . .

Traditionally, the famous interpreters and expositors of the meaning and purpose of the creative act (Aristotle, Quintilian, Horace, Longinus, Scaliger, Sidney, Dryden, Pope, Coleridge, Sainte-Beuve, Arnold, Pater, Sartre, Empson, Richards, Koestler, Burnshaw, among hosts of others) have intoned: to teach, to edify, to delight, to express, to communicate, to exhort, to exemplify. In our own time (though not for the first time), we might add: to insult, to titillate, to disgust and to excrete. Yet it has always seemed to me that most of these pronouncements served only as window dressing to the main nature of the act, much as concepts of romance, lust, spirituality, procreation, fidelity and need are invoked to form the façade for the sexual act. In either case, as in all promotional activity, a reductive process is employed as means to a false precision; the complexity of the experience has to be reduced to be described.

In lieu of definition, I throw out an eclectic harvest of answers from novelists to questions I sent them as part of a study of the creative process I conducted at the Annenberg School of Communications, University of Pennsylvania. Eclectic—for there is a wide diversity amongst the novelists answering.

Questions & Answers

1. Is the actual writing process with you characteristically conscious, orderly and controlled?

   Elizabeth Bowen: Really. I cannot tell you. Control—I suppose—varies from day to day.

   John Fowles: No. I believe in muses.

   Evan Hunter: It is controlled in that I usually know where I want to go. But writing is a form of fantasizing, and I do not know how one can effectively control a fantasy.

   Jerzy Kosinski: There may be a long period of preconscious development before I begin a novel. But the actual writing does not start until I am aware of characters, situations, or incidents which seem significant to me, and which I feel may be also significant to my readers. After that the whole process becomes quite orderly, each successive draft imposing more control over my material, aligning the characters and story more precisely with my original conception of the novel.

   Jerome Weidman: No. I write as well as I can, then go back and rewrite and rewrite and rewrite, frequently the same sentence a dozen times.

   Calder Willingham: Vague. Please define. Can't answer such a question. I'm boss.

2. Do you usually know "where" you're going next? Or do you, rather, "find out" (as one novelist has put it) where you're going, through and during the actual process of writing?

   Elizabeth Bowen: I am one of the finders-out.

   John Fowles: Both. Satisfying both methods is the trick.

   Evan Hunter: It's a combination of both. My outline may read "Son comes in, has fight with father, storms out." (Yes, as slight as that.) In the actual writing of the scene, they may kiss and make up. Which leads us to the next answer.

   Jerzy Kosinski: The basic topography of the novel is usually established before I put anything on paper; then, any new episodes or scenes are integrated with already existing material, and examined relative to my original idea of the narrative.

Jerome Weidman: I always know where I'm going next.

Calder Willingham: I find out. I do not write by scheme or plan except in broadest terms.

3. Have you ever had the sense of "being written," rather than writing? That is, have you ever experienced what used to be called "inspiration"—when things begin to flow through your mind that you have not planned, or even thought of before? Seldom? Often?

Elizabeth Bowen: Yes, on the whole, fairly often. There *are* dull days, when one has simply to hack along. Those hack-along passages, one re-writes (if one does not scrap them) on a better day.

John Fowles: Very often.

Evan Hunter: Yes, I very often feel that there is a muse sitting on my shoulder. I recognize, of course, that this "muse" is only the unconscious at work. But I am nonetheless constantly amazed upon rereading a page I supposedly just finished writing. And sometimes, I will type ten pages without once looking up except to put a new sheet of paper in the machine, and will be exhausted afterwards, and will look at the output in wonder. I suppose that's inspiration. I don't know what it is. When it happens, it's exciting as hell.

Jerzy Kosinski: Yes. But then I also feel that I have "been lived," that my life has progressed through a process of inspiration. My personal growth has depended on moments of increased awareness—enlightenment of a sort—of incidents that have or could have happened to me in the past, or of occurrences that may or may not happen in the future. I have been expanded not by events, circumstances and situations but by the heightened consciousness of myself in relation to them.

Jerome Weidman: Never.

Calder Willingham: Always when I write really well. But I am always in the typewriter chair—not someone else. I'm boss. [NOTE: Mr. Willingham inserted the word *consciously* in the question itself —*i.e.,* "or even thought of *consciously* before."]

4. When your writing is not coming easily, do you wait and "listen" (in the words of another novelist) for some word or image, some involuntary signal or "direction"? Frequently? Sometimes? Rarely? Never? If not, what do you do at such a time?

Elizabeth Bowen: On a bad day, I fiddle around. Or, as said above, "hack along," knowing that from this drab verbiage *something* may yet emerge, at a better time. But a bad day *is* a bad day.

John Fowles: Don't like that "listen." I try to analyze rationally what I'm looking for.

Evan Hunter: I usually start free-associating on paper. I talk to myself, I write notes like "Come on now, let's try to understand what this character is all about, okay? He's a guy who, etc., etc." I guess I'm really dredging the unconscious, searching for a springboard. It usually works. Nothing is so boring as sitting in a chair staring at a typewriter. I've trained myself to *stay* in that chair until something comes, rather than going out for a walk. If you know you have to be there, you might as well be there enjoying yourself. So you start writing, almost in self-defense.

Jerzy Kosinski: In my writing as in my life, nothing comes easily. I could wait forever for events to occur or for ideas to crystallize. I write only when I want to write; when I feel a different, stronger urge, I follow it.

Jerome Weidman: No. I forge ahead as best I can, which often is not very best, but somehow if I do that it starts to come again.

Calder Willingham: I rewrite and rewrite and rewrite, etc. etc. etc. Certain chapters of both my main books were rewritten 20-25-30 times. This sort of agony is part of the calling and separates the men from the boys. I *never* listen for "wrods" [NOTE: this was a typographical error in the original questionnaire] or *images!*

5. Some biologists and psychologists, theorizing about "the creative process," explain it as a physical process, in which the body becomes "heavy" with something it wants to excrete, causing a resultant tension that lasts until the words can be discharged. To what extent, if any, have you been aware of physical discomfort that is purged after you have gone on to write? Please illustrate specifically, if you can.

Elizabeth Bowen: Really, this question is too scientific for me. To me it makes non-sense. Can all you excellent people *not* stop this grotesque theorizing about "the creative process"?

John Fowles: A better metaphor is childbirth. Surely you mean psychological not physical.

Evan Hunter: To my knowledge, I've never experienced any physical discomfort while writing. There *is* a tremendous sense of elation when the work is finished, but I don't think this is physical. I should add what might be a point of interest here. I sometimes find myself reluctant to *end* a novel. I've been involved with it for such a long time that it has literally become another world, and it is painful to abandon it. The actual number of pages I complete each day when I am finishing a book is always less than at the beginning or the middle, an unconscious slowing down process.

Jerzy Kosinski: Words and ideas never well up inside me waiting to be discharged. The tension that spurs me to write exists before, during and after the actual writing process. For me, writing is simply an expression of energy which demands a high level of mental and physical concentration and which occasions certain somatic changes. The relief I feel after writing is not an extraordinary "literary" sensation; it comes not because I have produced words or generated ideas, but because I have accomplished a demanding task.

Jerome Weidman: I've never had this feeling. I feel fine while I'm writing. I feel terrible when I'm not.

Calder Willingham: Gawd almighty! Sounds like a case for Serutan. But I think there is such a thing. I have experienced it, a kind of blocking up and powerful release—but you *put* the blocking *there.*

6. Describe as fully and clearly as you can your experience and understanding of the creative *process,* as it takes place in you. Among other things, describe the emotional and psychological experience of and in writing. How do you *feel* when actually writing?

Elizabeth Bowen: Look here: this is an impossible and to my mind somewhat indecent question. All you good people really must leave writers *alone,* and not probe at us, if you wish us to continue to "create."

John Fowles: American heresy. I'm not taking my machine to bits. Leave it mysterious.

Evan Hunter: I'm sure that all of your queried writers will find this question the most difficult to answer. I'll try, but please excuse a certain amount of fumbling. I start with a definite idea (usually) of what I want to say thematically, and then I decide how to present this in terms of a story. I think. (Sometimes, I start with a *character,* and he in turn defines the theme and the plot.) In the beginning, I am conscious of writing. That is, I am aware that there is a blank sheet of paper, and that I am going to fill it with beautiful words that someone else is going to read sooner or later. As the story takes hold, I become more and more involved with it. I become an *actor* in the book, but an actor playing *all* the roles. The scenes become terribly real to me, there is no longer any thought of a reader, there is only the moment. Later, when revising, I will consider the effect of a scene on the reader, and will change or correct to achieve the precise reaction I want from him. But in the first draft (the only really *creative* draft), I am my own audience, I am the one engaged in brilliant dialogue or violent fisticuffs, I am *in* it and *of* it, and it is *me.*

Jerzy Kosinski: The creative process is one of conceptualization, which I define as an attempt to give shape to discordant experience. To write a novel is to create a pattern of dramatically significant events and people, in the hope that the reader will connect his own experience to the narrative one, will come to see his own life as a series of perceivable acts rather than a mass of irretrievable sensations. Thus, for me the creative process is circular: it begins with my own heightened perception, aims at reaching an unknown "audience" and finally, insofar as it may affect my readers, justifies my initial choice of words, incidents and characters. In short, the reading of my work by others is the ultimate legitimization of my writing.

Jerome Weidman: I feel great.

Calder Willingham: You don't want much! How can I answer this without writing pages and pages? I struggle and wrestle in the dark with my work, in terrible despair always *if it's going well.* The main feeling of the creative process is *struggle.* I feel courage and the affective emotions are crucial. Talent I take for granted.

7. Do you "control" your characters: make sure that they speak and act in harmony with the roles you have assigned them?

Elizabeth Bowen: I control them, within their ability to *be* controlled.

John Fowles: No. I leave that to geniuses like Mr. Spiro Agnew.

Evan Hunter: Yes, I sometimes control my characters, or try to. There is, after all, no protagonist without an antagonist and someone must be there to present the argument for the other side. Moreover, this must be done with the same energy and conviction as the argument for the side you favor. (I see I am also answering [#8]. Well, let's plunge on.) A character must also be controlled in order to keep the book from getting lopsided. Too many minor characters have a habit of stepping on stage and stealing the action, diverting the attention from where it should be.

Jerzy Kosinski: I begin with what I believe to be archetypical situations, the common denominators of everyday life, within which my characters have substantial latitude. The process of writing thereafter becomes reductive: my "control" consists not in making my characters act in harmony with pre-established roles, but in paring those characters down, insisting that they do not become "verbal replicas" of reality. My character begins with the maximum amount of idiosyncrasies and of personal history, and is gradually distilled and diminished, until only his or her "dramatic core" remains.

Jerome Weidman: You bet I do.

Calder Willingham: I am not an "architect" or "bookkeeper" novelist. I don't make "outlines" or "control" my characters, but write my books in a struggle of mind and spirit.

8. If you do this, what is your reason? To keep your established story line or plot from getting out of hand? To keep thematic or ideological content consistent?

Elizabeth Bowen: No reply.

John Fowles: No reply.

Evan Hunter: No reply (see question [#7]).

Jerzy Kosinski: I do this so that the reader may use my characters as receptacles and identify them in terms of his experience. Because I always condense my characters they never defy me. It is more accurate to say that I continually defy my own inclination to supply the characters with too much overt identification.

Jerome Weidman: I do it because in writing I experience a sense of superiority over the real world in which I am forced to live and where I have no sense of superiority at all. I cringe from taxi drivers, waiters, and the tax gatherer. But not in my work. When I'm writing they cringe from me.

Calder Willingham: I don't do it.

9. Do your characters ever defy you—that is, suddenly seem to assert themselves and do or say something out of line with your general plans for them?

Elizabeth Bowen: Occasionally, the refusal of a character to act *out* of character is to be respected. In that case one takes another look at the plot, and *perhaps* alters it.

John Fowles: Yes. Finest test there is that they're coming to life.

Evan Hunter: Yes, this very often happens. When it does, I let the character run wherever he wants to go. I can always curb him later. As Max Shulman once said to an actor portraying one of his characters on a television show, "When I close my eyes, you disappear." Often, when a character begins moving on his own, saying and doing things that were not contemplated, the resultant pages may be discarded but what was said or done will remain as an undercoating and will affect the character's later development. Nothing ever goes to waste. Since most of the writing process is unconscious anyway, it would be sinful to step on a character just when he's ready to make his move. The nice thing about writing is that you can be a slob the first time around—or indeed even the tenth time around. By the time the book is published, the resultant sparkling gem should appear as if it had been taken from the ground in its highly polished state. The scenes that were written and discarded, the character excursions that were later corralled are all somehow a part of the finished product, even if they do not show.

Jerzy Kosinski: [See question #8.]

Jerome Weidman: I don't recall that any of them ever did, but if it should happen I would slap them down at once. They are my creatures, not I theirs.

Calder Willingham: Yes.

10. Why do you write novels?

Elizabeth Bowen: Because I enjoy doing so. Which is as well, as doing so is also a way of making a living.

John Fowles: As poor substitutes for poetry.

Evan Hunter: I'm tempted to answer "Because it's easier than stealing." Seriously, I love writing them. It's something you do alone, unlike screenwriting or playwriting. The success or failure is exclusively yours. It's fun. It's exciting. It's ennobling.

Jerzy Kosinski: It is the best way I know of monitoring my own development, "that reality which there is grave danger we might die without ever having known and yet which is simply our life" (Proust). I am convinced that the individual psyche is steadily deadened by impersonal forces, and that one way of releasing the mind from its routine is by allowing it to become engaged in an imaginative experience. The novel is the most effective way I know of triggering that experience, precisely because it is the most demanding: unlike film and television, the novel exists only when the reader invests himself in the narrative world. The novel for me, then, is a form to which the reader supplies his own knowledge of the world, and through which he projects himself imaginatively beyond the limits of his own existence. The process of engagement cannot help but expand the reader's awareness of the relative value of his own life.

Jerome Weidman: I don't know any other way of life.

Calder Willingham: Because it happened I have a gift as a storyteller and also in order to support myself and 7 other people.

11. What is a novel?

Elizabeth Bowen: A story.—Look, I'm awfully sorry, but to answer this at any sort of length would involve an essay, or "piece," for which I should be entitled to charge you the anything from $1,000 to $5,000 I could get for that sort of thing from a magazine. Answering the rest of this questionnaire has been great fun, for which, thank you.

John Fowles: What I think it is; or any other novelist thinks it is.

Evan Hunter: If you save this question for the last one, you deserve not to have it answered.

Jerzy Kosinski: [See question #10.]

Jerome Weidman: The most extraordinary way of getting through your biblical allotment of three score years and ten.

Calder Willingham: A novel is a meaningfully inter-related series of events that occur as a result of the interaction of a number of recognizable or believable characters who exist in a specific place and time; these events are written down by an artist known as a novelist, hopefully in an entertaining, artful and vivid manner. The soul of the novel is narrative, the heart of a novel is its characters, its flesh and form are its style—and its existence as a work of art is to be found in the meaning or meanings it communicates to its readers— GOOD NIGHT!!!

This small sampling must suggest the bewildering variety of minds and attitudes involved in this activity. As Montaigne said, "Diversity is the most universal quality."

So much for generalities. Quite simply, my experience with writers bears out the validity of this observation. Writers are as various as people, and this means infinitely various.

Where to begin? I have just beaten a ragged tattoo in my head with this question, and a few faces, a few figures have emerged from the thickets of three decades. I've decided to let them come out as they choose: Thomas Gallagher, Aldous Huxley, Wright Morris. Why them? Simply because they're the first ones who showed up.

Tom, built like a bull, was once a spectacular running guard, in the days when Columbia had a football team. Built like a guard I would never want to see heading for me to take me out of the ball carrier's path. Square, shining face above a body so massive that it seems as broad as tall. His dazzling smile, his rafter-shaking laugh, his roar of dismay, the way he rises in sudden terrifying anger, fists balled, brow black as he bellows an imprecation.

A master of gallant loyalties, wild prejudices, fierce integrity. I'm remembering an encounter with H. L. (Doc) Humes, author of that fine novel, *The Underground City*. They were both to visit my New School novel workshop that evening, and we were dining together first. Over drinks in the restaurant Doc, who must have earned his name through having a diagnosis for every problem, began to needle me. Erratically brilliant, inventor, technician, philosopher sans portfolio, cofounder of *The Paris Review*, talented writer who was beset by an inability to consider finished any task he set himself—Doc was angry because I had not told him until the last possible moment (for various reasons, including the fact that he could not keep a secret) of my departure from Random House. The son of a wealthy, forbearing, bewildered father, Doc could not brook being left out of anything, and he was determined that I should pay for not making him my confidant.

He had a scattershot technique, and it was some time before Tom realized what was going on. One of Tom's most endearing qualities is his intransigent directness: deviousness, obliqueness, circumlocution are as alien and incomprehensible to him as the dust of the moon. Moreover, I was not much disturbed by Doc's acerbity, and largely ignored it. So it was not until he abandoned all dissimulation and opened a frontal assault that Tom caught up with him.

Came the outraged roar, the plunging to his feet that brought three or four waiters running.

"You miserable little pup," shouted Tom. "You can apologize to Hiram right now."

I have seldom seen a man shrink so rapidly as Doc Humes did then. He tried a feeble quip, laughed anemically.

"Apologize," Tom thundered, and then realized that Doc was terrified. "Why, you—you *thing!* You don't suppose that I would *hit* you, do you?" He snorted in disdain.

These rages were intensified when Tom had been drinking Martinis, which he loves past the love of pearls and fine rubies. But they are balanced by a customary gentleness, tenderness, equally and distinctively his. With a child, or with a man or woman he respects, the essential sweetness of his nature blossoms freely. His perpetual dilemma has seemed to me encapsulated in Isabella's words:

> *O, it is excellent*
> *To have a giant's strength: but it is tyrannous*
> *To use it like a giant.*

But, unlike Angelo, Tom needs no reproof to remind him of this. I have seen him cover his face with his hands; I have heard him groan in contrition over one of his outbursts.

That says it better, I think. He has always seemed to me larger than life—not just physically, but in terms of living out fully every emotion he feels, right before your astonished eyes, and without any apparent self-consciousness. This is never more evident than when he is surprised.

223

"You *did?* My God, do you *really* mean that's the *way* it happened? *Jee-zus!"* and a prolonged whistle. All this over what you had anticipated might elicit an expression of mild surprise.

I find him unremittingly lovable.

And now Gallagher the writer. To date three published novels: *The Gathering Darkness, The Monogamist,* and *Oona O'.* None of them in the accepted canon. All three the work of a superb craftsman and a generous, compassionate human being, written with delicate precision and warm understanding.

"Why?" Tom has roared at me. "Why?" and "Why not?"

I don't know. I don't understand, whether in terms of Tom or Sigrid de Lima, Evelyn Eaton, Gladys Schmitt, or others who seem to me among our best novelists. I tell myself that they were born at the wrong time, that current literary fashions, the predilections of the governing elite and the luck of the game are the contributing factors to their relative obscurity—or at least to their seldom receiving what I believe their just recognition. But I don't really know, and it's a question that plagues me past tolerance.

In Tom's case I am reminded of the oft-repeated assertion that male American novelists are incapable of creating a really believable woman character—that they treat all their women simply as sexual symbols. Like most generalizations, this one could bear some qualification, but I find it pregnant with truth, all the same.

Now consider Gallagher. His first novel centers on a family, deals at some length with the father, the mother and two daughters. But it is one of the daughters, Cathy, who dominates the book. This study of a passively rebellious, inquisitive girl who slowly succumbs to everything most corrupting in her environment makes, I respectfully submit, Henry James's rendition of this subject at once crude and artificial—an invention.

The girl in *The Monogamist* shares the central focus with a marvelously drawn older man suffering from the arterial restlessness of the aging. But she is equally convincing and touching in her rudderless, perverse addiction to sensation.

The title character of *Oona O'* demonstrates the catholicity of Gallagher's understanding of women. Oona is one of the few women in fiction who warrant the word *radiant.* From the opening pages one is caught up in the feckless course this quivering, giving young woman pursues in her determination to *live* her life. The account of her experiencing childbirth alone is masterly, and the way Gallagher captures in Oona that amazing combination of the everyday and the profound is unsurpassed in my reading.

But who has noted this, who has celebrated it? Reviews—and not too many of them—have praised Gallagher's skill in rendering the American-Irish, Catholic environment. Reviewers have found something of the somber, if not morbid, in the first two girls I have described, and have rejoiced in Oona's quality. But no one, to my knowledge, has done justice to his unique contribution to American fiction; no one has cited his work along with those of his peers, writers like J. F. Powers, J. P. Donleavy and Brian Moore.

I have wondered whether the fact that Tom seems to me an inheritor of the French naturalist tradition has told against him. Would he already have a secure niche in American literature if he had been a contemporary of Dreiser, Norris and Anderson? I don't know, but I do feel sure that Flaubert would have recognized him as a worthy disciple.

Gallagher has turned to the writing of extremely skillful books of reportage: *Fire at Sea* and *The X-Craft Raid.* He is concerned about supporting his family, but I find it hard not to believe that his relatively lukewarm reception has had a part in this change of direction and in the long delay in completing a novel on which he has worked off and on since 1957.

To move from Thomas Gallagher to Aldous Huxley must seem, to the unwary, a prodigious leap. However varied the critical responses to Huxley's work, and especially his fiction, his position seems unshakably secure. A superb essayist, a bold if highly partisan thinker, a bitter satirist and polemicist who turned mystic—he is an arresting and significant literary figure.

My acquaintance with Huxley was limited, but had an enduring impact on me. In 1945 we had a brief exchange of letters concerning an article of his that was published in *The American Scholar.* Within the next year he wrote me again, explaining that his son Matthew, who had been elected to Phi Beta Kappa in his senior year at the University of Colorado, had been forced to leave college early and had therefore never been initiated into the Society. In view of my connection with the United Chapters, could I see to it that Matthew, now in New York, be initiated in our offices?

I could and did. Matthew, Carl Billman, my successor as executive secretary, and I duly celebrated the mysteries, with our lone deviation from the established ritual an epilogue of brandy and cigars.

Only a month or two before, Harlow Shapley had suggested to me that I persuade Aldous's brother Julian Huxley to give the magazine, for publication, an address he had recently delivered. I could meet Huxley, Shapley told me, at a reception in his honor to be given shortly by the Independent Citizens' Committee of the Arts, Sciences and Professions. "Just go up and ask him," Harlow said. "I'll prepare the ground."

The moment came. When I was introduced, I stammered self-consciously that dusty phrase, "I don't mean to talk business at a social occasion, Mr. Huxley, but—"

I was interrupted.

"Then why do you?" The icy phrase, the glacial voice and mocking eyes!

So when Matthew said that his father was coming to New York and would like me to have lunch with them, I was literally terrified. If the famous humanist-biologist could be so pettily cruel, what would the equally famous and biting author of *Antic Hay* and *Point Counter Point* be like?

But of course I accepted the invitation. And met the gentle giant. I had envisioned an acidulous, skinny man with enormous trifocals and a tongue dripping vinegar. I met a man at least six feet four, with the broadest shoulders I have ever seen outside the arena of professional athletics. Quiet, courteous, possessed of that ultimate gentility that manages to put at ease the most awkward and insecure.

One eye was glazed over, unseeing, a wound. But the other contained life enough for two. He redeemed Cyclops. And even though that eye seemed piercing enough to rend my solid flesh and see at a glimpse the rags and tatters of my very soul, I was strangely content. It is all right, I remember thinking; he sees everything the way it is, so why not me, too?

Not long thereafter, in connection with a course I was teaching on the literature of the twenties, I reread *Point Counter Point*. I had first reread *Main Street, Winesburg, Ohio, U.S.A.* and others of that decade—all of which had tarnished sadly in the process. They seemed dated and, in some cases, trivially limited to the then current. *Point Counter Point,* on the other hand, had suffered nothing from the erosions of time. Among all these books I read, only it, *Sons and Lovers* and *La Condition Humaine* were as engrossing, as meaningful as before.

I wrote Aldous Huxley about this experience. He replied, in his spidery hand, that I was very kind, but that he knew better than to accept my evaluation of the book. "I would rather write novels than any other form," he said, "but I know my weakness. I am essentially an essayist; I lack the capacity to create in characters the illusion of life. The novelists I most admire inject so much life into their characters that it spills over, even beyond the book that houses them. That ability I wholly lack."*

In 1961 I made my only trip to Hollywood, staying at the Beverly Hills Hotel. I do not remember any other place or occasion to which I felt so totally alien. The atmosphere of the hotel, the swarming activity of the freeways, and the stern injunction of the local police not to take a walk in the evening all so intimidated me that I spent most of my week there entertaining writers in my *lanai,* as the patio outside my room was elaborately dubbed.

I telephoned Aldous Huxley, among others, and invited him to tea. To my surprise and delight, he immediately accepted, saying that he had never seen this renowned hostelry and would enjoy coming.

I awaited him with some excitement. In my incorrigible, unaging naïveté, I imagined his stepping out into the truly charming enclosure of the *lanai,* looking around with that piercing eye, and saying, "What a perfect spot for meditation."

He came, he looked around as I had anticipated, and said, with a rather incongruously mischievous expression, "What a perfect spot for an assignation."

When he left, I accompanied him back through the lobby.

* This, like many passages in this book contained in quotation marks, is not intended to be a precise direct quotation.

For days I had been aware of the sibilant whispers and staring eyes that attended the entrance of the most juvenile starlet, the most decayed character actor. And now, not a sound, not a glance at the majestic figure of Aldous Huxley. As Kurt Vonnegut is fond of saying, "So it goes."

So it goes. So it passes. And when all the little starlets are laid out in a subterranean row, toes to toes, wigs to wigs, in their old ladies' cerements, the Cyclopean eye will still look down at us in tender clairvoyance from the constellations of literature.

But I also believe that when, a generation or two from now, the *avant-garde* neoclassicists of 2013 will snicker as wearily at the geriatric persistence of the *New York Review of Books* as do its proselytes today at the "doddering antics" of *The New Yorker*—that then the name of Thomas Gallagher will still have meaning.

Somewhere between the Olympian reserved seat of Huxley and the obscure left-field bleacher residence of Gallagher, you will find Wright Morris.

His has been a most peculiar fate: to be cited, over and over again, as the great American writer who never gets his due. Lonely, piping voices here and there trill briefly this same message about now this writer, now another. But there has been a chorus about Wright Morris. The choirmaster has perhaps been Granville Hicks, one of the genuinely sound and modest critics of our time. But there have been many others chanting the same note of indignant lamentation.

This whole question of who has been neglected, who has been unjustly denied admission at the door of the pantheon, is probably inevitable, perhaps unanswerable. The very nature of the writer's enterprise is unlike that of any other profession except the other artistic ones. The part played by luck and politics in any given case is difficult to unravel; the validity of consensus as a means to final judgment is vulnerable. How do we know that the fact that Jones is lost and not rediscovered proves that his work was inferior? What we do know is only that his work never acquired sufficient force for a large enough number of people to win him a lasting place among the survivors. But I contend that a million Americans, for example, can be wrong.

By what criteria? Through what documentation and by what authority? None, of course, except my conviction (nor am I alone in this experience) that, about books, I know. In a sphere in which subjectivity is the instrument of creation, of response and of evaluation, there can be no absolutes.

It is at once the absurdity and the delight of the kind of book I have been invited to write, and am writing, that in it one may once and for all reject the strictures and confines of alleged objectivity, of precedent and external authority. I anticipate reactions of boredom, indifference and hostility without a twinge of apprehensiveness. My publisher has asked me to write this book without prescription, and I joyfully accept this extraordinary opportunity.

And so, inspired by the case of Wright Morris, I want to say a preliminary word about "getting one's due" and how it seems to have come about *at last,* in several prominent instances.

Along about 1956 I began to hear that James Gould Cozzens was "going to come into his own." I heard this from quite a few diversified people in the course of several months: after all, he had written many fine novels, chief among them and recently, *The Just and the Unjust,* but he had never had his deserved critical reception and certainly never achieved the wide sale that seemed appropriate to a writer of his stature *(sic)*. But now, now, he had almost finished a novel that was to be his masterpiece, and then, then he would at last *get his due.*

This prophetic statement was so persistent that at last I could still my curiosity no longer. I called his editor at Harcourt, Brace, Denver Lindley.

"Is it really that good?" I demanded.

"I haven't the faintest idea," he responded. "I haven't read any of it yet, nor has anyone else."

And then *By Love Possessed* swept the country. In the first week after publication there were more than a hundred reviews extolling its greatness. Jack Fischer, the editor of *Harper's* magazine, suggested that Cozzens be awarded the Nobel Prize. The book even received ultimately the cachet of being denounced as worse than mediocre by Dwight Macdonald and others of the New York establishment. As someone once said in another context, "Anyone Elizabeth Hardwick condemns can't be all bad."

In any event, *By Love Possessed* sold and sold and sold. It became, quite literally, the Book of the Year.

And what was it? A big, sprawling, uneven novel—at its best, engrossing; at its worst, turgid, heavy-handed and unimaginative. It inhabits the plateau long dominated by John O'Hara—the upper-middle-class American scene, where passion and poetry are masks worn by lickerish adultery and corporate loyalty. It was therefore, in my opinion, much inferior to Cozzens's best work.

The same pattern has since been apparent in the careers of Katherine Anne Porter and Saul Bellow. (I except the case of Philip Roth, because the advance hurrah emphasized almost exclusively Portnoy's peculiar brand of sexuality. Otherwise, I think he would belong in this cabinet.) Miss Porter, an exquisite craftsman in the short story, foundered with her *Ship of Fools;* Bellow, at his best a subtle and engaging novelist, capered about fatuously in that love affair with himself, *Herzog.*

Yet in each case the word went out ahead, spread even beyond the publishing world. At last Miss Porter, Mr. Bellow, would have her, his, due—in praise and shekels. And each did, although the early reviews of *Ship of Fools* did not accord it the adulation bestowed on *By Love Possessed* and *Herzog.*

What does this phenomenon mean? Can it be that some popular dowsing rod of the collective unconscious quivers in advance to indicate that a hitherto good novelist, with a "minor" reputation and modest sales, has all unwittingly succumbed to the American predilection for dressy mediocrity, and is therefore ready for membership in the Best Seller Academy, with the honorary degree of L.D. (Literary Distinction) ?

Of course I don't know. But it is interesting that each of the three novels in question is (in relation to the author's previous work) more pretentious, attended, as it were, by preliminary blasts of the trumpet: in Miss Porter's case, the medieval analogy, the sort of device entirely absent in her other work; in that of Cozzens, an outlandish vocabulary that struts words mined from some prodigious cavern below the sea bed; with Bellow (as might be predicted, a less conspicuous example) , the insistence on the hilariousness of the imaginary epistle, which is so overused as to suggest that it must project its inventor's spokesman beyond the limits of a character in a novel to the transcendent role of a character in cultural life, like a Don Quixote, a Pickwick or an Emma Bovary—who always stands *for one thing.*

At any rate, I cannot feel sure who vulgarizes whom in this process. But I think that an examination of it helps one to understand the peculiar plight of Wright Morris, who is *continually called to mind as neglected.* Wright, too, had his "big book": *The Field of Vision,* which won the National Book Award for 1956.

It was generally agreed that this had to be another such occasion as those we have been considering. Wright would now go on to be seated in his rightfully won place in the Circus Maximus, and from now on his books would *sell.*

Nothing of the sort has happened. Literary business continued as usual; Morris's novels sold little better than before; he continued to receive respectful reviews, but was seldom given the front pages, the interviews, the ballyhoo accorded those "home free."

Why? In the first place, Wright is (congenitally, I suppose) incapable of the big "come-on," the throat-clearing self-consciousness that hints at the possible presence of the Great American Novel. He writes about the shiftless, the inept, the eccentric, the mediocre—frequently with touching concern, though occasionally with avuncular sentimentality. When he takes a flier at the grotesque, the macabre without benefit of homely roots, as in *What a Way to Go,* the result makes one uneasy; it is comforting to dismiss the book as an aberration, not a part of Morris's main stream. So, too, with the caperings in the veterinarian's establishment of *One Day,* where he does use preliminary bugles, in connection with Kennedy's assassination.

But the main body of his work is set both in the dreary, dusty flatness of Nebraska, *pays triste,* and the exotic growths of a symbolic landscape most hauntingly presented in the opening paragraph of *Ceremony at Lone Tree,* a novel that is here to stay. Throughout, it shivers with that light (never on land or sea) uncovered on the first page, and through it trudge the lonely folk gathered for the ninetieth birthday of a man who cheats them by dying before they arrive—people seeking no grail, no final fruition, only the assurance that they need not be alone in the darkness. "That you, McKee?" is the ultimate human question, asked here much more simply and effectively than by those waiting interminably for Godot.

Hence, even if Morris's prize-winning novel comes closer, with its Fitzgeraldian overtones, to the recipe I have been concocting or examining, it (because he) is finally innocent of the Grand Manner.

Indeed, this is bound to be the case with a man who is terrified, beyond all else, of the possibility of being obvious. The first book for which I served as Wright's editor was *Ceremony at Lone Tree,* and I shall never forget the night I labored from 8:00 P.M. until 2:00 A.M. in an attempt to persuade him to introduce a few transitional hints here and there to help the reader make his way through his obliqueness, his determined reliance on the implicit.

"But it isn't a question of any danger of being obvious," I would cry. "Just a matter of pleading on my knees that you don't make your meaning here impenetrable."

He'd look at me with those steady shrewd eyes.

"I think I'll leave it the way it is, Hiram."

Wright had his own pact with his own tutelary deity—perhaps the Delphic sibyl? If on the one hand you so value your own subtlety, the impact of the unspoken, and on the other resolutely reject from the players on your boards all those in high places, all those resplendently beautiful or successful or obviously noble or courageous—then you cannot expect a place in the Big Show. It is far easier, for example, to refer to Kafka with knowing respect long after his death than to accept him as a great writer while he lives.

And Wright is of this breed. He has seen strange sights and stranger acts, has wandered through forbidding country. But these were seldom Gothic; rather, it is their homeliness that strikes one. It is the power (for good or evil, beauty or ugliness, understanding or ignorance) of the ordinary that fascinates him, and that he has constantly invoked—first in those extraordinary photographs of his, and then in his writing. He limits himself to the ordinary to prove that there is no such thing. Only when he deserts this, his true last, to seek strange effects strangely, does he go astray.

All this is evident in his person: his twinkling elliptical pronouncements, his somehow pixie camaraderie, his exuberantly sardonic affectation of plainness. He's a delightful wizard, who would be much more at home with James Stephens's philosophers and leprechauns than with American book reviewers, buyers and readers. . . .

To write about writers (quite different from writing criticism) is to wander, I find. And it is also, for me, to become angry—angry to a degree that astonishes me. Can I have kept all this, unexpressed, within me? No, not quite, for I remember more than a few times that someone has looked at me with what he perhaps fondly thought of as a quizzical astuteness, and said, "You don't really like contemporary writers, do you?"

Oh, but I do. Only I cannot understand why people cannot see how the John Cheever of the Wapshot books towers over John Updike, who gets most of the attention. Why do so few see, and fewer say, that Gladys Schmitt's *Rembrandt* is a majestic novel that doesn't shrink when placed beside Tolstoy's? Why have only a few people observed that Thornton Wilder's *The Ides of March,* in its complexity, sad wisdom and comprehensive vision, belongs on a shelf with *The Magic Mountain, Man's Fate* and *Swann's Way?* Why does no one write about Worth Tuttle Hedden's *Love Is a Wound,* and put it in its proper place in that *other* Southern tradition, beside the best work of Ellen Glasgow and Elizabeth Spencer (who, incidentally, seldom gets *her* due)? How can the critics ignore the rich and beautiful novels of Sigrid de Lima, especially *Praise a Fine Day* and *Oriane,* which I would invoke along with Virginia Woolf's *To the Lighthouse* and *Mrs. Dalloway* as bringing the quintessentially feminine to unrestricted universality? Why has Norma Rosen's subtle and searching work received so little attention?

But I am again lamenting the neglected. It might be more to the present point to examine the ingredients that seem to insure lasting fame to certain American writers whom I find preposterously overrated. The easiest syndrome to expound, I think, is that of those writers whose work and public personalities, or images, become so merged as to become inseparable in the minds of many observers. Take Ernest Hemingway, Scott Fitzgerald, Henry James, Norman Mailer.

Hemingway, Mailer. The aggressive, "athletic," self-consciously male image. I am not saying that their writings are similar, only that *they* are, in their various interpretations of this prototypical American role. Each won his original place in American letters through good writing, but slowly the integrity of the work slackened. Was it undermined by the writer's obsession with his public persona? It is, I believe, pure poppycock to pretend that Hemingway's *fiction,* after *Men Without Women,* is of any serious stature. Several years ago I spent four two-hour class periods with graduate students trying to *prove* that beside the authentic human dignity of Paul Morel's unhappy miner-father in *Sons and Lovers,* Hemingway's fisherman in *The Old Man and the Sea* is a figure of clichés and papier-mâché, as sentimentally drawn as a portrait of an old-timer in a soap opera. I convinced all but one student, by reading aloud passage after passage from both books. A year later, that one student wrote me, "I guess you were right, after all, but why did you have to come on *so hard?*"

I'm sure that there are complex psychological explanations of which I am not aware. But what surfaces, again and again, is the feeling of the child in Hans Christian Andersen's *The Emperor's New Clothes.* The later Hemingway, in work and life alike, seems to me a pathetic fake.* And Norman Mailer, in largely accepting Papa as the true father, seems to me strangely misguided. Norman has at least had the grace from time to time to play clown, to ape his own pretensions, to balance bluster with laughter.

Make no mistake—Hemingway could write, and so can Mailer. It has been, in both cases, the "perversions of the mind," the narcissism, the possessive need for the center of the stage, and hence to be on stage all the time, that has weakened the talent.

---

* There are exceptions, of course: characters, passages, sudden flashes of insight. And the narrative gift remained. I remember sitting up all night to finish *For Whom the Bell Tolls.* Yet two weeks later, thinking back to the experience, I retained a memory of one or two strong minor characters; all the rest were cardboard figures, manipulated through a Hollywood set.

The necessary fusing of word-skill with illumination and content and attitude that makes *good writing* has with them often been sadly dislocated.

When I speak of Mailer's reverence for Hemingway being misguided, I am not referring only to Hemingway's weaknesses, but to what seems to me a fundamental difference between the two. Hemingway was a chest thumper; Mailer is a nose thumber. His proper father is Henry Miller.

Scott Fitzgerald I think a good but limited novelist. As do most people, I consider *The Great Gatsby* his best book, but one that suffers badly from the lack of a third dimension: a past. It is finally *thin,* because it is difficult to feel with the characters in that imponderable way that makes one experience their lives, cease to read about them and live with them—if one has not shared their roots. And even if Fitzgerald's very point about Gatsby is his rootlessness, we must know more intimately the roots of his rootlessness if we are to have the ultimate experience with fiction that I have just been describing.

As for Fitzgerald's other work, some of the stories are certainly impressive. His first novel, *This Side of Paradise,* seems to me so crude and amateurish that my respect for Maxwell Perkins swells and swells—that he could see in *it* what its author might yet do. *Tender Is the Night* is slight. When one considers others who have dealt with problems comparable to Nicole's—Virginia Woolf, Dostoevsky, Conrad, Turgenev, to cite only a few—there is no need to labor the point.

The recent biography *Zelda* convinced me far more of the cruel suffering in the lives of the Fitzgeralds than does *Tender Is the Night.* It is obviously true that lives spent in triviality may contain profound anxiety, despair and terror. But increasingly Fitzgerald did not, in his writing, get down there.

Yet there he is in the Hall of Fame, with an epitaph from no less grave a presence than that of Edmund Wilson. Why? I think that again we are observing the merging of the public figure and the writer. Scott and Zelda Fitzgerald are the beautiful and the damned, are the prototypes of the plastic age, are John Held Jr.'s figures. They satisfy and satiate the public greed for the daring, reckless, wealthy, beautiful ones whom most will never know but envy to the point of worship and hatred. Yet finally they take these darlings to their hearts, because their tragic ends draw the venom from the sac of envy. Scott and Zelda rest in the golden mausoleum beside Marilyn Monroe and James Dean, Jimi Hendrix and Janis Joplin.

But, you may be complaining, I included in my list the name of Henry James. Surely his exclusively *literary* reputation is of a very different sort. Yes, it relates to the informed, the literati, the cultivated. But, I believe, it bears much the same relationship to them that these others do to the larger, more popular audience. The reverence for James is, beyond all else, that for someone who repudiated the blatant vulgarity of the American scene, and who has for long symbolized, as has no other American writer, sensibility, subtlety, sophistication, snobbish status. (How he would have hated such alliteration!) It has long been characteristic of American establishments to turn Anglophile as one unobtrusive way of expressing self-depreciation. I think that James and T. S. Eliot owe much of the adulation accorded them to this tendency.

Both were good writers, Eliot at his best (through "Burnt Norton") better than good. James, I think, was an excellent writer of very limited vision. His theoretical bias did Henry James the novelist a disservice. I once, without remission of sins, was required as a graduate student to examine (with other students) the nature of the revisions made for the definitive New York edition. I studied five thousand of these changes. One hundred seventy-four were cuts; all the rest were elaborations. There, I submit, is what was wrong with James and what is wrong with his idolaters. One may whittle a point until it disappears. At any rate, above all else, Henry James has been the high priest of the precious, the elite, the *raffinés* who deplore our commercialism and crudeness.

For decades the "limited point of view" that he expounded and practiced has been a shibboleth of both practitioners and theoreticians of the novel. One wonders how Tolstoy and Dostoevsky, Flaubert and Stendhal, Dickens and Thackeray, Melville and Twain, innocent of this means of creating the illusion of reality, have survived at all.

Top hats and bowlers . . . scones and crumpets . . . umbrellas and spats . . .

Sentimentality is rampant about those of us who have devoted much of our energy and time to working with young writers, whether as teachers or editors. To the delight of some and the disgust of others, a sickly aura of inspiration and sympathetic understanding has wreathed and defaced the work called "creative writing," in much the way that fashionable easy mysticisms cloud the athletic mind and disciplined life of the genuine mystic.

Some of the responsibility for such a misconception of the true nature of this work must rest with many of those practicing it. For example, at one point during the period I conducted a novel workshop at the New School, I was asked by two colleagues how many students in my class had completed novels during the academic year that was about to end. I gave the number, and asked why they wanted to know. They explained that they had decided to end the season with a banquet to which all those who had participated in the year's writing courses would be invited, and at which each student who had completed a novel or "book" of short stories would be asked to speak.

Just on the strength of finishing?

Just so. A tribute to perseverance, sustained effort.

Regardless of quality?

To try to select only the best would result in invidious comparisons and hurt feelings.

Why a banquet and speeches? Why not simply express to each student involved your honest appreciation of the time and work he had put in?

Oh, but this would be a public reward for persistence. It would give the fellow who might never achieve greatly as a writer, might never even be published, his moment in the sun.

Didn't it occur to them that they were doing him real harm by such a celebration? That they'd be giving him a false sense of achievement, and thereby set him up for a much greater disillusionment and sense of defeat later? That there was something downright immoral about inducing a conviction of ability not justified by the facts?

A glacial reaction.

I refused to participate.

I learned later that I had been denounced as a man corrupted by commercialism. . . .

Now these two men are, to the best of my knowledge, kind and decent. They are appreciators, not critics; they conceive of the teacher as a kind of therapist, and the writing course as creative therapy. Such an attitude and activity may well have a useful function; I do not find them appropriate to a program and group dedicated to the practice of imaginative writing.

Both in the classroom and the editorial office I have spent a lot of time with young writers. Teaching has always excited me; I find the impact of the minds of another generation challenging. I am not striking a noble stance when I say that in the classroom I learn as much as I teach. To extend these exchanges to editorial work seemed a natural development. To work in publishing while conducting a weekly writing workshop meant a meshing of interests that was productive. It meant that the students had an informed contact with the "book world" they hoped to enter eventually, and that the house I worked for had a first chance at publishing some talented new writers.

For there was abundant talent. The New School, when I worked there, was a vigorous and vital place, experimental, heavy with intellectual ferment. (No comparison with its former or present situation is intended; I speak only of the School as I knew it.) I first frequented it as a student, and was so fired by its atmosphere and its approach to continuing education for adults that I applied to its then president, Bryn Hovde, for a teaching post in its writing program. He referred me to the Dean, Clara Mayer, with whom I had several conversations.

I am amused when I think now of that dedicated and noble woman, and remember that my first reaction to her approximated terror. She seemed very severe, even Germanically pedantic, with her braids meticulously coiled around her head, her thick spectacles, her abrupt questions and her monosyllabic responses. I felt awkward, fatuous, and said things in a hundred words when ten would have sufficed. Twice I left her presence convinced that she thought me inadequate, maybe even foolish.

She told me about the program, which had been initiated by Gorham Munson, and it seemed clear that a workshop limited to the novel would add a new dimension to it. Yet, feeling as I did about the impression I had made, I doubted that she would take me on. When she telephoned me and asked me dryly whether I was prepared to start a week from Thursday, at the beginning of a new semester, I was able only to stammer yes.

Closer acquaintance and eventually, I am proud to say, friendship, revealed to me two things: I was preternaturally sensitive to being turned down, and I was not nearly so good a judge of character as I had thought myself. For Clara Mayer's terseness, her impatience with circumlocution, her apparent dryness, were all directly related to her deep involvement in the cause of man. She was constantly active in humane and liberal causes; the spirit that, working with Alvin Johnson, had engaged her in the bringing to the School of great refugee European scholars had since blossomed in other ways. I know of few people to whom the Biblical text "Well done, thou good and faithful servant" applies so fitly. And the years also have given me the chance to know her in a personal way, to become acquainted with her indomitable courage and her wry and mellow humor, to learn of some of her many deeds of individual kindness—the discovery of which by others flustered her as much as though she had been apprehended in a secret criminal career. . . .

But my present subject is young writers, and especially those who attended the New School. Many young writers drift or speed to New York after college, or even high school. In those years (the late forties and the fifties) most of them sought out the Village. Being lonely, and hungry for an audience, many attended writing courses, and the New School, with its location on West Twelfth Street and its more relaxed, less traditionally academic atmosphere, appealed to them.

The record of the early students in my small workshop (limited to twelve) was close to spectacular. For three successive years the American Academy of Arts and Letters awarded its Prix de Rome scholarship to a member or alumnus of the workshop: to William Styron, to Sigrid de Lima, and to Jefferson Young (who did not accept it). Others developed and received recognition more slowly. I think, for example, of one hefty, endlessly cheerful young man who sat throughout a year, hair unkempt, in short shirt sleeves, chewing lustily on the stump of a dead cigar. He did not talk a lot, and he did not turn in much writing, but what he wrote was always good. At the end of the term he stopped by and said, "Well, Prof, I really liked the course." I replied, "Well, Mario, the course really liked you, too, or it wouldn't have let your cigar stump destroy morale the way it did." This was Mario Puzo, of recent *Godfather* fame.

At any rate, word got around that good things happened to people enrolled in this course. I found myself beginning each new semester with the words, "Contrary to rumor, this course is not conducted by Dale Carnegie."

I was an instrument, a liaison officer in the establishment of this record, and that was all. One does not teach how to write; at best, as Thornton Wilder has put it, one can only teach how not to write. And the students at the New School, for the most part, were *ready* when they enrolled in the course. They needed, or at least wanted, a hearing, a critical audience, and this the course provided them, as well as an immediate access to publication. I was in the right place, holding down the right combination of jobs.

But it was rather a case of my seeking the job because I liked working with the young than my publishing a good many young writers because I taught at the New School. There is no other editorial experience so exciting as reading the work of a new talent. One has the sense of being at a frontier. I reread these last words, I hear them, and they sound pompous. But that's the way it feels. You've read fifteen, twenty pages, and they're *good*. You turn further pages anxiously—will they hold up? And then you begin to be sure, you forget to worry, and you're filled with an exultant sense of the wonder of recurring life, of the whole seasonal cycle of sap and buds and blossoming. Life renewed, life ascendant. This is the spur that keeps one constantly on the lookout for new young writers—on campuses, in magazines and even, occasionally, in newspaper stories.

One such experience occurred in the early days at Atheneum, when I read in the *Times* about the selection of Rhodes Scholars for that year. Among them was John Wideman of the University of Pennsylvania, where he had been an outstanding student and athlete. I then remembered that, a year or so before, my son Michael had brought me a copy of *Life* magazine containing a story, with pictures, about this extraordinary young black man—brilliant, handsome, athletic. A single line in the story said that he hoped to be a novelist.

"*There's* someone you ought to get for your list," Mike had said.

I had agreed that he sounded good, but had not followed up. Again in the *Times* story there was a brief reference to John's aspiration. It seemed, I thought superstitiously, to offer that second chance that one frequently doesn't have. I wired Wideman, asking for an option on his first book of fiction (as yet totally unwritten), offering a nonreturnable $250. A modest proposition, but he accepted, and from this "blind" agreement have come *A Glance Away, Hurry Home* and *The Lynchers,* three books that have established him as one of the really outstanding novelists of his generation.

Nor is that all. John is one of my dearest friends. He has a rich, complex nature, compact of passion and tenderness. He has many dimensions, not a dull one among them.

One of the problems that editors and publishers continually face in deciding whether or not to sign up a young writer is that so many have ready first a book of short stories, or, less often, of poems—genres that are notoriously hard to sell. Confronted with such a situation, the publisher's characteristic response is, "Write a novel. Then we'll see," or even sometimes, "I'll give you a contract for a novel, sight unseen, and then if that goes well and establishes you, we'll publish the stories later."

Hence the one most sure way to secure a writer of fiction of whose gift you are convinced is to face the almost certain loss of money involved, and sign up the book of stories. With Donald Klopfer's blessing, I did this with Reynolds Price. His agent, Diarmuid Russell of Russell and Volkening, told me, in that weary, condescending, nasal voice of his, that Chatto and Windus had acquired the British rights to the stories (Reynolds, too, had been at Oxford), but that all American publishers had given him the old routine about books of short stories, and that he and Reynolds had decided to stand firm and sign a contract for the short stories only. He commended me for my good sense; this time I was a good boy.

Then, a year or so later, I left Random House, and, because Price was bound by a *contract*, I expected to lose him permanently. Eventually I heard again Diarmuid's distinctive voice, only this time accelerated a little by anger. What he had to say went something like this: "You remember the short stories by Reynolds Price? Well, Random House has turned them down. Refused to honor the contract. And—" here he came unexpectedly close to snarling—"Jason Epstein told me not to bother him with that kind of stuff again. After *that*, do you still want to take a look at the script?"

I did. I found the stories remarkably good, and signed a new contract, for Atheneum. But the attendant irony was that one of them, new to me, was a long story, a novella, really, and Diarmuid (!) and I persuaded Reynolds to publish it alone first: *A Long and Happy Life*. It had a long and happy critical reception and sale, and the following book of short stories sold exceptionally well, somewhere up around seven or eight thousand copies. . . .

In 1967, Monica McCall, that gallant Scotswoman who is one of our best literary agents, sent me a script of poems by a young black woman named Alice Walker, a recent graduate of Sarah Lawrence, whose work was recommended by Muriel Rukeyser. Monica urged me to do that daring thing, accept a first book of poems and publish it *first*. Alice Walker, she said, wanted to write a novel, and if we published the poems we could certainly have the novel, too.

The poems were strong, some of them with a primitive vitality, others delicately evocative. Many dealt with the civil rights movement in the South of 1965 and '66, others with the poet's sojourn in Africa. Both Bill Jovanovich and I were impressed by them, but their quality did not insure the writer's ability as a *novelist*, and we had already committed ourselves to our "poet for the year." (This was our way of making sure that we continued to issue poetry: to have an agreement to publish one volume a year.) We finally, with real regret, decided against acceptance.

Some months later I was surprised to receive the script back, with a note from Monica saying that she had tried other publishers and all had balked at starting a writer off with a book of poems. She was still convinced that we were the people to do it, and hoped that we'd reconsider our decision.

The poems looked as good as ever. This time we passed them on to Melville Cane. His comment was that he had never before been so moved by poetry wholly alien to his taste. We decided to go ahead. In 1968, we published *Once* by Alice Walker. It has sold more than three thousand copies, a figure unusual for any book of poems. In 1970 we published her first novel, *The Third Life of Grange Copeland,* and both it and its tiny, fiery author were handsomely received. She will go on and on, Alice Walker will, and I look forward with joy to every moment of her fulfillment.

But the real "hero" of this piece is obviously Monica McCall. I have never heard of another case in which an agent not only stayed determined to sell a book of poems by an unknown writer, but made a *second* submission of it to a publisher.

There are of course many times when taking the risk on a new writer on *his own terms* does not work out to anyone's satisfaction. But I have often hesitated to commit myself on the strength of partial work, on fragmentary evidence, only to have the person in question develop into an outstanding writer—and one lost to our list through my indecisiveness or timidity. I am grateful, every time I think of these recurring situations, for one particular instance in which I hestitated and procrastinated and then made the right decision literally at the last moment.

In 1960, when Atheneum was only a year old, Marc Friedlaender and I took a trip to Cambridge. Each of us spent three busy days talking with many of the Harvard faculty. I think it was David Riesman who introduced me to a young graduate student named Kenneth Keniston. Keniston was much interested in the psychology of the new generation and before long submitted a paper to *The American Scholar* entitled "Alienation and the Decline of Utopia."

It was a well-written and brilliantly reasoned piece, and we promptly accepted it. I thought at the time that he would eventually be writing first-rate books, and that I must not lose sight of him. But it was only when I was rereading the article in page proof, in the very act of putting the issue "to bed," that I realized its caliber was so fine that in three weeks, when we published it, book publishers were sure to be after him. For this short time only, I had what amounted to an exclusive opportunity.

Remembering past omissions, I called him immediately, learned that he was shortly to be in New York, and arranged for him to stop off at my house in Westport on his way back to Cambridge. When he arrived I offered him a contract for his first book, which then existed, if at all, only in embryo. He accepted the offer.

Several months later he wrote rather diffidently that in the first few weeks after the appearance of the article he had received a dozen or more letters from publishers, each expressing a strong interest in publishing a book of his, and some of them ready to commit themselves on the strength of this one piece.

In 1965 his *The Uncommitted,* a study of alienated youth, received a glowing front-page review in the Sunday book section of the New York *Times.* It and his two succeeding volumes, *Radical Youth* and *Youth and Dissent,* have established him as a leading authority on the youth "revolution" that has shaken the nation in the last dozen years.

Working with young writers is tantamount to inviting a surprise a day. A few years ago several of us at Harcourt Brace Jovanovich read a sweeping and lively sociocultural study called *The Devolution of the People,* written by one Richard Silberg, of whom none of us had ever heard. The book was so comprehensive in scope, and so confident in approach, that we assumed its author must be an experienced scholar of forty or fifty. We decided to publish, and Mr. Silberg came to see me. He was twenty-one years old, wore his hair as long as I'd encountered, and was dressed in tight blue jeans and a sweater. He had been graduated from Harvard College only the year before.

But this was a case where I had not known I was dealing with the young until confrontation. While I was at Atheneum I accepted a novel, *The Garden,* by a nineteen-year-old writer named Kathrin Perutz. It was a delightful comic novel about the girls and faculty in a fashionable progressive college. I found it hilarious but thought it needed a good deal of revision. I met Miss Perutz, who looked more like the youngest member of the jet set than an author, and she declared herself open to any sort of revision I had in mind. She suggested that I blue-pencil the manuscript as I saw fit.

I spent some forty-odd hours on the process, and sent the script back to her, making an appointment to talk over the revisions once she had read what I had done. When we met, she said without embarrassment that she had decided that she didn't want any changes made at all! Well, it was good practice, and she was to turn out more good work.

This whole question of revision, whether with young or old writers, is of course a touchy one, involving delicate emotional equilibriums. Often, in the course of what seems to be a solid, useful exchange, the editor may graze an unsuspected raw spot, and the resultant scream of pain announces the destruction of the working relationship.

One of the most surprising and dramatic of these scenes took place while I was working with Jerome Weidman on his strong and successful novel, *The Enemy Camp.* I had first met Jerry, as I've said, when we moved to Westport, and we had seen quite a bit of the Weidmans socially. Westport was then a town, it seemed to me, in which you found your social niche (or it found you) in relation to your profession. Authors and editors and publishers entertained and were entertained by publishers and editors and authors. People in television and film work were apt to congregate, and those in advertising and public relations work. Of course there were some crosscurrents, some infiltration, but in this commuting community, never by a conventional businessman. At the most, practitioners of the "lively arts" consorted with those of us from the publishing world: writers, musicians, theater people, painters, photographers, actors, film directors.

It was a wholly new approach to (at least imputed) friendship to Mary and me—heady (in view of the prominence of many of these people), viviparous and tending to very "in-group" stories and conversations.

In this circle Jerry was an unofficial ringmaster. I suppose that it is fair to call him a professional funnyman, but he redeemed that genus by being genuinely funny. Quick-witted, unimpaired by illusion, a man who had made his way and enjoyed the place to which he had made it, he was a marvelous raconteur and master of the quick parry and rapier thrust in the exchanges of the cocktail hour—which in Fairfield County is a period of indeterminate length, as unpredictable as the duration of a baseball game.

His wit was sometimes cruel, no doubt because he had had to fight his way up with what weapons he had. His desire to be the center of attention was inordinate, but he at least almost always was amusing. And as we came to know him and Peggy more or less *en famille,* I learned what a devoted father he was.

His ego, like those of most, was indestructible in some respects, wholly vulnerable in others. Although I wasn't present I learned that he found the following exchange, in a round that he did lose, wildly funny.

The story goes that he had just completed editing a selection of stories by Somerset Maugham (a writer he greatly revered as a "real pro") for Doubleday, and on this occasion asked a friend his opinion of the book.

The friend replied that he thought it a very good selection.

"And did you like my introduction?" Jerry pressed him with an unwonted earnestness.

The friend is reported to have brightened up.

"There was just one thing in it I'd have changed," he said.

Jerry "bit" with a naïveté he seldom practices.

"Well," said the friend. "I'd have changed the opening sentence to this: 'A lifelong admirer of Somerset Maugham, I was born on the lower East Side. . . .'"

As a matter of fact, that lower East Side has served as the setting for Jerry's finest work. His nostalgia for it and for those who inhabited it results in vivid and often moving writing, softening effectively the foreground of tooth-and-claw Manhattan survival that he so often depicts. And this background is one clue to his unremitting devotion to Charles Dickens.

There is a little of this background in *The Enemy Camp,* but it seemed especially promising to me because Weidman was tackling in depth a theme he had only marginally dealt with in his other books. His subject was the self-destructive virus that goes to work in a person who has been subjected to racial or religious discrimination—in this particular case, anti-Semitism. Jerry's protagonist had bubbling in him a fierce and painful hatred and a thirst for revenge that he had fought to conceal from himself. But these emotions were, in the course of the book, coming to so poisonous a head that he was finally forced to acknowledge that he found the predominantly gentile world in which he lived the "enemy camp."

All this Jerry had probed with admirable honesty and fairness. And now he was coming to the end of the novel, and seeking a convincing way for his character finally to experience the full intensity of this hatred and thereby be purged.

The protagonist's wife, a gentile, had been portrayed throughout as loving, patient and understanding. So it seemed to me patently inevitable that he must learn the lesson at home, through some moment of illumination that would reveal to him how his own suffering had blinded him to her generosity of spirit, that *he* had made his own home part of the enemy camp and now could realize that the "enemy" was not necessarily encamped, drawn up in battle array, and—to oversimplify—could learn that people were people.

I have never been more astonished than at his reaction to this suggestion.

"No," he shouted. "No. That would make it *her* book. And it's *his*—it's got to be his."

We never again worked together very successfully.

Often, of course, such wounds are not articulated in the course of the work with the editor, if ever. Occasionally time and distance bring them out. A notable example is provided by my friend Walter Teller. Walter is the man who rediscovered and brought to fame Captain Joshua Slocum, the master mariner who sailed around the world alone. At Atheneum we published his *Five Sea Captains,* a collection of the logs of five masters in sail who wrote exceptionally well, and *Area Code 215,* a Thoreauvian journal knitting together the musings of a naturalist, Americana from Bucks County, and the exploits and opinions of native "characters." All this in a quiet, rich prose style.

Walter himself I have always liked inordinately. I have found him a man of deep passions and loyalties, which he packed away in such private depths that it often seemed to me that I could see his body quiver with their burden. It may be that I exaggerate, even have spun a psychological fairy tale about him, but I tell it as I experienced it.

At any rate, given this conviction, I tried to exceed my not extraordinary gift for subtlety and tact, and at the same time encourage the release and expression of the deeper emotional currents I thought could further strengthen Walter's work. That was, to use an expression I've heard Walter use, the day I threw my boomerang away.

When I urged him to tell me off if I was intruding upon emotional privileges that he had no desire to write about, he insisted this was not the case. But he continued in his established genre.

I know now that, right or wrong, I was offensively self-important. My determination to set Walter "free" was a piece of impertinent meddling. Quite probably I was experiencing some vicarious release in urging him to plumb the Dostoevskian murk of "his" soul.

Our writer-editor relation ended when I was unable to secure a contract for a project he had proposed, although, in an ironic twist, an extension of that same project was later accepted by the same publisher. Walter and I continued to see each other now and then, on Martha's Vineyard or in each other's winter homes. Then came two explosions.

The first occurred at his home in Princeton. I had asked him how his new work was developing, and foolishly added that it must be a relief to be working with an editor who didn't keep after him the way I did.

With everything well under control, he replied firmly, "It's very good. You and I should have had a fight long ago, but it wouldn't make any sense now."

That startled me into silence, but the theme was picked up again the following summer on the Vineyard. Walter is one of those rare people who carry their liquor gracefully. It gives him a fine sheen; he never regresses to hostility or wet-lipped garrulity or compulsive eroticism. (What does that do to my theory about his tension, his inhibitedness?) But this night he had burst the wonted bonds, and he drew me into a corner. We had never been friends, he told me; he had always found me insufferable even though he was inclined to like me, but now—now that I was no longer his editor, we could really be friends, and he would like to.

All in one long convulsive surge of words that almost literally blew me back against the wall. I don't remember what I had to say, but it wasn't much. He had opened a breach in me that was at first enormously painful, but in the longer range, salutary—cleansing and enlightening.

Which leads me to wonder what a book written about the incidents in this book, told from the other side, would be like. It's a rather sobering conjecture. There are those who would find inconsequential in their lives what I had stressed; others would relate a given episode from a very different angle of incidence; there are surely those who would simply remember me as an impossible son of a bitch. Hail and farewell.

One more generalization: both editor and writer have solid reason to be grateful when the other fights back, punching hard but cleanly, thus enabling both to clear their minds of irrelevant subjectivities, and to bear down on the *work*. Whether the editor is "at fault," or the writer, or more probably both, when one is all sweet agreement and gratitude, something will eventually blow—and hard.

I think of an author who must be nameless (at last!) since we still have a working relationship. From this writer I have received note after cloying note, telling me what a great editor I am, how thoughtful and generous I have been, and what an immense privilege it is to work with me. But once during the progress of each book there comes a telephone call from an outraged person, denouncing me for some ghastly commission or omission that has "destroyed my book." I pick up as many of the pieces as I can find, and the next exchange finds everything once more complacent.

I am at least grateful for the seasonal regularity of this phenomenon. More often, as in Walter Teller's case, the storm builds slowly, inexorably, hidden from sight, and then finally strikes me, unprepared, with the fury of a nor'easter. And when it comes from someone lacking Walter's integrity and deep sweetness of character, it can be a shattering experience. Perhaps, I tell myself ruefully later on, there were meteorologists on the job, sending out warnings that should have prepared me, but either their voices were too faint or I was too unimaginative; at any rate, I was not prepared.

I think of Randall Jarrell, who, I now know, was in his later years a desperately ill man, his great gifts poisoned by an emotional malignancy that took the horrifying form of sugary benevolence, laced suddenly, now and then, with infantile petulance or venomous spite.

I think of Randall Jarrell, and I think of the eulogies that spread over the literary landscape at the time of his death. Not just for the poet or essayist, but for the man. And I wonder about my own contrary testimony. But I also remember what Wright Morris once said about another writer, "To stay friends with ———, I read his books and avoid seeing him." Most of Randall's writing is excellent company.

We first became acquainted, I believe, in 1956, when he joined *The American Scholar* board. I was then at Random House, and Randall had previously, through Anchor Books, had Jason Epstein as his editor.

We had North Carolina experiences in common, though our widely differing estimates of people we both knew should have warned us of radical incompatibilities. But I found him devastatingly witty, and so long as his bitchiness was not aimed at me or my friends it suited the meannesses in myself.

The details blur for a bit; I remember, when he was poetry consultant at the Library of Congress, his driving me around Washington in his new Mercedes, taking city corners at forty-five miles an hour, driving up on sidewalks, all to demonstrate its extraordinary equilibrium, his eyes mocking me and his teeth flashing in his salt-and-pepper beard. He wildly loved sports cars;

he also loved professional sports of all sorts. He was Terence or Catullus watching at the Colosseum.

At any rate, we met at a time when he was restless, open to a new publishing arrangement, and when I left Random he decided to go with me to Atheneum. He stopped in to discuss the move during my last few days at Random House. I was expected on the West Side to talk with one of our prospective backers, Rupe Roth, and Randall walked over with me. It was Saint Patrick's Day, 1959, and we had a strenuous time crossing through the annual parade on Fifth Avenue. As we fought our way, explaining the urgency of our mission to policemen, Randall's hectic composure was unshaken. He continued throughout to expound whatever exegetic exercise then most occupied him, his head nodding and bobbing in characteristic emphasis, his white spatulate hands gesturing hieratically in the pale sunlight.

Jarrell's first book for Atheneum was a collection of poetry, *A Sad Heart at the Supermarket,* which won our first National Book Award in 1961. By this time my wife and I had come to know Randall's wife Mary, too—a handsome ruddy woman from the Southwest. They were a doting couple, exchanging new endearments and rather cloying pet names with every sentence. Watching and listening to them, I thought of two separate strands of ivy, intertwining so closely as to become indistinguishable.

On the day of the awards, my wife and I took the Jarrells to my favorite restaurant, Café Argenteuil. As we were seated, the headwaiter, the urbane and charming Breton Yves le Bris, launched Randall's day by saying, *"Monsieur le poète!* A champagne cocktail today, perhaps?"

I had not told Yves the identity of my guest; he knew. A cultivated man, he had a daughter who worked in one of the publishing houses, and many of his clients were publishers. But whether, through some uncanny divination, he knew that a champagne cocktail was the only liquor the Jarrells drank, or simply found it appropriate for a celebration, I have never found out. Yves keeps his peace, but his extraordinary antennae have brushed other occasions and guests just as felicitously.

This experience made Randall's day. The ceremony was long, and his rather embarrassingly intimate speech of acceptance was not its shortest portion. Then came a long cocktail hour and a longer dinner, toward the end of which, with conversation sagging increasingly, I asked Randall what had been for him the high point of the day.

For a moment he recovered his vivacity.

"Oh, the man at the restaurant!" he said fervently.

I should have listened more carefully.

Twice during the next year or two, we stopped off for a meal at the Jarrells' in Greensboro during trips through North Carolina. The first time was a Sunday lunch, made memorable by the presence of Eudora Welty—one writer who could in person disappoint no enthusiast. But the second time, we were alone with the Jarrells, and the atmosphere, which had been light and gay the first time, despite the habitual cooings and billings, was murderous now.

I have been riddled off and on by expert marksmen, but I remember no other experience to compare with this one. I had no sooner been handed a Martini (to be fair, an excellent one) than the attack began. It was two-pronged, and in retrospect it reminds me of the procedure in filling a tooth, when the dentist first uses the light high-speed drill, which is seldom painful but on occasion can be supersonically so, and then follows up, to prepare the structure for the filling, with a heavy rocklike drill that is reminiscent of the medieval mace.

Randall used the high-speed drill, Mary Jarrell the mace. His accusations, dripping with a poisonous sweetness, were like the darting pronouncements of a lizard's tongue—hers like the assault of a grizzly bear. Yet the predominant image that remains with me comes from the field of arachnology. I cannot be sure that Randall sat in a corner of the room on some sort of dais, but that's the way I see it now, with him ensconced in the center of a vast spider web.

What was it all about? Well, they cited every omission that an editor may be guilty of, in failing to provide "his" writer with any sense of his proper reverence for him. Some of the charges were true: I had neglected to send on review clippings with regularity; I had forgotten to look up a reference Randall had requested of me; I had sometimes failed to keep in touch with him for as long a period as three months.

Other accusations were true, too, but concerned my failure to render courtesies that I have seldom extended to any writer, such as having flowers in the hotel room when he came to town or taking him to the theater or opera.

I was totally inadequate to the occasion, soon gave up defending myself, and spent a thoroughly miserable several hours. One of the points they made stuck in my craw. Randall had taken me on in place of Jason Epstein because, although we seemed equally intelligent, I appeared to have a clearer idea that the editor was the secondary person in the relationship, there to serve the writer. This stuck in my craw, I say, because this was the position I had always held about the editor's job, and I became uneasily convinced that I really had been failing in my role, had become rather too full of myself in my new position as publisher and neglected my essential function as an editor.

And this realization made things still more difficult in the following months, especially in terms of Randall. There is a fine line between the editor's proper deference to a writer he values, and his enduring, if not abuse, at least an irritating condescension or arrogance on the part of the writer. I tried to walk in the middle of the path. When the Jarrells and I were simultaneously in London during the summer of 1963, I took them to the theater and then to dinner at the Connaught. But Randall was sulky, Mary impersonal. On the other hand, I did not buy them opera tickets or send flowers when they visited New York.

The end came before long. Randall had written a book for children that Macmillan was to publish, and he had discovered in his young editor there the kind of man who really appreciated him. He wanted to be released from his contract with Atheneum. In a conference that included several of us, he made no substantive points about any editorial failure or lack of promotional support from the house; he stayed with his previous complaints: no flowers, no opera tickets, no proper courtesies, no "appreciation." So we released him; ironically enough, within a couple of months, the young editor he found so satisfactory left Macmillan.

An unpleasant story to dwell on, from whatever angle. And when I think of Randall Jarrell's desperate and lonely death, the agonies he must have suffered, I stop, of course, and wonder about its inclusion in these pages. Yet I want to tell the story of my experiences as they happened, and such trying impasses, such conflicts of personality, are certainly an inherent part of that story.

A conflict of a very different sort, and one resolved quickly and decisively, concerns the several months during which I was Truman Capote's editor. When Bob Linscott retired from Random House, Bennett Cerf asked me to become Truman's editor. We met briefly several times, and then Truman asked me plaintively if I wasn't going to take him out to lunch. Or perhaps he complained to Bennett.

I said I'd be glad to lunch with him.

"Pavillon, of course," he said. "I wouldn't go anywhere else."

And so for the first time I lunched at Pavillon, literally horrified when I looked at the prices on the menu. Truman spent a little less than half the time with me, a little more than half at Elsa Maxwell's table. A friend of mine, who saw us walking down the street together after lunch, reported that it was one of the funniest sights of his experience. "Like Humpty Dumpty with Cyrano de Bergerac." I went to the mirror to re-examine my nose.

Truman always looked to me more like a most precocious boy. At the time, he affected a trench coat slung across his shoulders with only the top button buttoned and the sleeves hanging empty at his sides. I remember him standing in my office one day, observing me quizzically as I answered a long-distance call.

A moment before, he had asked me in that drawling lisp, "What do you think of the new stowy by J. D. Sawinger in *The New Yo-ker*?" Before I could answer him, the phone rang and I excused myself. It was a fairly long conversation, and several times before it was concluded someone entered the room and left a message on my desk. Each time, Truman accosted the person and asked the same question about Salinger's story. None of them had read it.

When I hung up, I told him that I also hadn't read it. What did he think of it?

He batted his eyes at me, permitted himself his favorite secret smile.

"I dunno," he said. "I haven't wed it either."

It occurred to me during this period that Truman probably found me as amusing and invertedly exotic as I did him. But when *Time* magazine asked him for a comment at the time of the founding of Atheneum, he described me as a nice, proper sort of commuter, with a family in the suburbs.

Between these two episodes I had offended him. He was almost ready with a book of stories to be called *Breakfast at Tiffany's*. The collection contained a beautiful Christmas story, about a little boy and his aunt, as simple and touching and masterly as Flaubert's *Un Coeur Simple*. I made this comparison to Truman, hoping that this deeply meant praise would make it easier to persuade him to rework the title story, which I found guilty of a kind of meretricious glitter that went ill with the masterpiece I have just described.

Not a bit of it. He was outraged, disgusted with me for finding fault with *Breakfast*. He hurried across the hall to Bennett and said, "I don't wanna work with Hiwum any more."

Fair enough.

Not so fair was the cause of the confrontation with another author, a clash that also involved Bennett. He had done some high-powered negotiating to sign Leon Uris, the author of the best-selling *Battle Cry*, paying him a handsome advance. Thereupon Uris had gone off to Israel to gather material for his next novel, eventually to be published as *Exodus*.

But when war broke out in Israel, Uris was forced to flee, and shortly before he returned to New York, Bennett asked me to act as his editor.

In a few days Uris called and came to see me. His breeziness was so outrageous as to be endearing. Perhaps the simplest way to convey his tonal quality is through an example of his sense of humor. We talked at first in a desultory way about his experience in Israel, both our backgrounds, and other introductory topics. Then he asked me where I would spend my summer vacation.

"Martha's Vineyard," I replied.

He cracked up. He thought that was the funniest place name he had ever heard. . . .

Before long, he made his modest proposal. He would like Random House to give him twelve thousand dollars.

As a further advance? The price was already pretty steep.

No. Forget the advance angle. Forget the contract altogether, for that matter. Just *give* it to him.

I was too shocked to say more than an awed, "But why?"

Because that was the amount he had invested and lost in his Israel experience. A house he had bought there, and other expenses. Hadn't he gone there for just one reason: to write a book for Random House, a book on which they would make a lot of money?

Although stunned, I offered the objections that anyone would have thought of, even said that I would be glad to see whether the partners would be willing to add a further advance, though almost surely not of that size.

He was adamant. He felt entitled to a *gift*, and he wanted it. Now.

I went across the hall, told the story to Bennett. The progress across his face of amusement, skepticism, astonishment, outrage and finally fury was epic.

He marched back to my room, barely managed the civilities, and then in a taut voice asked Uris if my account of his proposal was accurate.

It was.

"Then get out of this house," Bennett shouted. "Get out of here and never come back. Take your book anywhere you want. I'll cancel your contract, and I don't want any of the advance back. Keep it all. I don't care if your book makes millions of dollars. Just don't come near here again."

It was a magnificent scene.

Doubleday published *Exodus* and presumably made millions of dollars. But Bennett was true to his word: he refused the repayment of Random's advance.

The assumption of Universal Obligation by Lee Uris seemed cheeky. Ayn Rand made it imperial, by divine fiat—although she never acknowledged the authority of the Almighty.

One of the first things that Ross Baker made plain to me when I started work for Bobbs-Merrill was that my primary assignment was to keep Ayn Rand happy. She had become famous for *The Fountainhead,* published in 1943. But its enormous success owed little to Bobbs-Merrill, which had published it. Mr. Chambers disapproved of the book, which had been

256

signed by Archie Ogden, then New York editor for the firm. Bobbs had spent a comparatively small amount in promoting *The Fountainhead,* which had made its own way by "word of mouth."

Naturally, Ayn Rand was less than happy with her publisher, and when her editor and friend, Ogden, was fired, the estrangement grew. Nor was Ogden's successor, John L. B. Williams, by temperament suited to win her back. So Ross pinned on me that rigorous assignment.

I shall never forget (those words, again, but true) my first meeting with Ayn. A short, squarish woman, with black hair cut in bangs and Dutch bob, she wore a tricorne the exact replica of the one in the famous Bonaparte portrait—the sulky one in which he pokes around in his waistcoat with his fingers. She also wore a short cape that flowed in the breeze—in imitation, she was to confess to me later, of Supergirl.

Her eyes were as black as her hair, and piercing. We sat down for lunch at One Park Avenue, a place to which we were to return again and again because their eggs Benedict were good, and that was her invariable meal. I made one or two conventional remarks; she fixed me with those eyes and said, "What are your premises?"

Again and again, during the next decade, I was to hear that question—with anticipation when it was addressed to someone else, with discomfiture when to myself. For Ayn had built up a comprehensive systematic philosophy, which she calls Objectivism, and which, once you accept its first premises, is the most closely reasoned, rigorously logical and consistently interlocking world view and explanation since the great synthesis of Thomas Aquinas.

The basic premises are that *A* is *A,* which proposition she is at pains to explain to you she derived from Aristotle, and that man is primarily, characteristically and ultimately a rational being. Upon these foundations she has built a house of philosophy dedicated to the ideal of enlightened self-interest, and every room in it—her ontology, epistemology, ethics, politics, economic theory and psychology—is in perfect harmony with every other and with the whole edifice.

After that preliminary bow to *il maestro de colore che sanno,* her comprehensive philosophy is all hers, and through her efforts alone there has arisen a Randian school that has apostles and disciples and neophytes and sycophants all over the country. Even an Objectivist school of psychotherapy has developed, under the leadership of one of her early converts, Nathaniel Branden, although teacher and student have now split and gone each his/her own way.

To gather with her New York adherents, which I did several times, is a disquieting experience. I have rarely seen so many unattractive malcontents in one place at one time. It is then that one is fully aware of this woman's stature. She has been idolized and ridiculed, called a great thinker, a crackpot, a fascistic counterrevolutionary, a fake, but to me the truth is that her mind is all of one piece, a marvelous logical machine before which most computers and cyborgs would cower. And at such meetings, the very whining, toadying quality of the camp followers threw into brilliant relief the wholly dedicated, crusading, intrepid nature of the leader.

I speak of *her mind* being "all of one piece" and her *philosophy* as being a marvel of logical consistency. Her life, her emotions, her attitudes are full of inconsistencies. Her heroine in *Atlas Shrugged,* Dagny, flies a plane through the jagged peaks of the Rockies to reach her destination. Ayn Rand is terrified of planes. Her heroes, John Galt and Howard Roark, are rugged, fearless, massively decisive; her own husband, Frank O'Connor (no relation to the Irish writer), is painfully shy, sensitive, delicate. All her characters whom she respects (and there is no mistaking them) go their ways alone, proud, resolute, unafraid. Long before the threat of violence scared many New Yorkers from walking night streets, Ayn was fearful about leaving her apartment after dark, even when escorted.

Such discrepancies between what a writer depicts and what he lives are not unusual. One can dismiss them as compensatory. But the disparity is more telling when bound up with a philosophy that stresses so fervently *total* consistency, realism, logic and reason. Moreover, many of the unpleasant things she predicts in *Atlas Shrugged*—the collapse of our railroad system, the disintegration of our cities, the prevalence of violence—have occurred.

Yet the violence, for instance, was minimal at the time she was so timid about venturing out.

When all this is said, she remains a remarkable person, a formidable personality, and one whom I remember with genuine, if perverse, affection.

She set out, of course, but more or less *en passant,* to convert me. I think she believed me salvageable, although full of all those wishy-washy liberal humanitarian notions she despised: sentimental, vacillating and wrong-minded. Again I found walking the line between professional tactfulness and dishonesty excruciatingly difficult. It was one thing to be bested in an argument about "premises," for then I could—and did—go down to honest defeat. It was another for her to demand that I pledge allegiance to Objectivism, when I completely disbelieved her central concept of man's inherent and basic rationality.

Those arguments! One might make a casual pronouncement about the direction the weather would take. One might express an opinion about another writer. One might toss out a preference for the color red, for vodka Martinis, for a particular make of automobile. What were your premises? And in every argument in which she engaged, she emerged victorious, whether because her companion-opponent finally capitulated, or because he lost by default through exhaustion.

No matter with whom, or about what. First driving him to defensiveness with that all-impaling question, then catching every single point that admitted of any inconsistency, however marginal, and pressing on with more questions, at last to recapitulate and demonstrate the failure of the other's argument to "hang together."

Many are the people who laughed at my description of her dialectical invincibility, only later to try their hands and join me among the corpses on the Randian battlefield. In fact, it came to be for me a decisive criterion of honesty just how someone described his disputation with her. If he felt he had come off pretty well, I knew he belonged to the caste of *l'homme moyen sensuel,* given to *tonal* lying. If he boasted of total victory over her, I knew he was irredeemable.

Over our lunches at One Park Avenue, I came to realize that

259

the mission Ross Baker had assigned me would not be fulfilled. She had *had* Bobbs-Merrill. There was no point in urging her; *that* was settled. From then on, I felt freer to say just what I thought to her, and because this didn't win me any arguments we both enjoyed ourselves much more. So it was with a mingling of relief and regret that I said good-by to her when I left Bobbs for Random House. I had no suspicion that I was simply ending one chapter before beginning another.

Sometime in 1957 or '58, Ayn called me. After a gentle rebuke for not staying in touch, she informed me that *Atlas Shrugged* was completed. She had set up a series of lunches with publishers, having secured her release from Bobbs-Merrill. She was lunching with people from Viking, Knopf and a third publisher, whose identity I forget. She would have included Random House, for my sake, but it had come to her attention that Cerf and Klopfer were Communists.

For once, with Ayn, I simply laughed—uncontrollably, and long. Her patience snapped; she grew testy. I did not believe that they were Communists? What were my premises? *For once* I offered my premises without hesitation: their contrary and public affiliations, their publication of Whittaker Chambers's *Witness*, on and on.

"Well," she finally said, "that's very convincing. I congratulate you on having learned at last how to assemble and present your premises. You may be one of us yet."

Only a week later, Bennett, Donald and I had lunch with her, not at One Park Avenue, but at the old Ambassador, where she did, however, order eggs Benedict. She began by expressing her contempt for the other publishers with whom she had met. Only one, Pat Knopf, seemed to her even to have the makings of a man.

She addressed herself chiefly to Bennett, whose brisk, extroverted personality surprised and obviously attracted her. She soon challenged him. Suppose he lived in a truly enlightened society, one in which capitalism, individualism, self-interest and open competition of all sorts reigned. Would it not frighten him? Would he not withdraw from it?

Bennett launched his counterattack with joy. There was going to be no need to dissimulate at all. Withdraw? Be intimidated? He would embrace such an opportunity with delight.

What were his premises?

That he was smarter than the rest. That, starting with little, he and Donald had built Random House into a great publishing house, thereby proving that he needed no subsidizing, no special favors, no *help* of any sort to make his way.

She in turn was delighted and the rest of the lunch was full of verve. Within another two weeks she signed a contract, and I was again her editor. Bennett and Donald, with some hesitancy, had first explored the application of my contract with them, however. This would be a very long, high-priced novel, and expensive to produce—a large investment, even if it sold very well. Would I forgo my usual commissions, in the case of *Atlas Shrugged*?

I agreed immediately. I had felt all along some uneasiness of conscience. Ayn's philosophy, replete with social and political consequences, troubled me. Left to myself, I would not have published that book. Yet I had owed it to the partners to steer Ayn to them if I could, for she was a publishing catch, with "best seller" stamped all over her. I had been derelict of duty in that sense, not really having pursued her until she had taken the initiative.

Moreover, I believed that a publisher should publish books with all sorts of political and social coloration. Only I didn't want personally to make money on one so contrary to my own convictions. Yet, again, I was willing to act as her editor for Random House. So, in a muddled way, I split my allegiances.

How she would have laughed had she known the welter of contradictory reactions I was experiencing! And how well indeed I illustrated her concept of the softheaded, ambivalent, tortured liberal! This time I had no constant logical premises at all—at least that I can in retrospect discern.

So we worked on and on and on. After a few feeble attempts I gave up trying to suggest changes of any substantial sort, and became an apprentice copy editor, helping her to ferret out spots where she had inadvertently used within one paragraph two words that rhymed. This was an obsession with her: perhaps she was writing antipoetry.

Genuinely wasted time and energy, for at the conclusion of our sessions I turned her over to Bertie Krantz, recently moved from Crown to Random House and become chief copy editor and assistant managing editor, by whose capable hands the *formal* copy editing was conducted. And the book was published and prospered, on and on.

When I left Random for Atheneum, Ayn stayed with her successful publishers, quite rightly. But she approved of my striking out on my own, of course, though I think she wondered why I didn't make more of an effort to fight Bennett and Donald and carry her off with me.

The truth was that I was snobbish about it. Our proclaimed goal at Atheneum was to prove that a publisher could still make his way with a select list, publishing only works of high quality— and I did not think her books qualified. In her novels she wedded her ideas to a first-rate narrative skill; the pace of the action was usually fast, and she was proficient at suspense and the melodramatic, spectacular scene. But her style was drab, and although I respected her philosophy as one kind of arid intellectual triumph, a tour de force that commanded admiration even though she based it on an utterly false (as I see it) central premise—although that was how I felt in measured moments, there were times when I conceded that the world I lived in was most probably right, and she really was a crackpot, though of a noble sort.

Even now I can't write about Ayn Rand without feeling upset, unhappy with myself. I know of no other relation with an author in which I played such shamefaced ball, never being wholly for or against her, never saying right out all the things I believed about her book or her ideas or life in general.

Yet I must have done a partial, modified version of that ritualistic dance many times, with many different writers. Publishers' priorities versus those of the writer (because the persistent bromide, "Our interests always coincide. We both want the best results possible for this book," is so ambiguous as to be meaningless) ; concern about writers' egos versus honesty; tolerance for all points of view versus loyalty to one's own moral and political creed—these conflicts and multiple others crowd the editor's landscape. Most confounding of all, however, is that persisting doubt about a strong reaction against a book. To what extent is critical judgment (if there is such a thing, divorced from subjective associations) responsible, to what a masked visceral revulsion to something that strikes unbearably close to home?

I was chiefly responsible for Random House's rejection of two prominent books. The first was Norman Mailer's *The Deer Park*, the other Vladimir Nabokov's *Lolita*. (Both, interestingly enough, were eventually published by Putnam's.) I have already referred to the case of *The Deer Park*, but I want to return to it.

Rinehart, the contracted publisher, had decided not to risk the possible legal confrontations over obscenity and/or pornography, and begged out of the situation when the book was already in galleys. Mailer decided on multiple submissions to publishers, hoping, I suppose, that competitive bidding would bring him better terms.

Bill Styron called me to ask if Random House would be interested, and we were, of course. (Most publishers, for obvious reasons, dislike competitive bidding, but accept it when there's a real prize at stake.) At this point Mailer's literary stock had gone down somewhat, the vast success of *The Naked and the Dead* having been somewhat vitiated by the lukewarm reception of *Barbary Shore*. But he was still a catch, a young writer who had one spectacular success behind him and the time and vitality to produce another.

The Deer Park affected me as gray and dreary, one of the bleakest novels I had read in a long time. My objection to it, and to our publishing it, was not on the grounds that it was a dirty book (it seemed to me clearly serious, the work of a disillusioned idealist), but that it was a mediocre one. The word *gray* persisted in my mind: gray style, gray characters, gray outlook.

I said this to Mailer, who wanted to see me. We had lunch together, and I told him all this. He listened with his fighter's grin on his face, raffish, mocking, but genuinely interested.

He has recorded this meeting in *Advertisements for Myself*, where he misspells my name, credits me with being pretty honest, and yet believes that it was primarily my close relationship to Styron that was responsible for my reaction. And all the time he went on blaming Bennett Cerf, who, as I remember, wanted to publish it but was worried about its "dirty" passages.

In the present context, the point of the story is that years later I reread *The Deer Park* and had a markedly different reaction to it. I found it a good novel, far from dreary or bleak, and with a surprising but convincing strain of compassion for his unlovely and unhappy characters.

Now, why? I don't know. I search for a clue, and can't find it. Was my strong opposition related to something in my nature that I don't understand? If so, what aspect? Was there some element in my still relatively new relation to the partners at Random House that made me so obdurate? Again, and again, I don't know.

Lolita was a different matter. After its original publication by Girodias in Paris it was circulated amongst publishers in New York, argued over endlessly. Either Donald or Bennett was in favor of taking it, the other opposed. I think that it was Bennett who was positive, perhaps linking its publication to the pride he took in being the publisher who had fought and defeated censorship to make *Ulysses* available in the United States.

At any rate, I was asked to read and vote. From the beginning the book affected me strongly. I found the author's playful tone epicene, effete, *sick*.

I went on reading, revolted to the point of nausea. And then, about halfway through, I pounced like a cat upon what I now see as a rationalization of my emotional reaction—something that would base *it* on a responsible, professional judgment. As the tour of motels began, Nabokov and Humbert Humbert merged into a single entity. From presenting his character with "playful irony," the author had suddenly gone to the other extreme, lost control of his material and succumbed to the element in his own nature most closely akin to that of his hapless hero. It was a short step to convincing myself that Nabokov was a cruel and sadistic person who could maintain his self-imposed detachment only so far. *"Madame Bovary, c'est moi"* reached a sinister apotheosis in Humbert Humbert. I was so determined in my opposition to this book that the partners declined it, as Bennett often sadly reminded me.

When Putnam's published *Lolita* it became the toast of the literary world. I joined battle without invitation, and was hooted at from all sides. My unlovely Presbyterian origins were showing; I had no sense of humor; I was painfully literal-minded. My daughter Mary, who had studied under Nabokov at Cornell, rebuked me sternly: my picture of him was ridiculous; he was a great teacher and a wonderfully witty and talented man. And more than one person suggested that it was time to take inventory of my own psyche.

It did become a matter for self-scrutiny. As *Lolita* became more and more heralded, applauded as "ironic"—"symbolic"—"lyrical"—and, according to Lionel Trilling, "the most beautiful love story of our time," my rejection of it turned to something like hate for its author, whom I had never met.

I plunged into his other books. I was impressed by *Pnin*, which I thought a minor masterpiece, and liked some of the others. But I could not like *him*. I still found him cynical, arrogant, supercilious, pedantic and often boring. The eulogies infuriated me; I saw them as sycophantic, one more lavish example of American masochism. The point that was made about *Lolita*, over and over, was that, whatever else it meant, it was a devastating satire on our country.

The adulation reached its peak with the publication of *Pale Fire*. I yanked myself into place and started it three times. I never got beyond page twenty-two. In a way this was reassuring to me, for now I felt no rage; my rejection of this book was calm, almost weary. All the impatience I had known in the past with Henry James returned, reinforced. How mincing, how self-congratulatory, how condescending, how laboriously trivial—and how dull, dull, dull!

Nabokov remained for me a skillful, coldly intellectual, misanthropic minor talent, shining with pale illumination in our Alexandrian blue ceiling. But only recently I tried *Ada,* still grappling with doubts.

Ada brought me to a calmer perspective. This novel had its own peculiar vitality, it seemed to me, and I read quite a bit of it with pleasure, if not avidity. But the style—that much-vaunted style. Such extravagant images that the purpose of a metaphor—to sharpen one's perception of the original given—was ignored, the first impression destroyed. And the coyness of a single adjective, like "sly" or "subtle" or "daunted" placed before a proper name in a sort of attenuated *Time* magazine fashion! And the largest number of concocted or unusual words—strained, artificial, cumbersome—since Cozzens's *By Love Possessed!* The atrocious, simpering puns!

One friend says, "That's Nabokov, having fun." In the sense of exhibitionism, perhaps. But where did this reputation as stylist come from? He is not just baroque; he is rococo.

The intensity of my original reaction, however, remains unexplained. Am I some Stavrogin *manqué,* with a secret passion for nymphets? Am I simply envious of a man who could capture a nation by insulting it, tell such a story and win both a fortune and elite idolatry? I don't know. I don't know.

There has been a great deal written, even more spoken, about "writer's block." At times it seems almost to be considered a specific disease, with as exact a designation as, say, encephalitis lethargica or ventricular tachycardia. I claim neither perceptiveness nor originality in suggesting that it is rather a symptom of a psychic disequilibrium. This imbalance may of course originate in varied and disparate factors.

I have consulted no texts; I speak only from experience. That experience has led me to believe that this form of paralysis may come from a fear of completion, of termination—almost as though that act constituted a kind of death. Yet it may rather be a fear of *beginning,* of the commitment involved in setting down the words. There also may be a related fear of self-exposure.

Then there is the writer who can't begin, because she or he is simply overwhelmed by the multiplicity of possibilities. What William Faulkner found the promise of "going anywhere" is to this person a devastating need for decisiveness.

These suggestions merely graze the skin of the subject. But they may trigger off in the mind of the reader variants he has encountered. I want to mention only one further form of motivation. There are among writers, as among other people, perfectionists who make heroically stringent demands on themselves, on their work. These are not really "blocked"; they are rather insatiable in their pursuit of not simply *"le mot juste,"* but *"le livre juste."*

The most striking of these, in my editorial experience, is Paule Marshall. This woman, whose parents came from Jamaica to Brooklyn, first appeared, unheralded, at Random House in

1957. Appeared, that is, in the form of a manuscript, *Brown Girl, Brownstones,* which I accepted and Random House published with some success.

That sequence sounds simple, and long later still seems simple. There were talks and revisions, but for the most part, things marched. It was only with the second book, *Soul Clap Hands and Sing,* four novellas connected thematically, that I began to understand her tremendous drive to achieve, her resolute puritanical insistence on the very best that was in her, so that even a minor defection became a matter for shrieking, kicking pain.

I suppose that Paule is ambitious, in the literary sense—that, like every other writer, she would enjoy fame, adulation. But this is not the piercing goad. She wants, with every ounce of her powerful, proud, stubborn, flamboyant nature, to write a novel that takes life by the throat, squeezes it till its tongue hangs out, and then flings it in the face of the white world, crying out, "There! That's what I mean! See, you idiots!" This, despite—or along with—her public statement that she writes only for blacks.

This quivering, palpitating woman, compact of blood, gunpowder and iron inflexible will, makes in person an immediate impact. I cannot count the people who, after first meeting her, have said to me, "Formidable! Tremendous! She's beautiful, but she scares me." At such times I admire myself for being both her editor and her friend.

The full fury of her demands on herself and, incidentally, on those who work with her, did not appear until the long stretch between the appearance of *Soul Clap Hands* and the publication in the fall of 1969, of *The Chosen Place, the Timeless People,* of which the review in the Sunday *Times* book section said:

Not to mince words, "The Chosen Place, the Timeless People," in my opinion, is the best novel to be written by an American black woman, one of the two important black novels of the 1960's (the other being William Demby's "The Catacombs"), and one of the four or five most impressive novels ever written by a black American.

For seven Biblical years there was a shadow over the land, that of Paule Marshall. She wailed, groaned, cursed and then refused to speak altogether. She had dried up, she couldn't write, what she had written was meaningless weak trash, she would never write again, she was through. I argued, abstained, exhorted, withdrew, got angry, impatient, reassured her, scolded her. And there were long bouts of silence, between our encounters, usually held at the Argenteuil. On such occasions, Yves le Bris kept his exchanges with me to a minimum.

I believe that during all this time, only once, when Paule had reached the point where she needed an advance, did she let me see any of what she had done. I found it really good, and I think she half believed me. But for most of the rest of the time my attempts to learn what point she had reached, how much more there was to do, whether she was still on the first draft or had advanced to the second—were futile.

The monolithic nature of this "block" consisted not of being unable literally to write, but of being unable to write to her own demanding specifications. "No, soul," she would cry out in the manner of the heroine of *The Chosen Place*, "it's no use. It's all over. I can't write."

She can, does, will—magnificently. For which give thanks.

A much more complex "block" is that of John P. Marquand, Jr., whose first novel, *The Second Happiest Day*, published under the pseudonym John Phillips, was a Book-of-the-Month Club selection in 1949. I came to know Jack Marquand as one of the *Paris Review* group, which also included Styron, Peter Matthiessen, H. L. Humes and Tom Guinzburg. *The Second Happiest Day* had been published by Harper. There was a good deal of gossip about the Book-of-the-Month Club's choosing his book when his famous father was a judge. It was generally said J. P. Marquand had had no hand in the selection; the charges were of a venial, not a venal, kind.

But Jack's pseudonym was transparent to those in the publishing world, and he was not happy about the attention the whole matter received. Moreover, he felt his father's long shadow. How hard for a novelist to be the son of a famous novelist!

In the early days of Atheneum, Jack came to me and asked if he could attend the meetings of the novel workshop at the New School. This he did, fairly regularly, for several months. At the end of this period he told me that he would like to leave Harper and come to me at Atheneum. He found his "double" role at Harper (their author and married to a niece of the wife of Cass Canfield, the head of the firm) embarrassing, and he believed that he and I could work well together. I was delighted and, after a few exchanges, Harper released him.

By this time I had read much of a long novel on which he had been working for some time, a book he called *Bleat's Progress*. I found most of it, and in retrospect still find it, absolutely first-rate. There were two chapters in particular that moved me literally to tears, a rare experience for someone who spends his life reading manuscripts. But, except for one stretch written earlier, a long, overextended passage about the Village, all of it seemed to me genuinely *good*—complex, subtle, fully dimensioned, and superior in both depth and breadth to most of his father's work.

But Jack was *stuck*. He confessed to me once that it was true that his father's eminence contributed to his troubles, and that he was ambivalent about his father's work, feeling divided between loyalty and a need to surpass it.

Other factors contributed to his "block." When he returned to his novel after months of not writing he would find some of it, however good, no longer congenial to him. He was now between youth and middle age, and his point of view on many aspects of life was of course changing; it seemed to him that the book was necessarily going to be a Sisyphean labor. If he constantly rewrote, how could he get ahead with it?

As his editor, I have been a flat failure. No amount of interest and encouragement has had any real effect. I have encountered an unexpected and almost unique barrier in our relation. I like him and sympathize with him too much; I have found him one of the most generous and decent of men. When I keep after him about the book, plead with him to let me see more of it (for he has shown me nothing for some five years), the pain evident on his face makes me cut my plea short. I simply feel that he's had so much trouble with this book that discussing it is cruel.

There are two other books for which I have had contracts for many years, one since 1951, the other since 1960. When I signed a contract with Millard Lampell in 1951, I was at Bobbs-Merrill.

That contract has been resumed at Random House, Atheneum and Harcourt Brace Jovanovich. There was never much trouble in arranging the transfer because it has been years since Millard has submitted another word of it.

It is well worth finishing. The early chapters, depicting life in a dye factory in Paterson, New Jersey, might have been written by Zola. And the theme is a great American theme: an immigrant boy making his way, finally owning his own shop, and raising children who, in their sophistication, are alienated from him, as he, in his incomprehension, is from them. As projected by Millard, it would have become an inverted sort of *Death of a Salesman,* for he saw understanding and reconciliation at the end.

Meanwhile Millard has written plays, films, songs and television scripts, having done among other things a memorable adaptation of John Hersey's *The Wall* for the Broadway stage. But no novel.

The case of George Tabori is markedly different. He has moved from one medium to another, and may or may not return. I first encountered his work while I was on a sad mission to North Carolina. A dear friend, a really extraordinary woman named Mary Taylor Moore, was dying of cancer and wanted to see me. At the end of an intensely moving conversation during which her illness and impending death were never mentioned, she told me that she wanted to give me two books that she treasured beyond any others. They were Malcolm Lowry's *Under the Volcano,* then little known, and George Tabori's *Companions on the Left Hand,* to me still more obscure.

Much later, in the first year of Atheneum, when its unusual "birth" was attracting a number of writers, Tabori appeared one day at the suggestion of his agent, Phyllis Jackson, and discussed with me a novel he was beginning to conceive, a comedy about the adventures of a Middle European who, marrying an American widow, finds himself suddenly plunged into an environment full of rousing American children.

It sounded good, and a contract was signed. When I finally moved to Harcourt, George came along, only by now he was rather going to write a novel of suspense with psychological and philosophical overtones.

What has happened? Married to Viveca Lindfors* and step-father of Kristoffer Tabori, he has spent all his working hours in and for the theater—writing, directing, even acting. He has had a rich and varied career, in New York, London and the Berk-shires, but has not written a line of fiction. He still believes that he will, and for him I shall wait. Some compensation has come from the fact that I see him fairly regularly, and enjoy exuber-antly his friendship. This, in the port of missing novels, is unusual.

And it's an unusual friendship. This drawling, witty cosmo-politan, almost languid in manner and brilliant in thought, is a most unlikely comrade for me. I have sometimes wondered if I am not his only square friend. If so, it's a distinction I cherish.

But these are cases where novelists have been diverted in other directions. Another memory of a novelist in labor is the particularly distinctive one of H. L. Humes, known by everybody as "Doc."

A good-looking, sandy-colored young fellow with a nervous laugh that gained resonance only after he had been confronted by a question he had not expected, and had finally replied, "Well, yes, as a matter of fact, now that you mention it—"

Doc, it was immediately clear, was one of that vanishing breed, the Eccentric. Dazzlingly bright, he would often drown the originality of some proposal in a flood of words. He talked as fast and as much as Buckminster Fuller. Whether patenting a new burglar alarm or rattrap, mapping the celestial expanses, devising for his country an entirely new legal system, or pursuing some other of his encyclopedic ventures, he always gave me a sense of having the kind of near genius that could see in some-thing so simple, so at hand, that the rest of us paid it no attention, an applicability that he didn't pursue only because he had already been distracted to another project.

Quick, shrewd, unrealistic, impatient and convivial, Doc kept his own tabs on other human beings, measured himself alter-nately with solipsistic grandeur and with a whole barrelful of salt. He ignored all the amenities, especially those involving the

* They are now divorced, and George, remarried, is living in Berlin and has just announced that he is sending me the first draft of a new novel!

time and obligations of others. He found it as natural (when he thought about it at all) to show up at 2:00 A.M. as at 2:00 P.M.

He first came to me with some wild publishing project that I cannot even dimly remember. He had with him a friend whom he thought of and introduced rather grandly as his barrister. Of himself he said that he was the founder (*sic*) of *The Paris Review*. Whether or not this was true, he was at least an early participant in its mysteries. (One of his colleagues was to add, "as janitor.")

When I told him that I was not interested in his project, he showed not the slightest quiver of concern. "All right, then," he said. "How about a novel? I have one half finished," and cackled.

The manuscript was astonishingly good, but fragmented in a curious way. The putative opening section was complete, except for one gap that might require twenty or thirty pages of writing. A whole large middle portion was finished, and beautifully written. He had also completed another long sequence that obviously led to a climax and conclusion, but these were missing.

Call the three long portions A, B and C. Between A and B, and between B and C—voids of interstellar space. Galaxy A, Galaxy B, Galaxy C—splendid clusters of constellations. But the trips that had still to be made suggested the expenditure of light years.

Groaning, I signed Doc to a contract. I knew—or almost knew—what I was getting into, but what else was there to do when it was so good?

In the course of the next several years, Doc worked diligently but spasmodically. He turned day and night upside down, and he would appear in my office unannounced (he had a way of turning usually reliable receptionists and secretaries into his accomplices), no matter what was going on there, and, undisturbed by my obvious frustration, make himself at home.

On one occasion, when he had been writing at a table in the corner of the office and I was about to rush off to catch a commuter train, he said casually, "Look, lend me your key to the building. I'm really hot today and I think I can go all night. But I'll want to go out to eat, and I'll have to get back in."

To save an argument and catch a train, I gave it to him. The next morning, with some relief, I found him gone and the key dutifully returned. But when I had reason, several weeks later, to come to the office about ten o'clock at night, there was Doc, snoring on my couch. He had had a duplicate key made. When I insisted that he give it to me, he complied, with a grin. Only later did I realize that he would never have been satisfied with *one* duplicate key; in hopeless fantasy, a long chain of them danced before my eyes.

Somehow, at last, he had his novel complete, except for two chapters, not consecutive, from the middle. These he swore he could not do.

"Guess we'll just have to wait," he said complacently.

I was approaching despair. In a week, I was leaving for a long-awaited vacation. I knew that during that time Doc would remain in a seated position, sipping beer and holding forth, in prolonged and lusty monologues, for the benefit of whatever audience. Then, when I returned, he'd be hanging around my neck for another few months, if not forever.

Later that day I launched a harebrained conspiracy (what other kind would work with Doc?) with one of our outstanding young editors, Mary Heathcote. She had been assigned the redoubtable task of copy editing Doc's script when it was ready. I explained to her this last (I hoped) predicament, and enlisted her amused help.

First, I was to tell him that the book was now ready for copy editing, finished except for a few little touches here and there (like a couple of chapters). These he would do, under the head of copy editing, with Mary's assistance.

Incredible. But it worked. At first he eyed me with marked suspicion; then an unmistakable flash of cynicism crossed his face. Then a cautious hope. Finally, he chuckled exultantly.

"Really?" he exclaimed. "Gosh, and to think I didn't even know it!"

When I returned, the job was done. Mary's account of how she had cajoled him into sitting down and actually writing those chapters, under the guise of assisting her with the copy editing, was hilarious.

The Underground City was an extraordinary novel, huge,

sprawling, ridden with minor imperfections, but spilling over with abundant life, seething and churning with Doc's own vitality. Like so many others, it never had its due. . . .

I have often pondered Doc's disinclination to finish a piece of work. Sometimes I have thought it a matter of his having a low threshold for boredom. Again, that he was never satisfied with what he had done, and so long as the work was still in progress, he could always go back and "fix" this or that part. But increasingly I have come to believe that he simply dreaded completion—that it represented to him an end as final as death.

As though to disprove this theory, he hurried into a new novel, which he modestly called *Man's Life,* and insisted on having it published in a half-baked state. Then, after the wrangle over my departure for Atheneum, he disappeared from my life. I heard he was in London. Then nothing.

Departures . . . One of the focal points of the relation between a writer and his editor concerns their breaking up. Sometimes this occurs when an editor, voluntarily or otherwise, leaves one publishing house for another. The writer must then, of course, choose either to leave with him, if his contractual status permits him to do this, or to remain with his present publisher, feeling his primary loyalty to be that to the house.

Inevitably, if the relation has been a close one, and especially of long duration, the writer's decision to break it induces some emotional turmoil in one or both parties. Sometimes recriminations follow, sometimes frosty silences. If a real friendship, beyond the professional association, has existed, it rarely survives.

Some of the pain and resentment does not dissolve with the passing of time. It is not easy to accept rejection with grace; ingratitude (real or imagined) stings for a long time.

Among the partings I remember most vividly—whether sadly or humorously—are those with William Styron, Reynolds Price, Loren Eiseley, Aline Saarinen and Italo Calvino.

In the cases of Aline Saarinen and Calvino, there is a note of irony that I still enjoy. In each instance, I had negotiated a contract despite the opposition of one or both partners at Random House. Bernice Baumgarten, the peerless agent of the forties and fifties, had told me that Aline wanted to write a book about the great art collectors. She and I agreed that it had fine possibilities, and she asked for only a two-thousand-dollar advance. But the partners—I think it was chiefly Donald this time—were apathetic, and felt it was too risky a venture for even that amount. I finally prevailed, but only after really heavy opposition.

The Proud Possessors was an outstanding success; some twelve or thirteen years later it is still selling.

However, when I left Random House and called Aline long distance to the Orient to urge her to come to Atheneum, she balked. Random was her publisher and had done well by her. I don't remember now whether I succumbed to the temptation to tell her that "Random" hadn't wanted her, and had continued to stay skeptical about her book up to the point at which it was unmistakably clear that it was going to sell very well. If I did, it made no difference. Her loyalty went to the house, not the editor.

Calvino's was a similar decision—with a difference. I had to press hard to gain permission to sign up *The Baron in the Trees*. Fiction in translation, unless the author's name was Mann or Malraux, was not of great interest to the partners.

It was the first of Calvino's works to be published in the United States, and I can say without exaggeration that what modest success it had was exclusively through my efforts. Yet, when I talked to Calvino at the time of the forming of Atheneum, he promptly assured me that, grateful as he was, he would stay with Random. By then, he had been in New York for some months, and was fully aware that I—and I alone—had been his champion.

I asked him why he had made this decision.

He smiled. "I go back to Italy. When it is known that I am published by the publisher of William Faulkner, this will mean much more than being published by a new firm, however well considered here in America."

Much as I was irritated at the time, I respect his candor. He gave no equivocal excuse, and he has by now received his reward: all good Europeans, when they cross the Atlantic, are ultimately published by Helen Wolff.

There is also a humorous element in Reynolds Price's decision to stay at Atheneum when I left for Harcourt. I have already described the way in which he was released by Random and signed by Atheneum. But when the time came to publish his short novel, *A Long and Happy Life,* I encountered a new difficulty.

This book, like Jeff Young's *A Good Man* in the Bobbs-Merrill days, "had everything": a heroine, in Rosacoke Mustian, that one must love or turn into a granite monument; a supporting cast of authentic Tarheel humans; a wonderfully normal, uncomprehending young man named Wesley; and a message of hope for redeemable humanity.

This was, however, a much more sophisticated book than Young's. Its simplicity was finely honed, its myth so delicately and subtly integrated into the story as to stay invisible, until—long after one's first reading—it had been absorbed into one's very bones. Like most of the enduring works of fiction, it had sustenance for both the simple and the learned. One could extract from it in proportion to what one brought to it.

At our Atheneum sales conference, I tried to convey this sense of its rareness, to evoke an enthusiasm approaching my own. I failed miserably, perhaps because I was so intensely devoted to it that I found it almost impossible to achieve the "distance" that would convince the salesmen that there was professional expertise in this judgment. When I realized that my tone was one of pleading, I knew that I was not convincing my audience.

This meant that this lovely little book, with its word of deep faith in human potential—the kind of book so rare in our time—might go down the drain of oblivion, as had so many others I had strongly believed in. Indeed, that night I was plagued till late with the memories of those others which, in my opinion, had died stillborn through my inability to pierce the indifference and unimaginativeness of those who feel that a book is a book is a product.

The next morning I demanded of Bessie and Knopf that we postpone its publication, give me time to chart for it a fairer passage. As so often happens, anticipated opposition never developed. They were sympathetic; Pat sensibly inquired what I proposed to do. My psychic ganglia were exposed when I blurted, "Since no one believes me about it, I'm going to get endorsements from people whose *names* they will believe." I was infected again with the old editorial virus first encountered with Nat Wartels.

Pat assured me that if I succeeded, he would send out in advance to the book trade five hundred copies bound in paper, with the quotations I had secured on the cover. And he did: the names included those of Stephen Spender, Lord David Cecil, Eudora Welty and several others, equally well known, whom I cannot remember now.

Then luck joined the game, as it so often does. The difference made by plain coincidence in the fate of a given book, in the establishment of, or failure to establish, a particular writer, may be enormous. A month or two before the next sales conference, I had lunch with Jack Fischer, the editor of *Harper's* magazine. He told me that he was planning an innovation. For some time *Harper's* had been running periodically an extra installment. Usually this feature would deal with some large international or domestic issue, with a topical emphasis. Now, once, he wanted to do the same for fiction.

"What I'm looking for," he said, "is a short novel, not more than fifty or sixty thousand words, that can be published in full, just before book publication—and preferably one by an outstanding *new* writer, so that we will share with his publisher the honor of the discovery."

I offered to carry him back to Atheneum for one of those paper-bound copies of *A Long and Happy Life*. Fortunately, that didn't seem necessary to Jack; instead, I sent him one that afternoon. It was only two or three days before he made an offer for it.

So I came to the new sales conference with all this ammunition, and without any need to press for the book. It was now a *proved* success, before publication.

Inevitably, much of this story leaked to Reynolds. Therefore, when the break with Atheneum came, I was surprised and, I guess, hurt, when he said that he wanted time to think over the course he should follow. What came to mind immediately was his friendship with Harry Ford, the talented chief of production and art, who had followed Pat from Knopf to Atheneum. Through Harry, Reynolds had met many of the leading poets and novelists in New York, and much enjoyed being admitted to this circle.

Therefore, as time passed, I set about reconciling myself to losing him. But that summer (1964) I went down to the Tarheel Writers' Conference at Raleigh, and visited Reynolds as well. He was still undecided, but, in a gesture I misread, he took me to his mother's house to meet her. This was, from what I knew of Reynolds, unusual: I felt admitted to a circle of intimacy new to us.

I say "from what I knew of Reynolds," for I never felt that I did know him really well. (I suspect that he thought me a likable, flat-footed plodder.)

From Duke he had gone to New College, Oxford, on a Rhodes Scholarship. There he had come to know a number of distinguished British writers and developed a sophistication of taste and outlook that made him something of an exotic in North Carolina. Yet at home his manner was simple and courteous; he was devoted to his mother and brother (his father had died when he was very young) ; never, in my presence, did he suggest the sort of condescension to his more homely Carolina friends that often follows such extending of horizons. And in his writing he stayed with the simple small-town background that was his heritage.

When Reynolds first came out to our home in Connecticut, he was in his mid-twenties. He seemed frail, with a dramatic pallor and a lock of black hair that dropped over his forehead. We had guests; he was very quiet and seemed, although polite and thoughtful, a little removed from the gathering. I remember saying to my wife that I had a strange feeling that he would die young; in some elusive way he reminded me of John Keats. (I write this the more relaxedly, since it is obvious that he enjoys excellent health, and should live his full stint.)

In the fall of '64, after I had left Atheneum, Reynolds came north and we had lunch together. He then finally told me that he was staying on at Atheneum, and offered a (to me) unique explanation.

He and I loved each other. That was what he said. Because we did, and because nothing would affect that feeling, it would make no difference in our relation if we went separate ways professionally. And professionally it would be easier for him to stay put. I probed his reasoning a little, but not much; I have always been almost pathologically tender about being rejected, and this time was too startled by his reasoning to argue. And the only difference it has made in our relation is that it is now limited to occasional Christmas cards.

Yet there it is, this single passion flower of a reason for separation—*sui generis*—and there is no remaining sting to the memory, which still seems to me hilariously funny.

Not so with Bill Styron and Loren Eiseley. I suppose that if an editor has ever been known generally as so-and-so's editor, that was the case with Bill and me. For a long time, I heard frequently, "Oh, you're William Styron's editor." And I suspect that he became infinitely weary over hearing how much I had done for him. Indeed, he said this in the letter in which he told me he was staying with Random House.

What I *had* done was one central thing: I had believed that he was one of the most talented writers, not only of his generation, but of our time—and this when he was as yet wholly unknown. "So what?" as the banality goes. The fact that I literally staked my reputation as an editor on *Lie Down in Darkness* is to me—and I mean every word of this—quite simple, solid evidence that I am moderately intelligent and possessed of reasonably good editorial judgment. Supporting, promoting this book as a really outstanding one was the obvious thing to do; I was filled with joy at having such a work and such a writer walk in and say, "Here we are."

He had been told to come to see me in New York by his teacher at Duke, Bill Blackburn. He signed up at the New School for a fiction course in which he wrote several short stories, and then entered the novel workshop. When he turned in the first twenty pages of *Lie Down in Darkness,* I told him that he was out of place in a class, and took an option on the book for Crown. When I went to Bobbs, he followed, after staging an unusual sit-down strike at Crown until Nat Wartels would see him and release him. I remember that Bill told me he had taken his lunch with him, in case Nat held out until afternoon.

During the several years in which he worked on *Lie Down in Darkness,* the Haydns saw a great deal of him. He frequently visited us, and was really a *de facto* member of the family. Then, with only the final section of the book to complete, the situation in Korea worsened and, as a reserve officer in the Marines, he was called back to active duty.

This was crushing news. I inquired amongst publishing friends, and Jack Fischer told me of a brigadier general, an enlightened man who had an important part in reviewing cases of recall where unfairness might be involved. I asked Bill how much time he needed to finish the book, then called this man at the Pentagon, not without some trepidation. The general (I wish I could remember his name) was very courteous. A deferral of three months for the reasons I specified seemed to him entirely reasonable.

"In fact," he said, "it's the most valid grounds for deferment I've heard in a long time. If he's as good as you say he is. Are you sure?"

I was sure. He said that he must consult the others on his board; they were meeting the next morning; he would call me after their session, at 2:00 P.M.

The next day, at 1:58, the telephone rang. It was the general, who announced with obvious pleasure that the deferment had been approved. He had a favor to ask: a copy of the book when it was published. Who ever thought there could be such a general!

So Bill finished, and went back to the Marines. I began work on establishing the novel's quality in the house immediately. I had solid backing from several of its early readers, and especially from Ross Baker. We ordered an unusually large number of bound galleys, and sent them out to critics, hoping for support. Hoping? To me it was a sure thing. Maxwell Geismar, Howard Mumford Jones, Lloyd Morris and others responded handsomely. We began a campaign directed at the bookstores, sending a post-card each week on which was printed extravagant praise for the book, signed by one of these critics.

Hence there was telling support almost immediately, and Mr. Chambers's dour skepticism caused me far less concern than it would have if I had been forced to fight for it alone. That familiar snowballing process that accompanies the establishment of an outstanding new talent had begun, and there was no stopping it. Within a week after the publication of *Lie Down in Darkness,* almost everyone interested in books knew who William Styron was.

Bill was much feted—so much that I was frequently asked, "How will he survive all this adulation?" I always replied, "He'll revel in it, and finally go back to work. He has a sound core." And this was one of the times I was right.

I shan't attempt to trace the rest of his career; it is too well known, from *The Long March* to *The Confessions of Nat Turner*. When I left Random House, I of course gave him advance notice, and without making a full commitment, he indicated he expected to accompany me to Atheneum.

Twice thereafter, Bill came to Atheneum—once in the evening, so that I had the sense of participating in some sort of counterespionage. Each time he assured me that he would sign with us after Random House had published his next novel, *Set This House on Fire*. But on a third visit, when he and his lovely wife Rose joined Mary and me for an hour or so one afternoon, I began to have a premonition that he was changing his mind. He said nothing directly about such a change, but he appeared preoccupied, uneasy and impatient to get away to keep an appointment with Bennett Cerf.

The Styrons left for Europe that week, and soon I received a long letter from him, saying that he had decided to stay at Random House. He was grateful and appreciative, but he was tired of having people think and say that he owed everything to me; he wanted to stand on his own feet.

This was the chief reason for his decision—an understandable one. But there were other factors: his old friend from Duke University days, Bob Loomis, was at hand to be his editor. Bennett had entertained lavishly for him, and Bill, like Bennett, loves glamour and celebrities. Moreover, despite the largely unfavorable reception of his second full-length novel, there was no diminution of Random's regard for him.

Still, it was the imperative to leave the nest that mattered most, I think. At the time, what stung me was that he had chosen to go off to Europe before telling me, rather than doing so in person. But then I have always had a bias toward direct confrontations. It has frequently stood me in poor stead. . . .

I first met Loren Eiseley at Random House, after having published with joy in *The American Scholar* several of his beautiful essays on aspects of nature. Others of the same sort and caliber had appeared in *Harper's,* the *Atlantic* and elsewhere. That day at Random I proposed to him a book, composed of these essays but with transitional links that would make it a unified book rather than simply a collection. (Collections are notoriously hard to sell unless their author has already a large following.)

He agreed to make the attempt. We signed a contract, and during the next months worked together several times, and at length. Loren found the linking process difficult, and I believe that I helped him substantially. It was the last time he needed me in that capacity. With all the other books of his I published, he simply turned in the finished work; I found no need for editing.

Such a writer is rare. The only other of whom it has consistently been true in my experience is Gladys Schmitt. I don't believe that I have ever proposed the change of a paragraph in those majestic novels of hers.

But to return to Eiseley. At our first meeting I was surprised at his heavy and lugubrious manner, amazed at his circumlocutions. The master of that supple lyrical prose! In retrospect I find less to wonder at. The inner man of books and the outer one of social exchanges often do not resemble each other. I came in time to think of Loren's dichotomy (with proper acknowledgment to Rossini) as the Poet and Provost.

An anthropologist later to win renown with his book on Darwin, Eiseley was shortly to become provost of the University of Pennsylvania, a really uncongenial post from which he resigned after only a couple of years. Hence the designation. But I was not alone among his friends in finding him a man of ponderous melancholy. One of them named him "Schmertzy"—for *Weltschmerz.* A less kind comparison was to A. A. Milne's Eeyore.

Loren was a lonely and diffident man, who trusted few and was comfortable with few. My enthusiastic love of his writings made him easier with me than with most, I believe. He was also, I found, very raw to the touch. Once he either threatened to, or actually did, tear up his contract because someone he spoke to at Random House had shown him insufficient deference.

282

Little by little I learned a bit about his past, his strange and tormented childhood, and came to feel a strong sympathy for him. Eventually I painfully realized that I shared more of his vulnerabilities than I wanted to believe.

At any rate, the book was completed, entitled *The Immense Journey*. It contained the experiences and reflections of an anthropologist and naturalist who wrote like an inspired poet, whose philosophical contemplation of man and nature was haunting and moving.

Yet I could not persuade the powers at Random that it would find any sizable audience. I remember speaking for it with passion at the sales conference, only to have Lew Miller, the most elegant sales manager I have ever known, courteously cut me down. In effect, he said that I was right, that this was the best-written book on the list, but *that* was why it wouldn't sell. I jumped up again, saying that there were some books, wonderfully written, that had universal appeal, and these transcended the formulae for best sellers.

I lost, of course. At publication time advance orders were not much over a thousand copies, and the advertising appropriation was next to invisible. There were some good notices, but despite my plea, neither Prescott of the *Times* nor Hutchens of the *Tribune* reviewed it.

It had been published in August. Sometime in October, weekly orders and reorders began picking up. First fifty, then a hundred, then more than two hundred. All this with no further notice of the book. The third week I marched into Bennett's office.

He held up a hand.

"I know why you've come, and I'm disappointed in you, Hiram. I expected you last week."

"What are you talking about?"

"Eiseley. You want some advertising, and you'll get it."

It went on selling. Prescott and Hutchens both reviewed it with strong praise, and apologized for being so slow in getting to it. Dean Acheson ordered a thousand copies for Christmas presents. There was one week when the orders challenged those for John O'Hara's new novel, Random's current leader.

And *The Immense Journey* has gone on "forever." Published in 1957, the hard-cover edition had a sale of over a thousand copies in the year 1971, the paperback many thousands.

So Loren and I were off to a good start. There followed, at Atheneum, *The Firmament of Time,* and a contract for his autobiography. When I left Atheneum he wanted to come with me. The contract was an obstacle, but Bessie and Knopf had stated publicly that they would hold no author against his will. All they asked was the chance to dissuade him from leaving.

So Loren reluctantly (*he* hated confrontations) agreed to lunch with Mike Bessie. He told me about their meeting with a mixture of anger and pride. Or so it seemed.

"He was a half hour late. I was about to leave. Then in walked Mr. Bessie with his dapper little hat, his dapper little coat, and a lot of soft soap." Loren's anger stood him in good stead; he secured his release.

But a year or so after signing with Harcourt for his autobiography, he asked for a meeting with Bill Jovanovich and me, and proposed a textbook in anthropology. Such a book was being solicited by another publisher. Would we like to publish it? We would. Then he named the large price the other publisher would pay. Bill explained why it was too much, unrealistic. Loren left, obviously upset.

Thereafter he wanted his contract changed to make his first book one to be called *The Unexpected Universe,* with the autobiography postponed. We held separate contracts for them.

Later he kept telling me that he would never write the autobiography, and paid us back the advance—citing income-tax problems. He offered to release us from the contract altogether, but we declined, being ready to wait to see whether he might change his mind.

In the summer of 1969 I learned from some uninvolved person that Loren had a book coming out with Scribner's in the fall. I asked Loren what this meant. He replied that this was a "special case," that it didn't interfere with our arrangement, and that we had (true) no option clause. I agreed, but said I felt bad that, after all our years together, he had not even consulted me. He said that he knew I was on vacation, on Martha's Vineyard, and he hadn't wanted to bother me. (Before I had left New

York, I had given him my Vineyard number, urging him to call at any time.)

The Unexpected Universe came out, and did well. Then, the following summer, I received a letter from him saying that he had been offered a sum for that textbook that far exceeded what Jovanovich had been unwilling to pay, and because he really would never write the autobiography, he wanted us to release him.

This came like a flash storm: just before leaving the city, I had had a good talk with him (or so it appeared to me) and everything seemed in order. I consulted Bill, and he left it up to me. I felt it was hopeless: we gave Loren his release.

A year or so later, Scribner's published an autobiographical book of his.

I am haunted again by the subjective angle of incidence. Styron made a decision that he must have found difficult. Moreover, there was never any question of his being ungrateful; there is strong evidence to prove the reverse. Part of his reasoning in the letter was that he had twice gone with me to a different publishing house; if he did this a third time, it would only confirm the opinion he had often been exposed to—that he couldn't make his way without me. Add his liking for Cerf and Loomis, and the strength of Random House—and I think his decision a sound, logical one. Today we get together over a rowdy game of croquet now and then, but it took quite a while for the hurt to heal.

And I think a similar wound accounts for Eiseley's departure from HBJ. I believe that he felt utterly rejected the day that Jovanovich did not offer him the amount he wanted for the textbook. It festered; from time to time he would unexpectedly refer to it again, and at least once bitterly.

He was wrong to feel rejected over the textbook matter; what he expected *was* unrealistic. I was wrong in feeling hurt that Styron stayed at Random House; what I wanted him to do was unrealistic. But perhaps it is unrealistic to expect us to be realistic in matters of emotional ties, old wounds and loyalties.

Loyalty is a slippery subject. I wish now that I had not invoked the word so often. Easy to appeal to but hard to anatomize and harder to practice intelligently. There are honorable loyalties, but there are also stupid ones, destructive ones. And it is particularly self-righteous and futile to stress it in a relationship that involves careers, talent and business. An editor may be of real service to a writer, but he has chosen to offer that service because he is convinced of the high quality of the author's work. When the editor changes houses, he cannot expect the writer to change with him unless the writer believes that he will himself benefit from the shift. His reason may include a liking for the editor, but if it rests solely on that feeling he is acting foolishly and against his own interests.

Having dwelt on partings, and on rejections, real or imagined, I take pleasure in remembering an occasion on which the anticipation of loss was not warranted.

In the early days at Atheneum, William Goldman submitted a novel to me through his agent, Monica McCall. Goldman's first novel, *The Temple of Gold,* had been published by Knopf, but they had turned down his second, which was picked up by Doubleday: *Your Turn to Curtsy, My Turn to Bow.* Neither of these had sold very well, although *The Temple of Gold* was to have a long and wide distribution in paperback.

The new script was called *Soldier in the Rain.* I found it marvelously funny, and its chief character, Sergeant Slaughter, one of those really inimitable figures imbued with so much vitality and uniqueness that they seem to acquire lives of their own, without the circumference of the book in which they appeared. I accepted the book enthusiastically.

Goldman and I met, and hit it off well. I liked his directness and his sense of humor. We shared a fanatical love of baseball, and our sessions together were always full of talk and laughter.

Soldier, despite heavy promotion, didn't sell well. Bill took this handsomely, though he was much disappointed. He turned to film writing. He had already, in collaboration with his brother James, had two Broadway flops. His first film, *Harper,* broke his series of "failures," and eventually led to an even greater success, *Butch Cassidy and the Sundance Kid.*

In 1963 he finally completed a long novel called *Boys and Girls Together.* This was the only one of Bill's novels on which I did extensive work—not on the writing, but the arranging. He

286

told his story from the points of view of six young people who had come to New York to "make their way." He also dipped into their pasts, and after having worked so long and strenuously on each separate section, he had difficulty setting in order the mixture of time and points of view.

I took on this work during the period of strain near the end of my stay at Atheneum; the novel did not appear until after I had left. But the deal for the paperback edition was completed while I was there. It was a handsome one, and between it and his success with the films, Bill was at last "making it big."

Then came the final break at Atheneum for me, and a period, so painfully familiar by this time, of negotiating with writers. Who would go with me, who stay?

I did not see Bill for several weeks. First he was away, then I. I knew that the Atheneum partners were urgently pursuing him, and I felt pessimistic. How many times had I seen the change in a young writer once success had overtaken him? I braced myself for the change in Bill, yet I found it hard to believe that he would, *could* change. But many of those others had surprised me.

We met at lunch at Argenteuil. We ordered a drink. Then he turned directly to me.

"Well, Dad," he said, "where do I go and when?"

It has lasted. This man has since been paid the largest sum ever offered a film writer to do an original script. Although his books have not yet done too well in hard cover, except for his acerb critique of Broadway, *The Season,* his paperback sales have gone into the millions. Yet he has not changed. He is the same man, and I love and respect him.

Ongoing friendships between writer and editor are unlikely, precarious and rewarding. The primary risk, of course, is that the greater intimacy may injure the objectivity needed in professional collaboration. Yet I have experienced the reverse: a heightening of sensitiveness to the writer's work, a keener feeling for his intent, his peculiar vision, as a result of coming to know him or her better. Like most rare commodities, it is something to cherish.

Working with nonliterary people whose books are about their lives or careers requires of an editor a drastic reorientation.

Such people are almost always writing, or "writing," a book because they are well known and at least putatively of interest to a large audience. They are frequently highly conscious of their own importance, and demand deferential attention, but at the same time they may be capricious about keeping appointments. A few, a very few, write well; the majority need a ghost writer (whether or not acknowledged) or close and time-consuming editing.

Certain publishers and editors secure a great many "public figure books"—most of which emanate from the political circus in Washington. Cass Canfield, Sr., and Ken McCormick are two who have been particularly successful with such books.

I have worked on few of them. Few? I think of two: one by Jacob Javits, the senator from New York; the other by Paul H. Douglas, the senator from Illinois. They were widely disparate experiences.

The Javits book came to Atheneum because one of our backers, Richard Ernst, was close to the Senator. I don't remember clearly how I, rather than Mike Bessie, came to be the editor. But I do remember clearly my first meeting with Mr. Javits in his New York apartment. He had sent me a half-dozen chapters, and I had read them and taken many notes.

With him that evening was Richard Aurelio, then his chief aide, who later ran John Lindsay's aborted campaign for president. The Senator seemed to me ponderous, heavily judicious: in a curious way, *static*. In vivid contrast, I found Aurelio volatile, flamboyantly swarthy, and penetrating.

As our conference continued, certain facts were established, and certain impressions deepened. Aurelio was writing a first draft, Javits going over it and striking sections, paragraphs, sentences that did not satisfy him. Then Aurelio would rewrite. It was the second version that I had received.

Moreover, I found it increasingly clear that the Senator was a totally public man, not geared to informal editorial sessions. When I asked him questions pertaining to gaps in the material or apparent contradictions, he (at least that is how it struck me) would deliberate with every appearance of brooding thoughtful-

288

ness, then launch what seemed to be the opening of a public address.

As the conference bogged down in these florid generalizations, I began to be convinced that a book would be forthcoming only after many tortuous meetings over interminable months. Aurelio, who had mostly kept quiet, was obviously growing impatient.

At last I asked Senator Javits how he reconciled a passage on page *x* with one on page *y*. Both concerned his stand on foreign policy, yet one seemed at direct odds with the other. He paused even longer than usual, then wound up and delivered, after adjusting (this image came to me then, spontaneously) his eleventh mask of the evening.

I could never quote that speech, but the gist of it was that foreign policy was a weighty matter indeed, that what applied in one case did not in another, and that in a shrinking world that brought us face to face with all our overseas brothers, it was necessary to maintain a flexible and vigilant attitude.

Aurelio literally groaned, then gave forth with words that I at least believe I have "by heart."

"Cut the shit, Jack. Mr. Haydn really wants to help us with the book."

A twinge—of pain?—seemed to cross the Senator's face. Then he settled down to some plain and relevant exposition.

But I never came to feel that I knew him at all, although we had several more sessions, before Aurelio and I, apparently with Javits's blessing, began to carry out the hard daily grind of producing the book. I am sure the Senator did read all of it and check and revise it, but I seldom saw him.

I should add at this point that I respect his record, voting and otherwise, and that I believe him an able and effective man. But completely political. The procession of masks was not informative of the individual human being hidden away somewhere.

This metaphor reminds me, although there is a striking difference, of my acquaintance with Alger Hiss. When he was released from jail he spent a year or two in search of work, with little success. But he had some staunch friends, among them my friend Clara Mayer. She didn't claim to know all the rights of the famous Chambers-Hiss case, but—like Dean Acheson—she would not turn her back on a friend in adversity.

One day she called me at Random House and asked me if I would be willing to see Hiss. He was looking for any kind of free-lance editorial work, but even if I had none at hand, it would be good for his morale to be accorded serious consideration.

I found it difficult to say no to Clara, and I was, of course, curious about the man. After we set up the appointment I became fatuously confident that now I would know what the truth of the matter was. I actually believed that I was shrewd enough—or sensitive enough—to get at, not the *facts* of the case, but the nature of Alger Hiss—from one meeting!

Absurd. For the first ten minutes of our meeting, I was much impressed with the former president of the Carnegie Corporation. He was quiet, dignified and—most of all—bore himself with no trace of either defensiveness or aggressiveness.

More than an hour later, I was bewildered. Mask succeeded mask, role role, personality personality. There was a half hour during which our actual situation was reversed, as though *he* had granted *me* an interview. He asked me many questions about my work, suggested improved methods in running the editorial department, etc. All, no doubt, with an eye for how he might fit into the Random House structure. But the authority with which he spoke suggested that he was *in charge.*

Suddenly something brought this phase to an end, and he became gaminlike, elusive, answering my questions with the manner of a shrewd, precocious boy who was playing games and admiring his skill at them.

Another shift, and he seemed abruptly defensive. There were fear and suspicion in his expression, and he answered me in guarded monosyllables. This attitude passed like a summer storm, and he reverted to his original personality. We concluded our talk pleasantly, no hint of his (unconscious) other imper-sonations remaining.

It was I who brought the session to a close, with the plea that I must catch a train to Connecticut. He offered to accompany me down Madison Avenue as far as the Roosevelt, where I went underground to Grand Central. On the way I marveled that no one stared. No one recognized the man whose face had been prominently displayed, almost daily, a few years before.

We parted. Just before I entered the Roosevelt, I looked back. He was waiting for me to turn, for immediately he raised his hand and "waved" in an incongruous, stiff way, flapping his fingers toward me. Tall, thin, bony—the loneliest man in the world, I thought.

Because I had no work for him (amusingly, Bennett Cerf, that fiercely independent man, scolded me for having seen Hiss, warned me that such an association would do me no good) —because there was no other way in which I might help Hiss—it occurred to me that it might be good for that morale Clara Mayer had worried about if I asked him to lunch on the grounds that *he* could help *me*.

Sentimental, perhaps, but practical, too: I was working on a novel, *The Hands of Esau,* in which the central character was employed by a large foundation. Hiss's experience at Carnegie meant that he must be able to give me a good deal of useful information.

We had lunch. Two aspects of our conversation still impress me. We had barely sat down when he remarked that I seemed depressed, quite unlike the cheerful man he had seen several weeks before.

I replied that I was—that I was upset over something I had done that morning, something of which I was ashamed.

He shook his head.

"I know," he said sadly. "I have friends who say things like that—and feel that way. I can't understand it. I have never done anything of which I am ashamed. I always mean to do what I do."

It took me a while to recover from that statement, but when I did, I told him the way in which I needed his help.

For a full hour he gave generously of his experience: the organizational setup in a foundation, the methods employed in the making of decisions, the financial structure—on and on. It was a detailed exposition, yet utterly lucid, beautifully coherent. At its conclusion I felt as though I had been employed at a foundation for a decade.

The elegance of that mind! Only then did I feel the full extent of his tragedy. . . .

My experience with Paul Douglas has been of a very different order from that with Senator Javits. I have already described his debut at *The American Scholar* meeting. Massiveness is the first word that comes to mind; he is not only very tall, but broad and thick, with a short shock of white hair that somehow accents the effect of vastness. On that occasion he was expressing not only his astonishment that these intellectuals really said what they meant, but his joy.

This latter fact will not surprise anyone who has read his recently published memoirs, *In the Fullness of Time*, an astonishingly candid book from a prominent public figure. Its genuine honesty provides a refreshing contrast to all those wary, self-serving books that have come out of Washington.

I first proposed that he write such a book, to be published by my firm, when I was at Atheneum. He told me that he had already completed half a book of this sort. But he added that he wouldn't consider publication until he had retired from active service, because he had no intention of writing one of those "pious" formal autobiographies that turned the record into a bland and unrevealing recitation. Nor did he want to sign a contract until that time, but when he was ready he would give us first chance.

We met from time to time over the next few years, and he would tell me of his progress and repeat his determination to work it out according to his original plan. On one of these visits we were to have lunch in the Senate dining room. I appeared at his office at the appointed time, to find that there must be a delay. Paul was to present some new legislation, but his presentation was awaiting the completion of the oratory of his Illinois colleague and opponent, Everett Dirksen. We sat and chatted, and finally word was received that Senator Dirksen appeared to be "winding up." Or, Paul wanted to know, could he be "running down"?

He and a young aide and I went to the Senate Chambers, where I sat in the balcony with the aide. He turned out to be a very witty young man. The heat that July day had reached ninety-six degrees, and there was no air conditioning in the Chambers. As Dirksen droned lyrically on, pausing now and then to mop his florid face, the aide turned to me and whispered, "It isn't the heat; it's the humility."

Finally Dirksen finished, and Paul rose. I can't quote a word, but I shall never forget the impact. "The noblest Roman of them all" was how he looked, but his purport was a savage attack on "political favors" and chicanery in office, all pertaining to the need for new rules and checks in some governmental agency. He was a master at indictment, and his sharp, incisive style was like a sudden cooling breeze cutting through the humid air that Dirksen had produced.

At lunch later, I had the ambiguous pleasure of meeting and gawking at other senators: Kefauver, Humphrey and, finally, Jacob Javits again. Javits was very kind about my work on his book. After he left, I asked Paul what he thought of him.

"Jack's a good boy," he said. "He'll listen to reason."

I felt a bit abashed. . . .

When I went to Harcourt in 1964, Paul assured me that this made no difference in his intentions. Actually it made quite a bit, for I introduced Bill Jovanovich to him, and before long Bill (far better at this sort of thing than I) not only had secured for us a book of Paul's essays, *In Our Time,* but persuaded Paul to sign a contract for his memoirs, though with the understanding that they would not be submitted to us until after his retirement. And all went through as arranged. An outstanding book.

The four authors of books of memoirs on my list at Harcourt form a startling combination: Martha Graham, Paul Douglas, Anaïs Nin and Pearl Bailey. I have imagined the four of them, locked together in a small apartment in the manner of *No Exit.* . . .

I have seldom felt as honored as I did when Martha Graham's agent, Lucy Kroll, told me that she believed I would be the right editor to work eventually with Martha Graham on her autobiography.

I have known Lucy from my earliest days at Crown. Red-haired, brown-eyed Lucy of the subdued dramatic flair. I have never argued so long over a contract with any other agent as I have almost every time with Lucy. And I have no greater affection for any, either.

Our friendship has been constant, has endured through many difficult situations. The only time I can remember her really being angry at me was at the Plaza one night, when she thought she saw me dancing with a young girl. Her affection for my wife made her furious, she told me later, after she discovered that "the girl" was Mary with a new and different way of wearing her hair.

At any rate, through Lucy, we signed Martha Graham to a contract at Random House in the late fifties. Thereafter, thanks to her keen sense of loyalty and Lucy's firm stand, the contract was transferred, first to Atheneum, then to Harcourt Brace Jovanovich.

The original contract, for her autobiography, had to be renewed each time because she hadn't written a word of it. Directing her company, running her school, creating new dances, still dancing herself, taking the company on tours—she had no time for writing. During the years at Atheneum we lent her a Dictaphone, hoping she might be inspired by it to "talk" her book. This didn't work until much later, in 1971, when she began holding regular dialogues in this fashion with various interlocutors. As I write, we have transcripts of many of these, and the editorial work will soon begin.

During these fifteen or so years we have often lunched together, and I have often called at her apartment. She is perhaps the most electric person of my acquaintance. Her lithe movements, the force of those eloquent eyes, her habit of dropping her voice almost to a murmur when she has something especially incisive to say—all compel acute and sometimes dazzled attention.

Yet she never "puts on a show." You are aware that she is as marvelous an actress as she is a dancer, but however flamboyant she may seem at times there is a final sinewy integrity to her that would spurn with contempt that kind of artifice.

In preparation for those tape-recorded talks Martha gave me her notebooks from many years back. I had them typed, and sat down to read. It was a long and rapt evening. I stopped only twice—once to turn to Leonardo's notebooks, once to those of

Dostoevsky. Despite the differences of their subjects, I saw an obvious analogy: the artist at work, the creative process intimately revealed.

The notebooks display the sources for her dances, their transformations, the evolution of choreography. Her wealth of learning in mythology, literature, philosophy, theology and even anthropology is there, page after page, often in cryptic notations that fascinate even as they bewilder. The notebooks were published in the fall of 1973. . . .

Anaïs Nin is also *sui generis.* I first met her in the Village, when I was teaching at the New School. I invited her, as I did other writers, to visit my class and lead the criticism of student work. After a first selection had been discussed, she lifted a cool and imperious hand.

"Now that I have heard some of your work," she said, "it is only fair that you should listen to mine."

She read for the duration of the class.

At the time it seemed to me one of the purest expressions of ego I had ever encountered. I now regard it as a pure expression of the agonizing loneliness that attends the writer who receives little or no recognition. It was, I think, a valid act for survival.

Years passed. Anaïs Nin continued to struggle for the publication of her intense, fragile dream novels and stories, which include many of the technical innovations and surreal effects credited to others who "introduced" them later. Now and again she found a regular trade publisher, only to lose him with the next book. Once she printed her own book. Then, finally, that dedicated man, Alan Swallow, who ran the Swallow Press in Denver, took her on and issued, one by one, all her previous works as well as the new ones.

I met Alan only once, but we corresponded over the years. Whenever he felt that his budget did not permit him to take some book of good quality, he would send it to one or another of the New York publishers whose judgment he respected, and I was among them. Finally, not long after my arrival at Harcourt, he wrote me that Anaïs Nin was ready at last to begin publishing her multivolumed *Diaries,* about which the literary world had long heard, and which were awaited with eagerness because of her unusual "Bohemian" life and her close association with Henry Miller, Laurence Durrell, Otto Rank, Gore Vidal, Edmund Wilson and others.

Alan felt that this was too big a venture, too important an enterprise, for him to handle alone. He did not have adequate resources for distribution. So he inquired whether we would like to make it a joint publishing program. He said "program" because he anticipated at least eight volumes.

We agreed, signed a contract with him for the first volume, renewed it for the second, and would have so continued but for his untimely death. Four volumes have now been published, all successful in the hard-cover edition, all much more than successful in the paperback format. There are more to come.

I remember with great satisfaction the party for Anaïs given by Harcourt Brace Jovanovich and Frances Steloff, that indomitable woman, the proprietor of the Gotham Book Mart, on the publication of the first volume. The store was packed with people. Nona Balakian of the New York *Times* arrived with the copy of a glowing front-page review by Jean Garrigue. At last the literary world was paying full homage to Anaïs Nin. I remembered the hungry loneliness of that long-ago evening at the New School.

She wears acclaim with dignity, as she did neglect. An ageless woman, she enchants the young. I have heard them cheer, I have seen them kneel, I have listened to their words. In fact, I have asked a good many young women to explain this idolatry; it does not seem to me that her relatively subtle version of "women's liberation" bears much resemblance to their own.

"But she was the first," one answered with quiet insistence. "She was alone, and she did it."

And so she did. There are people who, in writing as well as conversation, denounce her vanity, her narcissism. I am persuaded of Anaïs's absorption in her art and her life. But to me a narcissist is one who is aware of others only as extensions of herself/himself. Such a charge does not apply to Anaïs Nin. I know few prominent writers who are so genuinely kind, so thoughtful about other—and particularly young—writers and artists of all sorts. She is always backing someone, recommending someone for a contract, scholarship, fellowship, sponsorship, writing in behalf of X or Y or Z. She even conspired with that able editor, William Claire, to devote forty pages of an issue of his magazine, *Voyages,* to a tribute to her editor, Haydn. Unheard of . . .

To be sure, she is the queen of her new world, the empress of the young. She has always possessed a hieratic sort of beauty. She laughed her strange tinkling laugh when I told her she looked like a Siamese cat. She knew that, she said, and reminded me of a passage in her work that says that of Sabina.

Perhaps more accurately, she is a priestess. I have thought that of Martha Graham, but her variety seems to me that of the Bacchae: it has a fierce ecstatic quality. Anaïs presides over an enchanted court of remote and exotic coolness. . . .

It is quite a journey from her to Pearl Bailey. My wife was enthusiastic about the Bailey voice and style from the very beginning of that spectacular career, and I had often heard her in night clubs and shows. But it wasn't until her debut at the Waldorf in the early sixties that I conceived of a book by her— her life story.

I had never published a book by an entertainer, and I was uncertain about procedures, awkward and timid. I believe I must have written her a half-dozen unanswered letters during the next year. Then, finally, through a friend, I had the opportunity to speak to her on another evening at the Waldorf.

She was amused and apparently pleased.

"So you're the man who wrote those letters. I kept thinking I'd see you some day, sweetheart."

But she was interested. There followed the most strenuous experience of my publishing life. There was no trouble getting Pearl to talk; difficulty centered in persuading her to stay with whatever subject I had introduced, to answer specific questions.

"I know, honey, I'll be right back to that, but first I've got to tell you . . ."

And those astonishing hands chiding, praising, condemning, grieving in counterpoint to her voice, weaving their own complementary tale.

Late sessions at hotels in New York, Philadelphia, Washington, after her show. I remember reaching the Shoreham Hotel in

Washington at 1:00 P.M. to keep a two o'clock appointment with her. At five minutes to the hour, her infinitely amiable husband, Louis Bellson, appeared to tell me that Pearl was tired and would have to postpone today's taping until after her show. One o'clock in the morning. I tried to sleep, failed, fumed.

But by this time a solution had been found. At the suggestion of Bill Jovanovich, an ingenious young editor named Wendell Shackelford joined our recordings. When I was too tired or disgruntled to keep Pearl fully interested, Wendell more than compensated. He ran the tape recorder, filled in silences, applauded, urged her on.

Wendell also did the close editing that brought order to the magnificent flood of words. Once he had joined me, my only real contribution was in giving the book a final over-all structure.

Aside from Pearl Bailey herself, the most extraordinary aspect of the whole undertaking was that Wendell and I were able to keep her unique flavor, her zest for her own kind of expression, in the text. For all our labors, it is her own book.

It had to be. That was what prompted me to try for this book from the beginning. I knew there wasn't a phony bone in Pearl Bailey, and I wanted the distillation of that fiery presence I had so often heard and watched improvising brilliantly on the stage: exhorting, mocking, promising, rejecting, scolding, seducing, talking to herself. And that was the title of her second book, *Talking to Myself*, on which Wendell also worked extensively. The first she had named *The Raw Pearl*.

Not a phony bone, I repeat. But complex! I think that we were treated, during those long hours of taping, to every mood known to woman—and each in all its marvelous, exasperating or inspiring richness. Pearl Bailey is a world.

These distinguished women have received many tributes—though none, perhaps, her deserved quota. I write those words, and I think "Who can measure *that*?" No one—except, perhaps, those who are long-time *inside* observers of a particular artistic world. I am obviously not such an observer of the world of dance, for example. In that of books, I think it easy to perceive that women writers have not received equal treatment with men.

Criteria? Doris Lessing, Mary McCarthy, Iris Murdoch,

Eudora Welty and Joyce Carol Oates may be accorded as prominent and long review space as Vladimir Nabokov, Saul Bellow, Philip Roth, Norman Mailer and John Updike. But whenever the outstanding novelists of our time are listed, the women's names do not appear. And when a young critic undertakes a study of a living novelist, it is almost certain that the subject will be a man.

The names I have just cited are to me not necessarily those of our best novelists,* but rather those of the ones, men and women, American and British, who are most often cited and who are surest of "front-page" reviews. When I list for myself novelists I think equally fine, or finer, but who have been neglected, many more women than men come to mind.

But one confronts an even more unbalanced picture when one considers the women who have worked and are working in book publishing. Except for certain well-defined precincts conspicuously labeled "for women only," few have found and been granted the opportunity to hold positions of real authority, to exercise fully their often brilliant talents.

One such exception, Helen Wolff, came to the American publishing scene from Germany with her husband, Kurt. I first met Kurt at a meeting of the American Book Publishers Council, and was immediately impressed with him. Here was one man whose presence lived up to his reputation. Tall, quiet, striking-looking, he carried a sort of glow that I find it hard to define. But even in a crowded room, and while maintaining silence, he was instantly recognizable as unusual and distinguished.

I never came to know him well, but I was a strong admirer from whatever distance. He had come to the United States in the early forties, having left Germany and the fine publishing house he had built to escape the era of Brown Shirts. And with the help of his wife, a French partner, Jacques Schiffrin, and Kyrill Schabert, he had made his new firm, Pantheon, one of the best in New York. An arrangement with the Bollingen Foundation to publish and distribute their learned series of books, and the acquisition of such best-selling authors as Anne Morrow Lindbergh and Joy Adamson had certainly helped his business. But

* In fact, I actively dislike the work of some of them, find others far inferior to their reputations.

the Wolffs gave Alfred and Blanche Knopf their first real competition for the European market, and Kurt Wolff's career culminated with his acquisition of *Dr. Zhivago* and Lampedusa's *The Leopard.*

I do not know the full particulars of the Wolffs' departure from Pantheon, but I do know enough about it to be sure that it was another of the not infrequent sorry stories about the forcing out, in an act of intramural politics, of an initiator and guiding spirit.

The Wolffs retired to Switzerland, and agreed to return to the American publishing scene only after William Jovanovich visited them and persuaded them to join the Harcourt publishing venture as copublishers. That is, they would have their own list, with each book indicated as a Helen and Kurt Wolff book, and a large share of autonomy, working exclusively with Mr. Jovanovich in directing the list.

Tragically, only three years later, Kurt Wolff was struck and killed by a truck in Germany. Only after much painful thought, and urging by Bill Jovanovich, who asked that the publishing arrangement continue, did his widow determine to move to New York and carry on alone. It was a fortunate decision for American publishing.

Helen Wolff is a gracious and charming woman. She has a keen and sensitive editorial mind, and her dedication to her authors is absolute. She lives only a block from her office at Harcourt Brace Jovanovich, and her apartment is a haven for European writers sojourning in New York.

What a list she publishes! Günter Grass, Uwe Johnson, Georges Simenon, Italo Calvino, Giorgio Bassani, Teilhard de Chardin, Karl Jaspers, Iris Origo, Bryher, Konrad Lorenz, James Morris, and Andrei Amalrik. She has been the prime mover in instigating and publishing the definitive translation of Casanova's authentic *Memoirs.*

She is an aristocrat among publishers, intolerant of meretriciousness. She is a scrupulous textual editor and works an incredible number of hours on close editorial detail. It is characteristic of the roundedness of her nature that so large-spirited a woman should consider the most detailed chore worthy of her best efforts.

Her modesty is humbling; her toughness, confronted by the enemy (greediness, cheapness, infidelity), inspiring. She sees as the bane of American publishing the balanced list, and deplores, in these terms, the Americanization of much European publishing. She cleaves to the ancient code (much honored in the breach) that books and their writers are the core of the publishing enterprise, and that those of us who have a hand in issuing and supporting them incur thereby a sacred trust, in which lies the reason for our pride and self-respect.

Once the decision is made to "take on" a promising young writer, Mrs. Wolff believes that it is a publisher's duty and privilege to stay with him, to see him through the ups and downs of the publication of several of his books, regardless of his record on the profit and loss sheet. And regardless of the possibility that a given one may prove too learned or *recherché* or specialized for more than a small audience, she can seldom resist a really good book. Her taste, though markedly individual, has attained a catholicity that insures breadth and diversity to her list. And "despite" all these idealistic practices, she maintains a going and growing business.

When she reads these words she will deplore their "extravagance." This because, knowing herself with rare honesty and perceptiveness, and finding herself a human being, with all the complexity that implies, she will not find such an account compatible with her stringent demands upon herself.

To be in her company, at any rate, is a joy. She is always aware of others, of their particularities, without losing sight of her own. She gives and takes, and where there is no response, maintains a forbearing silence. When she visited us several summers ago at our home on Martha's Vineyard, she left behind a sort of benignity that hovered around the house for several days.

Whenever someone you know only as a colleague becomes your house guest, you have an opportunity, of course, to increase your knowledge of that person more in a day or two than in many weeks at work. The role of guest is, I think, a sternly demanding one, even more exacting in its responsibilities than that of host or hostess. And it was as a guest that Helen Wolff revealed especially her breeding, sensitiveness and taste.

Crucial to the guest's role is, of course, the self-acceptance that enables one to be natural and relaxed. To such a capacity must be added an intuitive sense of when to assist and when to desist. This delicate timing Helen Wolff has to a superlative degree, together with an understanding of the central importance of reciprocity, the closely knit tie between self-respect and respect for others.

I have watched her with devout concentration on other, more public occasions. The private and the public person show a rare harmony. At the HBJ sales conferences, which she professes to dread, she sparkles with wit and grace. She is inimitably herself, never talking down to the salesmen. Yet she knows and accepts the fact that her task is to interest them in the books she is publishing, to "sell" them to them, and she seems to feel none of the stiff-necked resentment at "putting on a show" that handicaps many editors. She is at once of practical use to the salesmen and true to herself.

Different in tone and tempo was the evening she spent talking about European publishing to my class at the University of Pennsylvania. If on that occasion she had any sense of the need to perform a role, it was not evident. She captivated the students with her forthrightness, her clear unwillingness to give them a cut and dried exposition. Anecdotes, forceful opinions and her sharply critical view of current publishing tendencies won their unanimous enthusiasm. As one young man said to me after class, "Boy, does that lady tell it like it is!"

That *lady*. Right. New luster to old and tired terminology. The full force of Helen Wolff's achievement as a human being is rendered the clearer if one compares what I have written of her with Harding Lemay's portraits of Blanche and Alfred Knopf in his recent autobiographical book, *Inside, Looking Out*. While paying just tribute to their extraordinary and distinguished achievements in publishing, he stresses the tyrannical and arrogant uses they have made of those who have worked for them. Power may corrupt, perhaps most often does, but Helen Wolff is a shining exception to that time-tarnished yet still partly valid maxim.

I cannot resist repeating one of her infrequent stories about the frailties of others, to round out the comparison with Blanche

Knopf. One day, Helen told me, they were lunching together. Blanche was at her most imperious. She sent her Martini back because, sensitive as the princess with the pea under her mattress, she could smell in it an alien and inferior brand of vermouth. She caviled at the menu, could find nothing to suit her. Finally, the waiter turned to Helen, whose patience was almost exhausted.

"I'll have *Bratwurst* and lentils," she said. . . .

She told me once that she thinks of herself as a plain woman. Although thoroughly feminine, she makes few concessions to the traditional wiles of cosmetics and finery. She always looks elegant, quietly well dressed. There is in her features a lived-in humaneness, an admixture of gentleness with strength. And there is at times that often invoked but seldom realized "inner light" that transfigures her face, makes it radiant with some further dimension of life. I saw it so, for instance, one late afternoon at the Vineyard, when she was surrounded by her family and holding one of her grandchildren on her lap. Laughing, head thrown back, she was beautiful, and the whole gathering became golden.

She is the truly great lady of our profession.

When I began to write about women in publishing, I mentioned that there were "certain well-defined precincts" to which they are usually dispatched. What are these areas?

First, that of books for children. Here their authority has been all but absolute. Of all the heads of houses I have known at all well, only Mr. Chambers had the audacity to challenge the opinion of his editor of children's books. Nat Wartels would leave a hot session, in which he had told off everyone in sight, to become soft-spoken and deferential to Beatrice Creighton, the then children's book editor for Lothrop, Lee & Shepard. Bennett Cerf might fume over something done by his editor, but, with certain limited qualifications, she ran her show.

Of course the core of the matter lay in the fact that almost all of these men knew little or nothing about books for children. It was one field in which they had to rely, almost exclusively, on the judgment of women. A disproportionate number of them were excellent and brought in a good profit, so the obvious course was to cherish them and leave them alone. And as a matter of fact, to upset that delicate balance was to risk bringing down upon yourself a whole society, so intermeshed were the activities of children's book editors with those of librarians, teachers, reading experts, etc.

I have the only partly informed opinion that this is no longer so unquestionably true, although women do continue to dominate this realm. Walter Retan of Random House is still, so far as I know, the only male editor in chief in the field.

A second traditional role for women has been in publicity, sometimes extending over into advertising and promotion. Most characteristically, however, it has been limited to publicity, presumably because the job requires charm. To discuss publishing lists with book-review editors over lunch, to entice columnists and interviewers (whether on the air or in print) to select a given publishing house's authors for their programs and columns —these tasks require tact and intelligence, but especially charm.

Now and then some extraordinary woman brings an imaginativeness and dedication to this job. Such a one is Hilda Lindley of Harcourt Brace Jovanovich. I will gladly risk the charge of partisanship; Hilda is unique in my experience. She is never content with a routine performance; she reads, then *studies* each book on the list until she is confident that she has exhausted the different possibilities of approaches to promoting it—no matter how small the appropriation may be in a given case.

To the editor, who is accustomed to pleading with everyone who has a hand in selling and backing the books he has edited, this is exhilarating, unusually comforting. If he is himself at all perceptive, he learns quickly that behind Hilda's ready laugh and outgoing nature is a sensitive and reflective mind, a passion for her work, and a flexibility of approach. I have known other excellent people in this work, but never her equal.

Women are also to be found in the production and art department, but only rarely in charge. And that about tells the story, except of course in terms of secretaries and clerks and a very occasional woman high up in fiscal matters.

"About tells the story," in the sense that the key positions in administration, editorial work and sales are so seldom allotted to women that it almost seems safe to say never. A majority of women college graduates who are interested in publishing want to be editors. They are very likely to be disappointed.

Another qualification: almost all *copy* editors are women. (A to-be-expected variant is found in Mr. Chambers, who trained men—very well, too.) The demanding task of the copy editor is to know everything, including where to find out what she doesn't already know. She painstakingly goes over every line in the manuscript that the editor has given her, and inserts the order of consistency, correct usage and accuracy. She is held responsible for misquotations and errors of fact. She marks the manuscript for the printer, using the symbols that direct him. She—but enough.

The good copy editor is an artist of the first rank. Yet there is a tendency among all but the really informed to consider copy editing a subordinate job, actually inferior to "regular" editing. This is the grossest sort of ignorance. The kind of work Bertha Krantz, Roberta Leighton, Patricia McEldon, Lucy Wilder do is of equal or greater importance to the health of a book than that of most of the original editors.

Yet, in the hierarchy, it is not conceived of, and only rarely paid for, in these terms. And as one reviews these distinctions, it is apparent that in publishing there has been practiced widely a sort of male chauvinism, as it is now called.

As with most "male chauvinists," it has not, I believe, been maintained consciously. Rather, it has been taken for granted that women belong in certain roles and not in others. A brief anatomy of these roles reveals a tired pattern. As editors of children's books—the maternal role. As publicity directors—the seductive. As art and production workers—the appropriate concern for the decorative. As copy editors and proofreaders—properly devoting themselves to the smaller details, while leaving the imaginative flights and the large decisions to male editors.

Increasingly, one finds female "editors" in trade departments for books for adults. Many of these are "promoted" from the task of copy editing and proofreading. Some are advanced from the position called "reader"—meaning the person who reads entirely from the "slush pile" of unsolicited and almost always unwanted manuscripts. Very occasionally, a secretary becomes an editor.

But even those who attain an editorship are seldom yielded a commensurate authority. In my time at Random House, the copy editors were a very talented group, young women who, in their close editing, made a considerable difference to the final book. When I left, I proposed to Donald Klopfer that he make one of them, Mary Heathcote, a full-fledged editor. He listened to my praise of her, and decided to do it.

She was grateful. But I warned her that not so much had been accomplished as seemed to have been. She now had the title and a raise. Well and good. But she was still a woman; it would be interesting to see whether the partners would give her the same credence as her male colleagues, on the strength of whose recommendations they often approved books they hadn't read.

A couple of years later Mary answered the question by leaving Random and, in the next five or six years, going to first one, then another publishing house, finally preferring to free lance.

Outstanding women editors who achieved eminent posts? Blanche Knopf—another matter. Helen Wolff, also with a husband and with a distinguished background in Europe. And there have been a few women publishers who brought their own money into the business. Elizabeth Lawrence had a long and honored career at Harper, but I know of it only as an outsider. During the twelve years that Margaret Marshall and I both worked at HBJ, she was certainly a respected member of the department. Helen Taylor held a responsible post at that meteoric short-lived firm, William Sloane Associates; perhaps she was editor in chief. Then she went to Viking as a senior editor: one heard less and less of her. Louise Townsend Nicholl brought E. P. Dutton more editorial distinction than it had before or since, yet she was forced to retire before she wanted to.

Things are improving, but it is hard to escape the conviction that, as with black people, women are being sought in greater numbers now because in all sorts of ways and in all sorts of occupations, they are forcing men to *acknowledge* them as peers, even if they are not so *treated*. For consider the younger ones: who recognizes the names of Berenice Hoffman, Judith Jones, Dorothy Parker (no, not *that* one), Genevieve Young, as readily as those of Bob Gottlieb, Aaron Asher and Michael Korda? The men's front yields only foot by foot.

Not too surprisingly, the situation in the magazine world has been a much more open one, and for a long time. From Marianne Moore and Helen Walker on, women have regularly held key positions in magazine publishing. One reason, of course, is the number of these publications designed for women readers, yet the distinguished women who have held top posts in general magazines far outnumber their counterparts in book publishing.

Perhaps the evenest situation in the American book and magazine world is to be found in the literary agencies. Bernice Baumgarten, Mavis McIntosh, Elizabeth Otis, Mary Abbot, Carol Brandt, Patricia Myrer, Marie Rodell, Monica McCall, Lucy Kroll, Joan Daves, Cyrilly Abels, Wendy Weill, Candida Donadio, Lynn Nesbit, Phyllis Jackson, Elizabeth McKee—one could go on and on.

Reverting to publishing houses, the record is better in England. I think immediately of Ruth and Livia Gollancz, of Diana Athill, Barley Alison, Elizabeth Stockwell and others. And especially of that splendid woman, Norah Smallwood of Chatto and Windus—of whom my daughter Miranda, after staying several days in her London apartment, wrote, "She is something else!"

What does all this mean? Does it have a meaning? Perhaps it is to be found in the history of book publishing in America in this century. The slow shift from "the gentleman's profession" to the new, more vigorous, flamboyant and, in many instances, the more commercially minded breed beginning in the twenties, through the process of "going public," to the new inundation of the business by the huge conglomerates—this progression has meant that this peculiar profession-industry has always been in the hands of men (however otherwise different, each generation from the others) who conceived of women in stereotyped terms. First as ladies, then as hostesses and enchantresses, and perhaps finally as consumers, secretaries, Bunnies and integers.

An editor can rarely evaluate with accuracy the competence of another editor. He can form an opinion of that editor's taste and interests from the books he acquires for his publishing house. If they are colleagues, he can appraise another's style and judgment from presentations of books at sales conferences. But the bone and sinew of editorial work are usually displayed only when writer and editor work together. How can anyone else know how much and what that editor contributes to the final shaping of the book in question?

Editorial work includes the study of the text of a given manuscript; the attempt to grasp, with imaginative precision, the writer's over-all "intent" (including, sometimes, themes or counterpoint of which he is not consciously aware), and to establish where he has fallen short; and, finally, the give-and-take of the process of revision.

There are those who consider such work an intrusive meddling with the author's creation. Many British publishers and many British editors take this position. It has amused me that they, from Victor Gollancz to Fredric Warburg, have harangued me, among others, on the preposterousness of this practice, yet have owed many of their successes with books of American origin to the fidelity and patience of American editors.

It is true that an editor can, and sometimes does, meddle with a writer's work. The attempt to grasp another's intent, and help him fulfill it, is often bumbling and presumptuous. How, in such a task, to disentangle the editor's subjective preoccupations and emotional prejudices from his inquiry into the nature of the work at hand?

This difficulty is inherent in the act of reading. Fulfillment for any reader, whether in the traditional role of exploring and understanding the writer's *meaning,* or in the contemporary variant of responding to what the book *does* and *how* it does it—fulfillment for any reader must originate in a willingness to permit an invasion of his mind, as Georges Poulet has put it. If he does not resist, and insist upon his own critical independence, and if he does not find in the first few pages anything jarring, rasping or even threatening to his emotional equilibrium—then he will give the book he reads a real chance to establish its world. Criticism can wait.

But the editor's job is also to read critically—whether the manuscript in question is one being considered for publication, or one already accepted and in presumable need of revision. How to achieve contradictory goals?

I have done very little theorizing about this matter. But I have reconsidered what I have actually practiced. I find that my more or less instinctive procedure has been, when reading a virgin script, to let go, to allow it to invade my mind, to float on its current as much as I can, and to let response come or not come. On the other hand, when reading a manuscript under contract, delivered by the writer for publication, I become exacting, challenging. I take extensive notes; I deliberate; I measure the performance against the author's "intent" as I have construed it.

There follows a meeting with the writer, and an exchange about the proposed revisions. The editor must walk a thin line between remaining firm on changes he considers crucial and "taking over" the book. If he is really to be useful he must remember constantly that he is the party of the second part, that in this dyad he is the subordinate.* As the truism goes, it is his function to act as catalyst and as sounding board. It is not his book; he is the reader and consultant, not the writer.

Periodically, editors seem to feel the need for camaraderie. A new lunch or dinner group is formed. It is carefully explained that this is not a *club,* that there is nothing exclusive about it, just a small group of friendly people who happen to work as editors in publishing houses. It is stressed either that this provides a great chance for shoptalk, or that one mustn't fear that one will have to talk shop.

I first frequented such a group in the late forties. I entered publishing in the fall of 1945 and in a year or so was invited to "a monthly lunch group." I have forgotten details, but these gatherings, held in the pleasant Wine Room upstairs in Pierre's Restaurant on East Fifty-second Street, were chaired by John Farrar. The group was small; I believe I was the seventh to join. It included Helen Everett, now dead; Mark Saxton, now with Gambit in Boston; Robert Giroux, now a partner of Farrar,

---

* In this connection, I was recently amused to read that Eugene McCarthy, considering an editorial job with Simon and Schuster, was quoted as saying, "It [being an editor] may be an escape that won't be satisfying, but anyway I may try it. It's a little like being God. You know you can say to the writer, as God said to Adam, there's the earth, now name all the things in it—put it in writing, and I'll decide whether you've done well or not." (New York *Times,* October 14, 1972)

Straus & Giroux; Harold Strauss of Knopf; and Marshall Best of the Viking Press. Others who joined us shortly were, I believe, Ken McCormick of Doubleday and Tom Wilson, back from the wars and soon to become the distinguished director of the Harvard University Press.

I was immensely flattered at the invitation. For years I had naïvely dreamed of entering publishing, but the only way I had "entered" was by having the first four novels I had written rejected by a majority of the publishers in the country. And now, to be sitting in this group, a member, under the genial leadership of John Farrar, awed me.

Not for long, because awe was not relevant to this happy fellowship. It is customary when old, etc. . . . But like most clichés, this is not untrue. I do feel a warm and sentimental glow, remembering those lunches. The talk was spontaneous and good, the food excellent, and Pierre himself announced the menus in his mock magnificent style. He would say such things as "Then we have the *ragoût de boeuf* Pierre, which is delicious. It contains chunks of seasoned beef, left over from last week's prime ribs. Or perhaps you would prefer the bouillabaisse. Particularly tasty. The chef and waiters stand in a circle, at equal distances from a large bowl set in the center of a table, scrape the remnants from last evening's plates, and toss them into the bowl. Not the plates."

It can't be written properly. I cannot imitate Pierre's courtly manner and the rich, unFrenchlike rolling of his *r*s.

The talk was spontaneous, I said. And it was, though not easily so, since John Farrar liked to prepare a topic for discussion—some aspect of editorial work. He relished such occasions and such a ritual. It was a little as though we were enacting the Symposium in modern dress. (There were a few other differences, too.)

At first, everyone would defer to him, and make a contribution or two on the appointed subject. But gradually, the impact of several cocktails and the general sense of well-being would overcome the strictures of a formal theme, and the talk would range broadly from publishing gossip to the state of the nation and to arguments about the merits of various writers.

John seemed to me a strange but very likable man. His

mannerisms were delicate, confidential, his intonation alternately placating and complacent. There was something hieratic about him. Yet he also was capable of shy, generous impulses, rarely spontaneous kindnesses.

He was always championing younger men and sponsoring newcomers to our world. This explained to me my own admission to the group. But it also led before long to many more admissions, until the group and its meetings became unwieldy. Even before it was stretched to that extent, John was going through ordeals about which I know nothing, and patently losing his precarious hold on himself. There was one lunch at which he suddenly stood up and launched a speech, in which he quite superfluously denied being a Communist and in a loud voice denounced the conspiracy against him.

I found him a tragic man. After a brilliant stay at Yale, he had edited the best literary magazine in my time, *The Bookman*. He became a partner of Farrar and Rinehart, and later a founding partner of the firm now known as Farrar, Straus & Giroux, of which he remains chairman of the board. I have not seen him in years, but I hope and believe that he has reached some serene plateau.

Helen Everett contributed a special *élan* to the group. The only woman, she enjoyed our admiration, as we enjoyed her wit and grace. Widowed early (her husband had been an executive officer of Little, Brown), she had carried on both in book and magazine editing, with considerable success. There was an underlying sadness to her, but in our company she was charming and gay.

I found Best, Strauss, Giroux and Saxton interesting, each in his own idiom. Mark Saxton, fair and tall, a handsome man, was at once shy and possessed of great nervous energy, which would now and again break through his reticence. Both he and Marshall Best seemed to me patricians. I think I was once garrulous enough to tell Marshall that his head should be on a Roman coin, to which he wryly replied that he would like to keep it on his neck. An intensely serious man, he has always escaped solemnity. Urbane, thoughtful, quiet, he is, I believe, one of our best.

I found it difficult to talk to Harold Strauss; we seemed to miss each other in an exchange. But I enjoyed listening to him and watching him hold forth. A most articulate man, he came to a discussion with a peculiar eagerness, and as he listened to someone else, one could sense the urgency of his need to cut in, the tension under which he restrained himself. Then a rush of words, forceful, pertinent, and yet somehow, to me, delivered from an oblique angle, so that I caught myself tilting the head of my mind, trying to right the focus for myself.

The Wine Room group still exists, but I think there must be sixty or seventy members. Over the years other groups have come together and disbanded, and I even had a hand in starting one, with Mike Bessie. This, a dinner group, included Erskine, Ken McCormick, Giroux, Burroughs Mitchell, Denver Lindley, George Brockway, Tom Wilson, Evan Thomas, Walter Bradbury of Doubleday and Paul Brooks of Houghton Mifflin.

A word about several of them. Ken McCormick has been editor in chief at Doubleday since the Civil War.* He has made it a lifetime job. Immensely likable, he has an unmatched earnestness of manner that sometimes puts off people who remember the young folks' minister in their childhood Sunday school. But he is friendly, decent, a puzzler about life, I think, who hides his philosophical questions under a hearty good-fellow exterior. And he has been a dedicated and effective worker in the cause of publishing, books and reading.

Denver Lindley, a Scot Highlander, is a man who has always appealed to me. Tall and thin, he looks austere, a bit Grant Woodish. He is another whose passionate nature is held in, but hinted at by the rigidity of his carriage. A gentleman, he has been known to play Hotspur on occasion, with resultant fireworks. He has done brilliant translations of Mann's *The Confessions of Felix Krull* and Remarque's *The Black Obelisk*. He has won the respect and affection of the writers he has worked with.

Tom Wilson, a Southerner, died of a heart attack several years ago. As someone in publishing said of him, "We have lost one of our best statesmen." Tall, gracious, with an infectious laugh, he was always good company. And he was of that rare breed: those who are both good editors and good publishers.

* Only recently he has retired to a post as consulting editor.

312

Your basically editorial editor rarely makes a good publisher; your professional publishing man is apt to be uninspired, though sound in a business sense, in his selection of books and in his work with authors.

Tom could do both these things, and more, too. His grave, measured voice, with its Southern mellifluousness, was listened to with respect at the industry meetings, whether that of the American Book Publishers' Council or of the American Association of University Presses.

Our acquaintance dated from 1940 or 1941, when I was teaching in Cleveland and, with two associates, preparing an anthology for freshmen for Reynal and Hitchcock, whose college editor Tom was. Shortly thereafter, he became director of the University of North Carolina Press. When he left there for Harvard, he recommended me as his successor, which pleased me although I did not accept.

In 1960 or '61, we at the new firm of Atheneum decided that the only way we could build with dispatch a paperback list was to persuade the Harvard, Princeton and Stanford presses to give us first chance to issue the paper editions of their hard-cover books, in return for giving them a regular outlet. I made the journey to Cambridge, where Tom listened with his usual grave courtesy, and then acted in his usual decisive way. The deal was completed rapidly.

Tom's and my friendship was the sort that meant, however infrequently we saw each other, we immediately resumed a sort of perpetual dialogue. He had a stylish mind. Its agility made one forget his physical massiveness. And he was persuasive. He even persuaded me to regress to insisting on an olive in my Martini.

A peculiar irony attended us in those last years. I had been at Harcourt only a short time when William Jovanovich's book, *Now, Barabbas,* was published by Harper & Row. Tom was chosen to review it in the New York *Times,* and he wrote a mixed review, with some praise, but expressing disappointment, as I remember it, that Bill hadn't grappled with more of the central publishing problems in the United States.

Bill fired up, and there was a spirited exchange of letters. Bill thought that Tom was indulging that frequent vice of reviewers:

313

asking of the writer the kind of book he had no intention of writing. He found Tom either obtuse or willful in saying that the essays on Milovan Djilas were not relevant to the concerns of writing, publishing and reading.

Hostilities were terminated, but the breach wasn't healed. As a result, when I attended, with Bill, the international publishers' meeting in Washington not long after, I had the temporarily sad experience of seeing Tom, as Bill and I approached the group he was with, turn away, without even a greeting.

I know that mostly he did not want to embarrass me, and wrote him so. Then, not long after, he was newly troubled over a matter that concerned me.

A month before my departure from Atheneum in 1964, Tom got wind of developments, and paid me a visit on Chappaquiddick Island to hear the story. We sat up high on the widow's walk of the house, and talked long, looking out at the incredible view of ocean, sound and bay. Within the next year Bessie and Knopf would want a replacement for me at Atheneum, although not as a partner. Tom had just retired at Harvard, and they sought him out.

The first word I had of all this was from Tom. The envelope contained a formal announcement of his joining Atheneum (one not yet released), across which he had scribbled in a fierce hand that he knew what they had done to me, but that he didn't want to retire, and this was his chance to "go on." He hoped that this would make no difference between us.

It did not. We continued to meet from time to time for lunch. The last of these lunches was two weeks before his sudden death. I remember asking him how it was going at Atheneum. He said, "All right," then hesitated and added that it was very hard, once you had held complete authority at one place, to defer to others for final decisions. Afterward, I watched him walk down the street, jaunty beret and brisk, powerful strides, until he was out of sight. . . .

One goes on and on, not always with sadness. Ben Huebsch, after Perkins the senior editor of true distinction, first with his own firm, then and finally with the Viking Press, was the editor of James Joyce and countless others. Ben of the eager eyes and bubbling voice, over whose shoulders lay an invisible prayer shawl—the nearest thing to a saint I found among editors, yet such a joyous saint. I shall never forget a strange Publishers' Lunch Club Christmas party. The theme of the program was dirty stories—for Christmas! And Ben had been appointed to tell one of them. I don't remember the story, but it went on for some time, was wistfully, mutedly funny. When Ben finished and sat down, someone called out, "But, Ben, what's dirty about it?"

He clasped his hands to his head in mock distress.

There was Pat Covici, John Steinbeck's beloved editor, who also did his final work at Viking. I came to know him because my agent, Mavis McIntosh, heard that Viking was looking for someone to do an Elizabethan reader in their Portable series. Urged by her, I wrote a table of contents for one, and Pat chose mine among those submitted by several competitors.

When I went to see him, I found a likable, inquisitive, grizzled man somewhat my senior, who searched my face with bright eyes incontestably birdlike. He appraised me; I heard later he thought me "a nice professor."

"Listen, do you know why I chose yours?" he asked. "Nobody's ever heard of you, and Mark Van Doren submitted a synopsis, too. But yours is really fresh. I don't know a quarter of the selections you listed. They must be good. But listen, I won't take it unless you include a poem by Nicholas Breton—something about 'Lullaby, babe.' "

The earnestness. The poem was included. Later, someone said, "Pat Covici? He's a Rumanian horse thief." Lullaby. Cabbages and kings.

Before concluding the roll call, I must mention one more editor whose judgment I have been privileged to observe. Dan Wickenden is extraordinary. Two ways. A novelist himself, who has not written much since he went into editorial work, he has a most sensitive—nose? feel?—for the identifying distinctions of different authentic talents. He and I have happened to read the same manuscript in a number of cases, including one by my daughter, whom he did not know to be my daughter, and his evaluation was always precise, just, thoughtful.

The second way? An unusual gift for kindness that never

degenerates into condescension or sentimentality. A sure touch, born of understanding and sympathy. A rare man. . . .

All these people. All these editors. I find myself wondering what I am reaching for, in setting down in brief their portraits. Some archetype? If so, these pages prove failure; I can find no mean or norm in those I have described. Indeed, their diversity is as great as that to be found in any professional group—perhaps greater.

And perhaps their only sure similarities are ones sufficiently simple and clear-cut to make describing them superfluous. But I will risk the obvious. First, a genuine love of books. The most purely literary editor will on occasion become fiercely commercial, as he turns the pages of a manuscript and visions of sugar-plums dance in his head. But day in and year out, his richest excitement and his surest pleasure will be instead to read a script that he finds good: strong in wisdom, illuminating of the human experience, possessed of the gift of style—that sureness with words that dazzles or satisfies through the unusual juxtaposition of the usual. I find the true editor a votary of a sort—his creed that of the word and the book.

Another quality that I am sure is shared by every good editor is a belief in his own judgment, his own taste. I do not mean a fatuous egotism. Nor do I mean that any of these men is free from self-doubts and periods of indecisiveness. But it has been my experience that able editors decide for themselves the value of a given work, aware that sometimes the consensus may go against them, but convinced that this is the only way to come to grips with a manuscript, and the only way to remain fresh in this work.

Those I have known who freely declared that they had an especial talent for sniffing the wind and sensing the present predilections of the great Public, that putative amorphous They, the book readers of America—those have not impressed me. Those who perpetually look elsewhere for guidance eventually find they are turning to figments of their imaginations.

True, there are subjects that seem consistently to appeal to many readers. (Here one had better leave fiction alone.) Nature, sexual behavior, outstanding public figures, doctors and medicine, food and health, inspirational books—one could go on and on. And there have been and are fashions—for mountain climbing, the twenties, World War I, etc. But for the editor who will build his list for the most part of the enduring staples of literature—fiction, biography, memoirs, history, essays and belles-lettres (with an occasional wistful bow to poetry)—for such an editor the choice must be made on his own. It sometimes becomes a lonely activity. Then it is well to remember how much lonelier the writer's work is.

I have often been asked, as I suppose all editors have been, "How do you select a book?" It has been this frequent curiosity that has led me from time to time to study the process. But I have come up only with two rather simple guidelines.

I have taught myself to ask the question, "How much do I want to turn the next page?" Sometimes the answer is easy, sometimes not. When it isn't, I decide that some worry, ailment, distraction or preoccupation may be blocking my receptiveness. Then I do something else for a half hour. On my return to the manuscript, I usually need to read no more than a page or two before I feel sure.

If the verdict is negative, I then ask myself a battery of questions about the possible ways in which this script is unsatisfactory to me, whether it may not have redeeming qualities (however unappealing to me) that offset those I find dull or superficial or heavy. I am apt, I think, to give such a book too much "the benefit of the doubt" and to read on long past the point at which I really know I will not make an offer for it. It is a foolish waste of time and energy.

Less foolish, if only because there is some enjoyment to it, is reading through a bad book simply because something about it intrigues one. It may be atrociously written, or preposterously sexy or predatory, or sensationally plotted: whatever pulls you on, groaning and remonstrating with yourself, must come from some perverse vitality in the script.

Why not take it then? Won't other readers have similar experiences? It is at this point that my second guideline proves helpful. Whenever possible, I wait about two weeks before making my final decision about a script I have read. I then ask myself: what's left? The bad but readable has always faded out.

The book I have felt confident I would eventually take usually is there—as clearly as just after reading it. But there are exceptions.

There are also talents so outstanding that no delay is necessary or even defensible. I signed William Styron after reading twenty typewritten pages of what became *Lie Down in Darkness*. . . .

One day at Atheneum, a manuscript came in, accompanied by a brief note from Ivan von Auw of the Harold Ober agency. Its substance? "Little, Brown-Atlantic and Knopf have turned this down. I think it's fine."

I was curious. I respected those two houses, but I also respected Ivan. We had at that time a small bedroom (the one in which I set the mattress on fire) on the fourth floor of the brownstone on Thirty-eighth Street, and I was spending the night there. I took the script up with me about ten o'clock. I read it through—until 3:00 A.M. In the morning I astonished Ivan by calling him and telling him we wanted to publish it. It was a first novel, *The Morning and the Evening*, by Joan Williams. It later won the John P. Marquand Award for the best first novel of the year.

Such experiences are rare. But I find them always to be trusted, and my worst misses have happened when I have delayed too long and reversed a strong initial experience. While with Bobbs-Merrill, I was reading at home one day. Someone in the family would come into my study every hour or so and say, "You're still laughing? It must be wonderful."

Yet for reasons I can't recall (probably I don't want to), I procrastinated. I had several colleagues at Bobbs read it; they did not find it as funny as I did. Finally Ross Baker, the director of the New York office, refused to read it. "I don't need to," he said. "You usually know and trust your own mind. If you're so uncertain, I don't need to read it. Let's turn it down."

It was *No Time for Sergeants*, by Mac Hyman. . . .

Trust your own mind. For an editor, there is another commandment equally important. Tell the truth. Forever a middleman, caught between his loyalty to his authors and to his company, the editor must temper his truthtelling with some tact and some reticence. Yet better he should be blunt and even rude than a truth-shader, to say nothing of a liar. Your honest opinion about the chances of a given book, whether you are talking to its author or to your employer, is crucial. I have known an editor to become so entangled in the nets of his own deceits, reassuring promises and contradictory statements that he eventually looked like Laocoön.

At bottom the motivating drive must be, is, fear, insecurity. If there is little trust in self, in one's own judgment, it is inevitable that one overreassure others, hoping blindly that one's prophecies will actualize. It is one form of covering one's head and waiting for disaster to go away.

Why so much fear? Book publishing does not compare, in terms of summary and mass hirings and firings, with advertising or television or the movies. But a fair share of it goes on; outsiders are always asking, "Why do editors keep changing houses?" Writers complain, "By the time I finish a book, my editor has always left my publishing house."

This migration has various causes: personality differences, laziness, insubordination, the failure to build an impressive list. But only one major one: the failure to produce a good share of the year's profit. I am sure that at least two-thirds of the dismissals of editors happen because the man in question has not been able to acquire books that sell well.

This is the nub of the *editorial* editor's problem. Being a *bookman,* he is eager to develop a list of genuine distinction. The other sort of editor I have described briefly I would call a producer. He seeks, finds and publishes books largely on the basis of their probable commercial success, estimated on past records, subject matter and current fashions.

But the bookman won't do it that way. Perhaps he *can't.* At any rate, if he is to survive and continue his sort of work, then he must know his own mind, trust his own judgment. And he must stand and deliver, whether to writer or to employer or to colleagues, the truth as he knows it. He must seek that happy kind of vulnerability that is substantially fearless, because it has left nothing hidden.

Throughout the years that this book covers, Mary and I have shared friendship with Jerry and Rees Mason. In New York, in Connecticut and on Martha's Vineyard, we have spent many warm and happy hours together. Jerry and I have also worked together in publishing. Long ago, he initiated Maco Books, a series that included books on dogs, horses, hunting, fishing, cooking—on and on. With his colleagues and an expert in whichever field, he would produce a complete book, then turn it over to a traditional publisher for distribution. For a while Bobbs-Merrill had the exclusive distribution of Maco Books, then Random House.

Thereafter Jerry founded the Ridge Press, and has since produced a great many diversified books, most of which have illustrated his conviction that a message is best conveyed in our time through the wedding of picture and text. (He feels that most publishers are living in the nineteenth century.) He has continued to produce complete books, but for distribution he turns now to one publisher, now to another—in each case, to the one he believes most competent to sell the book in question.

The firms I've worked for—and I—have gained a good deal through association with Jerry—and one, Random House, would have gained a great deal more had I been able to persuade one of the partners to walk with me four blocks to take a look at the *Family of Man* exhibition. The famous and beautiful book made from this collection, and eventually published by Simon and Schuster, Jerry had previously offered to Random House and me.

At any rate, it's been a long association and a close friendship. So when Jerry, having heard that I was working on this book, asked to read some of the manuscript, I was happy to turn it over to him.

Pitched halfway between indignation and dismay, his voice rattled the telephone.

"I think it's terrible," he said. "Who wants to read about all those publishing people? I know them, for Christ's sake. It's just reporting. And your tribute to ———, why, it's like a piece of public relations. I thought you were going to write your auto-biography, memoirs—I don't care what you call it, but give us something of yourself, your thoughts, your *real* experience."

Well. I rocked on my heels for a few days. Jerry called again: "I mean an inner book."

Myself, my thoughts, my *real* experience . . . I think they're there—here. Only confined to my professional life, revealed through my report on it. Such has been my intention ever since Bill Jovanovich persuaded me to write this book.

So I share only one of Jerry's doubts: who wants to read this book? who wants to read about my encounters with these people?

I don't know. But my thinking, or rationalization, runs like this. I have known, however fleetingly in many cases, a multiplicity of people who have left their mark on our literary, cultural and intellectual history. They are certainly worth writing about; surely some will find them worth reading about.

Why use the form of portraits, profiles, vignettes and anecdotes? Because that is my way—derivative from my lifelong infatuation with people, people, people . . . faces, faces, faces. . . .

Why include stories that show people at a disadvantage, naked in fury or stealth, in selfishness or greed, in fear or deviousness? Because these are bone and sinew, tendon and blood of us all—of the human animal, along with the blessed redeeming things.

Why tell? Why tell? Why tell at all? Because I am a teller. I experience and I tell about it. Others tell in paint or brick or wood or stone or music, I in words. It is my last, my only means of expressing my vision of some aspects of what it means to be human.

Why explain now, in this passage? Because I have been reliving my life experience in publishing, and now I want to examine the way in which I have recorded it. I write always to find out.

One of my two idols (the other belongs to almost everybody) is Michel de Montaigne. In his essay "On Repentance," he writes, "Authors communicate with the people by some special extrinsic mark; I am the first to do so by my entire being, as Michel de Montaigne, not as a grammarian or a poet or a jurist. If the world complains that I speak too much of myself, I complain that it does not even think of itself."

I want to come to grips with my life, with my self. Ever since God tapped me on the shoulder with an admonitory finger, six years ago, that has been my obsession. Having been "promoted from immortality to mortality," and already a full-fledged member of the geriatric community, I have to ask myself the inevitable and universal questions: What has it all meant? Has it meant? Why? Or why not?

Someday, I may write the book Jerry Mason wanted to read. But for perspective I chose, first and now, to look outward, fully aware that the way I looked would be self-revealing and that I could hardly display others as I see them without displaying myself also.

So the montage has rolled on, is still rolling. I see Padraic Colum, Paddy of the inexhaustible sweetness, sitting in his shirt sleeves at a table in a Woods Hole restaurant, while all around him, on chairs or on the floor—young people. . . . I see Katrin Lamon (Martha Albrand to the world) at a lunch table—gallant explorer of life, staunch friend. . . . David Garnett's ruddy, smiling face under a blue beret . . . Maurice Sterne, fighting off cancer of the bone for nine years while he finished his memoirs. I hear him call me back, that last visit, to kiss me good-by. Not a word . . . Friends, with whom one may share silences as well as words: Gus Day, Rom Linney, Don Frame, Evelyn Eaton, Ken Keniston, Sigrid de Lima, Ed Hodge, Bob Lumiansky . . . and hear the chuckle of that unlikely and delightful man, Aaron Sussman—an intellectual advertising agent! . . . I see the broad grin of Arnold Zimmerman, and hear the patient exhaustion in his voice over my utter inability to understand tax returns . . . and see again the marvelous medieval court jester face of Jay Williams, experience again the generosity of his companionship.

Stanley Burnshaw at croquet, face alight and mallet high, after one of those incredible long shots . . . Luciano Rebay and Phil Hallie, insouciant duo on a long weekend of walking, canoeing, poker and beverages, vying for chef of the week—*ciao*, Luciano, *ciao*, Filippo . . . Peter Boynton, that vivid spirit, raising the first Martini in a silent toast to living . . . Edmund Wilson gleefully spraying the wash-basin mirror with his urine, in derision of someone's pompous statement . . . Wilson, snubbing me coldly at Wesleyan cocktails by denying he knew me, then at dinner crying out, "Oh, I say, Haydn, I remember you now!" while spewing *Sauerbraten* over the two men between us . . . Wilson enraged at the attenuated abstractions of a phenomenologist, shouting out, "Bullshit and poppycock."

People. Faces. I come to Henry Beetle Hough, that strong and gentle man who, with his wife Elizabeth, ran the *Vineyard Gazette* for many years, and brought joy, truth and edification to our island. The champion of birds and trees and dogs, the lover and defender of the whole continent of nature, a man who cherishes the traditional and welcomes the radical, who has made of his whole life a dedication to justice and freedom. Who writes quiet wise novels and chronicles made, as though carved in stone, to last.

Yet with so wry a humor, so genuine a humility, that he is incapable of even infinitesimal falseness or self-aggrandizement. The man who, asked by an envious acquaintance if he was going to let Haydn rent his coveted house, Fish Hook (the end of the line), for the rest of his life, replied, "Oh, I should think a bit longer than that."

Yes, to Henry Hough, that good and faithful servant of the Lord, who has overcome the world, and to all the Houghs: George, that "master of the quiet days," and Clara, bright questioner and happily chiding critic, full of the juices of life—and to all their clan. And to the legendary father of that clan and to his house with all the great trees surf-sighing in the evening wind, amen.

And behind that search outward that also turns inward, I wonder about the weather of mortality. I sense a tie between commitment and mortality—between knowing really who you are and *being* that you—and accepting the knowledge of your own eventual death.

I think that the fear of not having lived has a great deal to do with our hidden, masked terror of death. And one has not, I submit, fully lived if he has not attained a proximate knowledge of his own character.

And that leads to another question. Is self-knowledge accessible to the contemporary person I am tempted to call Spastic Man? Spastic, because with the exception of single, inconclusive encounters, I have met no live human being without tensions, conflicts and tics—whether visible or clearly implied. I have found no one at peace, at rest—no one in sustained equilibrium. Most of the people I have known at all well have carried so heavy a cargo of these tensions that I do not see how we survive the days of our years.

But I specified a *live* human being because it is clear to me that many, perhaps most, people are not alive in the sense in which I am using the word, and hence may give the illusion of calm. Alive? That is: fully aware of the civil wars within oneself, trying to deal with them and those animal compulsions we all share, seeking (because for him, whichever individual, this is what it means to be a human being) as much self-knowledge as one can absorb and use toward fulfillment.

One can often recognize those who have given up the battle. Having found their conflicts, their impulses in two or more directions at once, unbearable, they have withdrawn from the participation that I have been describing. Their eyes are opaque, there is a special air of coolness, remoteness, about them; they are the often hypothesized mechanical men of the future, thinking but not being able to identify—or to identify with—their own feelings. These are to me the most obviously defeated. And ironically, their distance often enables them to be very objective and wise about all but their own problems.

But there are other sorts of people who have also given up the search, and unless you come to know them quite well you would think them among the happiest of mortals. There is, for instance, the self-distracter, who skims merrily along the surface of life like a hummingbird or a dragonfly.

He* distracts himself to keep, on the one hand, from being aware of the tensions that are inevitable for the *live* man,† and to keep from looking, unblinking, into the depths of self—his origins and his potentialities. Eventually novelty becomes the goal of his life. He must move from place to place, from occupation to occupation, always in search of the new.

But the person who most successfully evades the whole problem I think of as the egoist, defined by *Webster's New International* (in that traditionally helpful way of dictionaries) as one given overmuch to egoism. Egoism, however, *is* defined—as "excessive love and thought of self; the habit of regarding oneself

* This pronoun, here and hereafter, is defensively followed, not inadvertently. Do you want me to say she/he or he/she?
† Likewise.

as the center of every interest." The egoist, then, smothers our problems. He is, almost to the point of solipsism, a successful narcissist. He is seldom aggressive or boastful, but he is so fully in love with, absorbed in, himself that whenever someone else is really hostile to him or even indifferent, he either does not recognize it, or is astonished. Most of the time he unconsciously takes it for granted that everyone else is enjoying him as much as he enjoys himself. Indeeed, he is not always sure that there *is* anyone else—until he needs reassurance, as he does desperately from time to time. Cut off his source of supply then, and he is lost, trapped, suicidal. . . . There are other varieties of the unalive, but these must suffice for now.

But who then is the *live* person? He whom I would term the conscious person, the person who is determined to *find out* (I cannot stress enough the centrality of those simple words) ; to endure as best he can the pain of being a man or woman; to discover its complementary joy; to live fully his own experience.

Easy to say, hard to come by. There are several great passages in Bergson's *Creative Mind,* as majestic to me as the best of Lucretius or Dante, and they are pertinent to what I am trying to say:

But nowhere is the substantiality of change so visible, so palpable as in the domain of the inner life. Difficulties and contradictions of every kind to which the theories of personality have led come from our having imagined, on the one hand, a series of distinct psychological states, each one invariable, which would produce the variations of the ego by their very succession, and on the other hand an ego, no less invariable, which would serve as support for them. How could this unity and this multiplicity meet? . . .

The truth is that there is neither a rigid, immovable substratum nor distinct states passing over it like actors on a stage. There is simply the continuous melody of inner life—a melody which is going on and will go on, indivisible, from the beginning to the end of our conscious existence. Our personality is precisely that. . . . [Yet] we have no interest in listening to the uninterrupted humming of life's depths.

The problem is to learn how to get in there to look and to listen, and then come out into the external world—how to go back in again and come out again. A cycle of renewal. The other day someone said to me that he was interested only in people who had looked in, had been appalled and had forgiven themselves in order to get on with life. But I think he is wrong. Such an act of forgiving is too likely to be a tipping of the hat in polite acknowledgment and a turning away with no intention of exploring again. It is not so easy to forgive the appalling, especially if one finds it in *oneself*. I think instead that one must, to stay within the borders of distinctively human life, and to be fully alive—one must, with whatever Pascalian vertigo, look back down into that murky broth of self again and again, not to forgive but to understand, which will perhaps, paradoxically, lead eventually to genuine self-forgiveness. One must, in short, invoke that darkness, listen and record—and then go out, to see the stars again.

Montaigne was fully aware of all this long, long ago. I have learned more from him than from contemporary psychologists. Morality, he believed, depends chiefly on psychology, on learning what we are and what we may justly expect or hope to be, and how we can implement this hope. Moreover, he was very conversant in his own way with man's animal origins and nature. "It is still man we are dealing with," he says in the essay called "The Art of Discussion," and "his condition is amazingly physical." From the earliest essays he stresses the value of the study of self.

We must probe the inside and discover what springs set man in motion. . . . I who spy on myself [most] closely, who have my eyes incessantly intent on myself, as one who has not much business elsewhere—I would hardly dare tell of the vanity and weaknesses that I find in myself. . . . Others always go elsewhere, if they stop to think about it; they always go forward; as for me, I roll about in myself. This capacity for sifting truth . . . I owe principally to myself.

The central importance of self-study for Montaigne is that it teaches us to *live*. He approves Socrates' view that, without this, all other knowledge is a waste of time. "I make no account," he writes, "of the goods that I have been unable to employ in the service of my life. . . . I have put all my efforts into forming my life. That is my trade and my work."

Montaigne is almost always very clear. In forming what he calls his *judgment,* he is honest and shrewd. He comes, indeed, to a great deal of self-knowledge, but he stops short—for that is *his* nature—of those depths of feeling that are so rare for most of us, so hard to describe or define, and yet are to anyone who has ever experienced them the established source of the energy of his life and the nearest, in my opinion, that man may come to a true *celebration* of life.

These are perhaps religious depths, or at least so interpreted throughout history by seers and priests and those we call visionaries.

Mysticism, you may say. True, if you will, but not the most familiar sort—rather a physical mysticism. Its most superficial level for me is discovering that my body puns. I learned this through having at different times a stiff neck, blood in my eyes, nausea, and a weakness in my knee which made me limp. When I caught the pun, in each case the symptom disappeared within a short time. But in this dialogue, to which, I find, very few people attend, one sometimes suffers considerable pain. One had best listen well or be unaware of the whole business. This fact came to me most clearly when I had an infection of the middle ear that didn't respond to this sort of exorcism.

It is probably arbitrary to divide the human world into two camps, those of the dry well and those of the full well. But something like this is part of my experience. After my first (and late) encounter with an unreasoned sense of my own identity, my separateness, and at the same time my interconnection with all other living, growing things, the words "the wet green world" kept recurring in my mind and I felt an exuberance, a joy in life wholly alien to any previous experience. Where had I been all those years? In some sterile clinic, I told myself. I could almost smell its disinfectant, antiseptic corridors, see its barren white-painted rooms, empty of all life, filled with the odors of medication and preservation.

This was true, but in another sense I had been in the Deep Freeze. My flesh had never been informed of me, my heart had beaten like a clock, the fluid in my veins had been as static, as glass-encased as though captive in a test tube.

But now life moved, raced, echoed through me. I could feel hatreds, jealousies, intolerance, self-pitying complaints, falling off me like dried, flaked skin. There was oil in the new skin that lay beneath. . . .

Did it last? No. But it comes back now and then.

Shakespeare, Dostoevsky, Goethe knew and wrote of this experience—far beyond my capacities. I think of it (with man added) as Darwin's tangled bank.

Bergson has described this experience admirably:

Thanks to philosophy, all things acquire depth—more than depth, something like a fourth dimension, which permits anterior perceptions to remain bound up with present perceptions, and the immediate future itself to become partly outlined in the present. Reality no longer appears then in the static state, in its manner of being; it affirms itself dynamically, in the continuity and variability of its tendency. What was immobile and frozen in our perception is warmed and set in motion. Everything comes to life around us, everything is revivified in us. A great impulse carries being and things along. We feel ourselves uplifted, carried away, borne along by it. We are more fully alive and this increase of life brings with it the conviction that grave philosophical enigmas can be resolved, or even perhaps that they need not be raised, since they arise from a frozen vision of the real and are only the translation, in terms of thought, of a certain artificial weakening of our vitality.

And Matthew Arnold:

A bolt is shot back somewhere in our breast,
And a lost pulse of feeling stirs again.
The eye sinks inward, and the heart lies plain,
And what we mean, we say, and what we would, we know.
A man becomes aware of his life's flow,
And hears its winding murmur; and he sees
The meadows where it glides, the sun, the breeze. . . .

And then he thinks he knows
The hills where his life rose,
And the sea where it goes.

So much for the source, the forces of renewal. What about the conduct of life? Surely a different matter. Well, all distinctively *lived* life is commitment. This frequently, when carried out in practice, is like riding one of those jolting machines intended to make one lose excessive flesh. But to be fully or even mostly engaged in the rough-and-tumble, the push-and-pull of life, is to be vulnerable.

And all around us we find people in masks and armor. I want

to distinguish between the social mask (there is, after all, no need to be intimate with everyone, or to tell everything you know) and the self-mask, the product of long years of attrition. Sometimes, after a period spent with a person whose mask (in this sense) is so old that it is cracked, I think of him afterward as alone and tugging desperately to remove it, only to find that it's stuck forever.

Somewhere along in the thirties of every life, at the latest, both Orwell and Camus have said in their different ways, each of us begins to acquire the face he deserves. If one wears the mask or masks perpetually, is there only a blankness under them?

The masked person leads a life of paranoiac (however dulled) strategy and maneuver. What will so-and-so think of him? How can he get his own way without appearing to do so? How can he keep Jones from learning how insecure he really is? But deeper than these are all the moves he makes to avoid the force of the direct impact of other personalities. I have known many people, any one of whom so departmentalized his images of himself, or so alternated his masks—like wigs—that whenever there were at the same time two or three other people with him, toward each of whom he was accustomed to present a particular different mask, these juxtapositions threw him into a panic close to hysteria.

We cannot regain our prelapsarian innocence, but it is possible to have a sufficient acquaintance with oneself, to have risked a sufficient exposure of that self to others, that one may feel oneself, however complex and divided, still at least raggedly *one* in the midst of many. Life as strategy and maneuver is ultimately terrifying; the engaged and vulnerable life is full of pain, but ultimately fulfilling, the practice of a genuinely humanistic ethic.

What are some of the inner conditions that one must learn to live with to attain any considerable share of that fulfillment?

One I am sure of is to accept what I think of as our mixed motivation—to be honest about it and to accept it. By mixed motivation I mean that we may often, perhaps must always, be simultaneously motivated by self-serving and by helping or caring for others.

Consider generosity and the need to be liked or even loved. Take the desire for complete honesty, and exhibitionism; or self-denial in the interest of something beyond self, and self-effacement. I do not mean that there is no difference between the two elements in each of these pairs. To the contrary. But I doubt if we can disentangle each from the other in many cases, nor do I believe it worth the effort. What I think is important is to understand that, even in what seems to be the noblest, or the worst, of acts, there must be some ambiguity of motivation.

To feel that one's motives are regularly and exclusively altruistic is to believe oneself other than human. To believe that one is exclusively motivated by self-interest (consider the self-destructive tendencies, the predatory animal rending himself) and to be ashamed of that self-interest is futile and debilitating. . . .

I have spoken of the sometimes desperate need to learn to balance one's tensions. I dream of peace, of some ultimate tranquility, but I know that I shall never find it: that is not within the reach of most of us. Indeed, when one considers the strength and ferocity of some of our compulsive drives, one might think of each of us as winding himself up early in the morning, to follow the day's prescribed round.

There is no aspect of this compulsiveness that so discourages me in myself as my trivial and rigid habits of tidiness—those repetitive cycles of doing small and necessary but unimportant chores in exactly the same order that I have done them before. If this were efficiency, I could accept it; but it is not. Frequently, it takes me longer than if I performed them in a casual and unpremeditated way.

A further and more devastating version occurs when one discovers oneself re-enacting an old drama with a new person or persons—ones for whom the plot is not appropriate. Do we ever have done with our mothers and fathers and brothers and sisters? Sometimes I think the only proper definition of neuroticism is the failure of effective memory, the inability to recognize these repetitions and deal with them.

Finally, however, we come to those larger and most frightening compulsions. Let's use the old names: covetousness, lust, wrath and pride. Are these instinctual? pre-human-history in origin? I do not know, but I suggest that most unjustified anger comes from irrational claims we make on others and are not granted. I think of an experience of some years ago. Seated in a train, I was reading a morning newspaper. Dwight Eisenhower (not yet president) had been given some extraordinary citation and decoration. The stock market was up, my favorite team had won yesterday's baseball game, a book that I had a hand in publishing had made the best-seller list. There was a prediction of continued sunny, pleasant weather. All this—but I found that I had become irritable, and now my irritability was mounting into a savage fury. And yet only a few minutes before, I had sat down to read the paper, feeling content and amiable. It took me the rest of the trip to fasten at last with a snap of recognition on the fact, yes, *fact,* that Eisenhower had received altogether too many medals and it was time that someone gave me one. Moreover, it had better be a good one. . . .

Similarly, an overriding sense of fear, when one can see no realistic explanation for this diffused anxiety, often comes from suppressed guilt over a quite specific act. It is then, although its message is blurred, a form of self-castigation.

Again, quite often, after one has spoken or acted violently, one is assailed by a sudden anonymous fear and may dismiss it as fear of retribution. But most often, I think, it is rather terror over the discovery of the predatory animal within oneself.

All these human miseries! With pride, false pride (the instinct for dominance), still the ultimate matrix. No wonder many people resign from life. How much to indulge, how much to control? How much to cajole or circumvent? It must be played by ear, with vigilance and flexibility and a striving after effective memory. These forces in us must have ventilation lest they explode lethally, and that ventilation, most of the time, must take place within the narrow confines of the human skull. It is a difficult discipline.

But then much of human life *is* painful. I think of Melville Cane's "I have lived with my pain."

I find that a great part of living with one's pain is sustaining one's considered resolutions. As the annual joke goes, heroic resolutions are easy; sustaining them and fulfilling them are not. This discipline results, with many of us, in daily irritability. The solution, I think, is to find ways that are convincing to oneself to consider so sustained an effort a challenge, not a denial of self.

One thing is sure: the old ideals of a muscular will are not congenial to many of us any longer, except when applied to worldly ambition. I have known only a few people in a long time who take the expression "free will" seriously. It is as though there has been a consensus that our individual wills are infected, if not dead—or have been, from the beginning, a fictitious concept. But I would suggest, whatever the terminology, that the kind of self-discipline that is possible and fulfilling comes from extensive self-knowledge, and more from the sense within oneself of growing—and finding that growing a source of liking oneself—than from a muscular concept of self-mastery. One key, surely, is not to make one's resolutions on too heroic a scale. Yes, perhaps a man's reach should exceed his grasp, but not by so much as to make failure inevitable.

The tough core of these problems is exercising conscious choice—not essentially between good and evil, which lack, after all, a universal definition, but rather between two goods, two desired ends that are incompatible. Often it is the choice between the value of the moment ("Oh, stay, thou art so fair") and the long continuity stretching before one. Whether it be glory or recognition in opposition to principle and conscience; whether it be only a man's share of comfort and peace opposed to what he feels to be his responsibility—it is the most grueling of human disciplines. . . .

The contemporary humanist I am implicitly invoking faces an ideal of responsibility most difficult to attain. That is: to believe one's every act has importance to oneself and to others, without becoming obsessed with self-conscious evaluations.

I do not mean that one should or could consciously initiate every act with this realization, but only that if one pursues self-knowledge down some of these paths, one will eventually be living in an emotional and intellectual climate that will enable one much of the time to have such a sense of responsibility to oneself and to others without consciously thinking of it very often.

And finally—the two-pronged concept of responsibility leads to the Thou half of Martin Buber's dialogue between I and Thou.

332

Day after day, hour after hour, we misunderstand each other because we cross well-marked boundaries; we blur the sense of *you out there* and *me here;* we merge, frequently very sloppily, the subjective with the objective, in various ways. We make of the other person simply an extension of self, either through the attribution of our own thoughts and attitudes to the other person or by too facile a decision about his nature, after which we go on responding to him as though he were the character we have invented. Or we force him/her into the role of surrogate for some member of the original cast. Or yet again, we have built up early in life a mythical community wholly subjective but now often imposed on the outside world of empirical actuality. We re-enact, re-enact, re-enact.

The often invoked injunction to respect—and not to use—other people is insufficient. We must *listen*. To explore, to find out the quality, flavor and substance of another person's mind, of another personality, is one of the joys of life. All of a sudden one is no longer alone in his self-engrossed cell. But to attain this joy we must listen—instead of being busy preparing a reply, while uttering that most uninspiring of human sounds: uh-huh.

At the very least, life as dialogue can be amusing, entertaining. Listen for the key words and phrases. If a man repeatedly introduces what he has to say with "frankly" or "I am going to be honest with you" or "to tell the truth," one must infer that this assertion and repetition have a particular significance. The red semaphore is blinking.

I use simple examples and necessarily few. One of the most egotistical and even tyrannical men I have ever known always, in introducing his opinion about a decision to be made, used the words—and I mean *used*—"I, *for one,* am . . ."*

These ambiguities of meaning are interesting, amusing and helpful in understanding a little more about other people. But open listening reaps a better harvest than that. For when there is a real engagement between two people who find that they have something to say to each other, and the capacity, the curiosity, to listen both imaginatively and carefully—then there is a rare

---

* Yet, as I have already said, these generalizations, too, can be misleading, as I have found in the cases of Donald Klopfer and Lew Miller.

communication and response. There is an unguarded sponta-
neity in such dialogue. Life spreads its wings.

What persuasion, what enticement does such a way of life
offer? I suppose, in addition to the respect for truth, it is the
appeal to challenge and response. Life as response, life as experience—not life passively endured. For the great enemy is apathy,
indifference, callousness, the failure to engage. . . .

I know that I have no more than introduced, hinted at, the
possibilities in such a way of life. I know too little. I have learned
too late. I cannot consistently keep the scales from my eyes. But I
take comfort in these words of Montaigne:

> Others form man; I tell of him, and portray a particular one, very
> ill formed, whom I should really make very different from what he is if
> I had to fashion him over again. But now it is done. . . .
> I cannot keep my subject still. It goes along befuddled and stagger-
> ing, with a natural drunkenness. . . .
> If my mind could gain a firm footing, I would not make essays, I
> would make decisions; but it is always an apprenticeship and on trial.

Tuthill, July 25, 1973

Index

Gumpert, Martin, 61

Haas, Robert K., 77–78, 80–82, 86, 98, 103–05
Halliburton, Richard, 44, 56
Hallie, Philip, 157, 322
Hallinan, Nancy, 38
Hamilton, Jamie, 68, 71
Hamilton, Walton, 187
Hamish Hamilton Ltd., 71
Hands of Esau, The (Haydn), 291
Hanger Stout, Awake! (Matthews), 144
Happy Generation, The (Kormendi), 62
Harcourt, Alfred, 137, 143
Harcourt, Brace and Company, 140–41
Harcourt, Brace and Howe, 4
Harcourt, Brace & World, 8, 92, 139
Harcourt Brace Jovanovich, 28, 92, 137–45, 197, 242–43, 244, 270, 284–85, 293, 295–98, 306
Hardwick, Elizabeth, 229
Hardy, Thomas, 214
Harper & Brothers, Publishers, 108, 109, 110, 112, 268, 269, 306
Harper & Row, Publishers, 130, 139, 313
Harper's, 207, 229, 277, 282
Harris, Mark, 73
Hastings, William T., 182, 200
Hausman, Louis, 118
Haydn, Hiram: on agents, 13, 56; with Bobbs-Merrill, 23–24, 32, 36–38, 41–59, 61, 63–80, 256–60, 269, 279–80, 318; as copublisher at Harcourt, 138–52, 197, 242–43, 244, 270, 284–85, 293, 295–98, 313–14; with Crown, 5–13, 17, 19–21, 24, 26–32, 37, 50, 61–63; as an editor, 24–25, 58–59, 232, 245, 247–98 *passim*, 317–18; on editors, 28–29, 37, 91, 249, 262–63, 274, 307–09, 316–19; on European writers, 59–68, 275; on Jews in publishing, 31, 70; Makers of the American Tradition series, 75, 169; on man, 323–34; as partner at Atheneum, 39, 72, 73, 106, 113–35, 240–41, 242, 243, 245, 248, 251–53, 262, 268–69, 270, 274, 275–78, 281, 284, 287, 288, 313, 318; with Phi Beta Kappa Society and *The American Scholar*, 4–5, 158–209; on publishers, 28–31, 37, 105, 241, 262; with Random House, 16, 74, 77–106, 112–14, 117, 241, 254–56, 260–62, 263–65, 266–67, 270, 274–75, 282–84, 290–91, 306, 320; on reviewers, 74; on sales departments, 28, 37, 276, 283; as teacher, 3–4, 38, 109, 197, 237–40; Twentieth Century Library, 13–16, 17, 21–22, 65, 75; on women in publishing, 298–307; as a writer, 13 and *n.*, 17–19, 32–34, 65, 197, 229; on writers, 59, 67, 91, 213–22, 228–36 *passim*, 249, 266, 274–87
Haydn, Jonathan, 97–98, 193–94
Haydn, Mary, 265
Haydn, Mary (Mrs. Hiram), 17, 41–42, 52, 68, 71, 78, 102, 110, 116, 117, 122 and *n.*, 123, 132, 142, 188, 193, 194, 199, 246, 251, 278, 281, 294, 297, 319
Haydn, Michael, 94, 241
Haydn, Miranda, 94, 307
Hazlitt, Henry, 164, 165, 182, 187
Heathcote, Mary, 273, 306
Heckscher, August, 156
Hedden, Worth Tuttle, 20, 29–30, 233
Held, John Jr., 235
Heller, Joseph, 39, 66
Hellman, Lillian, 158, 176–77
Hemingway, Ernest, 56, 191, 234–35
Herrmann, David, 111, 123, 124, 125, 127
Hersey, John, 157
Herter, Christian, 116
Herzog (Bellow), 230
Hicks, Granville, 228

345